Kudos

"For Jack's many fans, the stories recalling episodes of his 45-year, personal evolution from cattle rancher, to emerging naturalist and conservationist, to renowned environmentalist will be equally enlightening and entertaining. This book will appeal to all ages and a wide range of readers…tourists, naturalists, environmentalists, natural history students, local history buffs and anyone who has had the pleasure of experiencing the natural Costa Rica that Jack has worked so hard to foster and protect.

Dorothy MacKinnon, travel writer – *Fodor's Guide to Costa Rica, Insight Guide to Costa Rica, Tico Times*

"Because of Jack Ewing and people like him we are sure to see the return of the tapir and jaguar to this extraordinary biological corridor, keeping this part of Costa Rica truly the 'rich coast' as it was meant to be. *Where the Tapirs and Jaguars Once Roamed* is a must read for those that love Costa Rica and those yet to discover this beautiful country."

Pat Cheek, Quepolandia

"The Costa Rican conservation story is a fascinating one and Jack Ewing has been an incredibly effective participant in its success. The book gives a very real and personal context to it. And he's a great story teller as well. I loved it!"

Richard Andrus, Professor – Binghamton University, New York

"*Where Tapirs and Jaguars Once Roamed* transports the reader into Costa Rica with an intimacy born from the author's life there and with a vividness that would be difficult to match even seeing it for yourself. It is fascinating and personal, never dry or academic, yet by the end there's no denying it's a thoroughly educational read."

Ray & Sue Krueger-Koplin, Toucan Maps Inc.

ALSO BY JACK EWING

*Monkeys Are Made of Chocolate:
Exotic and Unseen Costa Rica*

Where Tapirs and Jaguars Once Roamed

Ever-Evolving Costa Rica

JACK EWING

foreword by PAMELA HERRING

PixyJack Press
INC

Where Tapirs and Jaguars Once Roamed:
Ever-Evolving Costa Rica

Published by PixyJack Press, Inc.
PO Box 149, Masonville, CO 80541 USA

print ISBN 978-1-936555-55-0
Kindle ISBN 978-1-936555-56-7
epub ISBN 978-1-936555-57-4

Cover artwork by Jan Betts.
Unless noted otherwise, interior illustrations by Jan Betts, photos by Jack Ewing.

Library of Congress Cataloging-in-Publication Data
    Ewing, Jack, 1943-
      Where tapirs and jaguars once roamed : ever-evolving Costa Rica / by Jack Ewing.
        pages cm
      Includes bibliographical references.
      Summary: "An ecological and social history of southwestern Costa Rica, from the land formation of Central America to present day"-- Provided by publisher.
      ISBN 978-1-936555-55-0 -- ISBN 978-1-936555-56-7 (Kindle) -- ISBN 978-1-936555-57-4 (epub)
      1. Human ecology--Costa Rica--Corredor Biológico Paso de la Danta. 2. Corredor Biológico Paso de la Danta (Costa Rica)--History. 3. Nature conservation--Costa Rica--Corredor Biológico Paso de la Danta. 4. Ewing, Jack, 1943---Travel--Costa Rica. 5. Costa Rica--Description and travel. I. Title. II. Title: Where tapirs and jaguars once roamed.
      GF522.C8E95 2015
      304.2097286'7--dc23
                    2014042300

To my wife Diane -
Still beautiful after 40 years in the Costa Rican jungle,
and 50 years with me

NICARAGUA

CARIBBEAN SEA

La Cruz

Liberia

Tortuguero

Santa
Cruz

San Jose

Cartago

Limon

Puntarenas

Los Santos
Reserve

La Amistad

Isla del Coco

Quepos

Manuel
Antonio

San Isidro

Hacienda Baru

Uvita

Dominical

Palmar

Sierpe

Cortés

Terraba-Sierpe

San Vito

Piedras Blancas

PANAMA

★ National Capital
✪ Provincial Capital
● Cities
— Roads
░ Protected Areas

Golfito

0 10 20 30 40 50

Kilometers

PACIFIC OCEAN

Corcovado

Gulfo Dulce

Puerto Jiménez

Contents

Part Three

Foreword

"As Jack spoke with us, I saw a special peace in his eyes. I want the type of peace Jack Ewing has."

Mariela Araujo, Student – University of Texas at Brownsville

Each year I bring my students to Hacienda Barú in Costa Rica for their class, "Living, Reading, Writing Nature." It is not the beautiful land or the mighty Pacific Ocean, nor is it the monkeys, sloths or toucans they wish most to see. The main attraction for the students is Jack Ewing. They ask, "When do we get to meet Jack?" They have read his book, *Monkeys are Made of Chocolate*, and are amazed one person can make such a dramatic change in a country, and that his message is reaching around the world. When we return home the students become ambassadors for the protection of Mother Nature and become involved in local sanctuaries and organizations to make positive changes in their communities.

A door opened for Jack and Diane Ewing when they were a young married couple. Their trip to Costa Rica was only to be a four-month adventure, yet it became a life-long passion that has helped restore the face of Costa Rica from farmland to rainforest. What if Jack and Diane had not taken the Costa Rican opportunity?

When Jack realized the damage that had been done to the rainforest, he made an incredible change. He stopped the destruction of habitat, banned hunting, and began re-growing the natural jungle. As you read this book, you'll see it has been a long journey.

It takes devotion and sacrifice to be committed to such a venture. Jack, Diane, and their children lived in a jungle house for eight years without electricity or running water. At times the only way to town was on horseback so Diane and her horse Chopo swam the Barú River to get necessary supplies.

Jack tells us that at nearby Manuel Antonio, the rainforest—the very reason tourists have come to Costa Rica—is being destroyed so they may have fancy places to stay, dine and play. At Hacienda Barú, however, Jack has ensured that the natural beauty and wonder of the rainforest is what his visitors will experience. With his leadership and his partnership with Steve Stroud, others have become determined to see the Path of the Tapir Biological Corridor come to fruition. Recently when the highway was widened, they persuaded the Ministry of the Transport to include wildlife bridges and tunnels—the first to be built in Costa Rica. Their great success in saving wildlife has caught the attention of other environmentalists throughout the country and beyond.

How does one acquire the peace found in Jack Ewing's eyes? A person must find an important passion and live by its calling. One must see the results and know what has been done is worthwhile and valuable for all time. It is something that will ignite passion in others.

UT Brownsville student Gus Hernandez says, "Jack is courageous, patient, kind. I could feel his passion. He taught me to be more appreciative of life and be open to opportunities. The rainforest he is protecting helped me see life anew and welcome new adventures and challenges. I can say I left Costa Rica a changed person."

Jack Ewing teaches us that if we open our hearts and eyes "every day we will see something we have never seen before." Because of Jack's vision, determination and leadership, the dream of the Path of the Tapir Biological Corridor is unfolding. One day we will see tapirs at Hacienda Barú.

Pamela Herring
University of Texas at Brownsville

Preface

A visitor traveling south along the Pacific coast of Costa Rica will experience a diversity of landscapes, from cattle ranches, farm land, and tree plantations to crocodile-filled rivers and lush rainforests. They will observe the high-rise condos of Jaco and the beautiful landscape of Manuel Antonio marred by an overabundance of hotels, restaurants, and all variety of establishments dedicated to the entertainment of tourists.

Traveling south from the Quepos-Manuel Antonio area the visitor will encounter vast plantations of oil palms as far as the eye can see up until arriving at the Savegre River. The river itself, though large, is not remarkable, but even before entering the bridge spanning its width, the change in landscape is notable. On the south side of the bridge, a mere 200 to 300 meters to the left, a small rainforest-covered mountain range rises up from the flat lowlands. This coastal ridge forms the backbone of a natural corridor which is one of the few places on our planet where biodiversity is increasing and has been doing so for the last 30 years.

This is the story of a place on the south-central Pacific coast of Costa Rica which is today known as the Path of the Tapir Biological Corridor. Eighty kilometers long and averaging 15 kilometers in width, the corridor is bounded to the west and north by the Savegre River and the Los Santos Forest Reserve, and to the south and east by the Pacific Ocean and the Rio Grande de Térraba. In the middle, where three regions meet, is a small town called Dominical and a river called Barú. As the story unfolds the significance of the three regions and how they have affected the way people live and use the land will become clear.

The Path of the Tapir is characterized by a narrow strip of coastal lowland and two small mountain ranges—the coastal ridge and the Tinamastes ridge—both of which run parallel to the coast. It is bisected by 11 rivers which originate within its bounds. Estuaries where mangroves thrive branch off near the mouths of eight of those rivers where they empty into the Pacific Ocean. Large extensions of mangrove are also found at the rivers on each end of the corridor, the Savegre and the Térraba. To the northwest the beaches are straight and open, sometimes sandy, sometimes rocky, but always incessantly pounded by the Pacific surf. Southeast of the Barú River, rocky points and coves predominate, the exception being the Ballena Marine National Park with its sandy coves protected by the rocky reefs extending outward from Uvita Point to Ballena Island and several smaller rock islands.

The Path of the Tapir Biological Corridor is a place where tapirs once roamed, but have been locally extinct since 1957 when a hunter shot the last one. To some people Baird's Tapir *(Tapirus bairdii)* resembles a small cow and to others a large pig. This is Central America's largest land mammal, as high at the shoulder as the waist of a tall man with a mass equal to that of a couple of linemen from a Super Bowl Team. Its head is big and elongated with a nose that might be described as a sawed-off trunk or a lengthy upper lip. This prehensile snout grasps the foliage that forms the tapir's diet and pulls it into its mouth. Each foot would cover a dinner plate. All four feet have three functional toes and the front feet each have a vestigial forth toe high on

Illustration: Georgie Wingfield

the outside. These digits are really hooves, making the tapir an ungulate, the only one in Central America with three toes.

Although tapirs no longer roam in the corridor that bears their name, they may still be found at both ends. The dream of the Path of the Tapir Biological Corridor project is that people will work together to restore natural habitat, especially along rivers and streams, thus connecting larger protected areas of rainforest. The ultimate sign of success will be the migration of tapirs into the corridor from the Los Santos Reserve on the north and Corcovado National Park in the south.

In the early stages of researching the different aspects of this story, it became apparent that the geological forces that formed Central America as a whole and this region in particular have continually exerted a powerful influence on the place and the people who have inhabited it. As we will see, a single geological aspect, the coastal ridge, played a major role in the way humans have used this land since they first arrived in the Americas. With this in mind, we will begin 15 million years ago when the forces that created Central America were already moving the first pieces into place. We will see how once the connection between North and South America was complete, species from each continent migrated across the land bridge, mixed and concentrated in Central America. Later humans entered the picture and the spectrum of flora and fauna changed as did the landscape. This is the story not only of a place, but also of those who inhabited the place, how they lived, and how they used the land.

The historical happenings that took place prior to the last century were necessarily gleaned from written sources; the stories about indigenous people represent my portrayal of how people may have lived at that time. The people in the last century of this story are real. Their stories were told to me in personal interviews and, in most cases, their names have not been changed. Some of them are still alive and well. A few of the details, such as thoughts and conversations, were created for the purpose of making the story more readable.

The last section includes stories of me and my family, how we came to Costa Rica in 1970 and ended up living at a cattle ranch called Hacienda Barú, located near the town of Dominical in the middle of what later became known as the Path of the Tapir Biological Corridor. It tells about the people and organizations involved in the creation of that corridor project, and how Hacienda Barú has evolved from a cattle ranch into an internationally known ecological tourism destination.

This is the story of a place where tapirs and jaguars once roamed and may someday return. 🐾

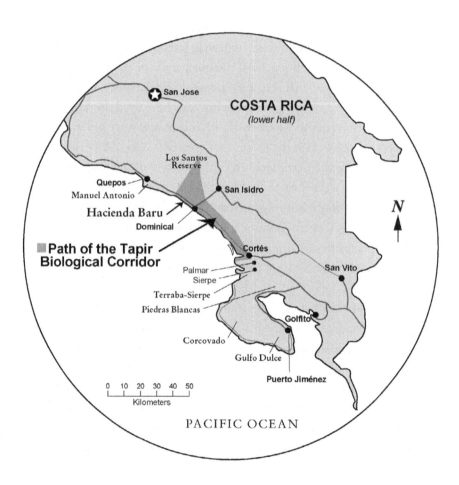

"You Make Mistake, Maybe We Die"

An Unforgettable Flight

These days everybody knows that Costa Rica is a Central American country located between Panama and Nicaragua, but there was a time when it was fairly common for people to confuse it with Puerto Rico. I once made that mistake myself. Little did I know that I would end up living here for most of my life.

As owner of Hacienda Barú Lodge, I meet lots of people and am often asked the question, "How long have you been here?"

"Forty-four years," I reply.

"Wow, what did you do, come here on vacation and never leave?"

"Well no, it wasn't quite like that."

My introduction to Costa Rica was in 1970, and my reasons for coming here had nothing to do with a vacation, rainforest conservation, or ecological tourism. At the time I was in the cattle business. Fresh out of Colorado State University with a degree in animal husbandry, I went to work for my father but found, as have many other young men, that working with Dad is sometimes difficult or impossible. I ended up managing a cattle farm in Ontario, Canada. As it turned out, I couldn't get along any better with my new employer than I did with my father. At the time it didn't occur to me that my own immaturity might be a big part of the problem, but that's a different story. Regardless of who was right or wrong, I decided it was time to look for another job.

The fateful phone call came one night during dinner. "I'm exporting about 150 head of cattle to Costa Rica," said the voice on the other end of the line, a man named Ken Allen. "We'll truck them to Miami and fly them on down from there."

"Costa Rica?" I replied, "that's an island in the Caribbean, isn't it?"

"No," he laughed, "Costa Rica is in Central America just north of Panama. Anyway, I need someone with your ability to help me get the cattle down there, take care of them, and keep them healthy until I get them sold. I figure it will take about four months. I can offer you a job for that long, but I can't promise anything after that."

My wife, Diane, and I talked it over and decided to accept the offer. We weren't happy where we were and Costa Rica sounded like an interesting experience. I called Ken back the next day and told him that we would accept his offer on the condition that Diane and our daughter, Natalie, could go too. He agreed.

We moved into a house on Ken's farm in a place called Flesherton, Ontario, and began vaccinating, worming and preparing the cattle for shipment. In early December, the first 37 head were loaded on a large truck which set off for Miami. A day later, with three feet of snow on the ground, Ken, Diane, Natalie and I drove to the airport in Toronto and boarded a flight to Miami to meet the cattle.

When we arrived in Miami the cattle were already in the international quarantine station where they would remain for testing over the next three days. If everything went well they would then be certified free of any contagious diseases and cleared for international shipment. We checked into a hotel near the airport. The next day Ken left for Costa Rica on a commercial flight. We were to wait until the cattle were released from quarantine and then fly down in the same plane with them. It sounded like fun.

The following day, December 12, 1970, was Natalie's birthday.

We celebrated it at the hotel. The dining room staff brought a chocolate cake with four candles and we all sang "Happy Birthday." Afterwards, it was off to bed. Tomorrow was the big day.

The air cargo company owned only one airplane, a DC-6. The owners and crew were exiled Cubans. The pilot and his wife, both of whom spoke broken English, picked us up at the hotel at four o'clock in the morning. On the way to the airport they stopped at an all-night diner for sweet rolls and coffee. The cattle were on the plane when we arrived.

Originally designed to be a bomber in World War II, the DC-6 wasn't quite ready for service when the war ended. It was a four-engine propeller plane with a cruising speed of about 500 kph and a maximum altitude of 7,600 feet. It could carry a payload of about 18,000 kilos.

"How do we get on the plane?" asked Diane. "I don't see a ramp."

I looked the plane over. "I guess we climb that ladder going up to the cockpit door."

The pilot's wife offered us some of the fare she had bought at the diner. After we ate she took us to the plane. She held the ladder while Diane climbed up. The copilot carried Natalie up the ladder, delivered her into Diane's arms and then came back down. I went last.

The cattle, 37 head in all, were divided into four pens. The weight distribution was important, and they had put the heaviest ones up front. Sturdy nets were draped over the pens. This, I was told, was to keep the animals from smashing into the ceiling or flying around the interior of the fuselage if the plane were to hit a sudden down-draft. There was one bench-seat for passengers immediately behind the cockpit, which we assumed was for us. Diane and Natalie sat down. I walked over to the door and looked down.

The crew and other company representatives were standing beside the plane, talking animatedly in Spanish and gesticulating excitedly. I wondered what they were discussing. My Spanish was rudimentary at that time. The pilot walked over to the foot of the boarding ladder and called up to me. "How much these cows weigh?"

"32,674 pounds," I answered.

"That is official weight, no? From three days ago, no? They eat and get fat, no?"

"No," I said, not quite as sure as I sounded, "that's not right. These cattle came from Canada and subzero temperatures. They have heavy coats of hair. They've been cooped up in the quarantine station for three days, sweating in this tropical weather. They probably weigh less now than they did when they arrived."

He gave me a skeptical glance, walked back to the crew and resumed the animated discussion. Eventually one of the men got a portable scale out of the back of a pickup truck, placed it in front of one of the wheels and towed the plane a few inches until the wheel rolled up on the scale. One man read the scale and did some quick calculations with a pencil on a clipboard—hand-held calculators hadn't been invented yet—and they all went back to the discussion. Finally everyone seemed to agree. They said their good-byes and the crew climbed the ladder.

The pilot looked at me with a grave expression. "I hope you be right about the weight," he said seriously. "You make mistake, maybe we die."

A thousand thoughts went through my mind: *Maybe the cattle do weigh more than I thought. They had a long truck ride. Maybe they were empty when they weighed-in and are full now. But no, they have really been suffering in this heat; they have to weigh less. What if they do weigh more? Will the plane really crash?*

We taxied to our runway and, after a short wait, the pilot proceeded to rev up the engines. All four propellers roared. The pilot released the brakes. The plane shuddered and started forward, the vibration increasing in intensity as we rumbled down the runway. We rolled and rolled, and then we rolled some more. My imagination was working overtime. *What's happening? Are we going to make it? Are we going to crash at the end of the runway? No, they wouldn't risk it. Would they?*

The caution lights at the end of the runway flashed past the window. The vibration changed pitch. The fuselage trembled. We were airborne. We dropped back to the runway and bounced. *Wait a minute. We're not supposed to bounce on takeoff.* We were airborne again, and this time we stayed up. The plane ascended slowly, but we were flying.

Diane remembers a magical pink hue to the east where the sun was thinking about peaking over the horizon, and the pitch black night dotted with twinkling stars to the west. We banked, came around and straightened out over the ocean, now clear of brightly lit Miami. The navigator stood up and gave Diane his chair, which was more comfortable than hers. He stretched, laid down on the floor and went to sleep.

After about 30 minutes we saw more lights below. "We no talk on the radio here," said the pilot. He rolled his eyes and pointed down, "Cuba! Fidel know we here, they shoot." He cackled with laughter. We were beginning to get the idea that the pilot liked to pull our leg.

I went back and checked the cattle. They were calm, but hot. The temperature was around 35 degrees Celsius (95°F) and the relative humidity near 100 percent. Diane had undressed Natalie down to her underwear. I stuck my head in between the pilot and copilot. "Could you turn the air conditioning up a little? The cattle are really uncomfortable."

"No air conditioning," smiled the pilot. "Weigh too much. We take it out so we carry more cows."

We whiled away the hours talking, dozing, staring out the window, and wishing for the time to pass more rapidly. After five hours of not moving a muscle, the navigator suddenly opened his eyes, stood up, stretched, and indicated that he needed his seat back. We were over Costa Rica.

If you've only flown in commercial planes and think landings are a "piece of cake," you should try it while sitting practically in the cockpit of a DC-6 full of cattle. As we descended, the humidity condensed and started dripping from the ceiling. The pilot and copilot had to wipe the fog from the windshield with toilet paper. We joked about it raining inside the plane.

Once they cleared the windshield the pilots began making preparations for landing. I recognized the procedure, but couldn't see where they intended to set the plane down. After a few minutes I noticed a short, narrow black ribbon in the distance. *They can't possibly hit that tiny thing, can they?* As we continued our approach, the black ribbon grew and eventually started looking a little more like a runway. With every gust of wind the plane turned slightly to one side or the other, and my heart jumped clear up into my throat. Just as I was becoming convinced that we might actually be able to land, the cattle got restless and started moving around. The plane rocked a little from side to side. My heart sunk from my throat down to the pit of my stomach.

Through all of my anxiety, the crew appeared to be utterly unconcerned. Somehow they held the plane straight and level, countered every gust of wind and movement of the cattle, and got the airplane right down to the ground just where it was supposed to be. We hit the runway and bounced. The cattle shifted. We bounced again. The third time we stayed down, rolled to a stop and taxied over to the cargo area where two cattle trucks were waiting. The navigator opened the doors. We had arrived safely at El Coco International Airport (now Juan Santa Maria International Airport), a 30-minute drive from San Jose, the capital of Costa Rica.

A forklift carrying a wooden chute drove up to the DC-6 and maneuvered one end of the chute onto the floor inside the back door of the plane, and then lowered the other end onto the bed of a waiting truck. We started unloading cattle. Ken was there, as were his Costa Rican partners. Once two pens of cattle were loaded on the first truck, the process was repeated with another truck. Finally we climbed down from the plane and took our bags to Customs Inspection, which consisted of two tables and two inspectors. We opened our suitcases, got the nod, and walked out. In all of the confusion, nobody took us through Immigration, and we drove out the cargo gate without having been officially checked into Costa Rica. As you might imagine, this caused us considerable delay and confusion the first time we wanted to leave the country.

It was about three o'clock in the afternoon and all we wanted to do was sleep, but that was not to be. The cattle were taken to a farm halfway between the airport and San Jose, in a place called Heredia, where they would stay for the next two weeks. It took several more hours to get them unloaded, fed and settled down. Then we went out to eat with Ken's partners, and finally, around ten o'clock we got some sleep.

As cattle were sold, new ones arrived, five more planeloads altogether. Before the four-month contract with Ken was finished, I was offered a job with a meat packing company that owned several large ranches and about 10,000 head of cattle. In the early 1970s I worked on a big ranch on the Caribbean side of Costa Rica, near a town called Siquieres. Diane and Natalie lived in San Jose, and I traveled back and forth every week. Our son Chris was born in 1972. That was the same year I first visited Hacienda Barú, which the meat packing company had leased for fattening cattle. In 1976 I left the packing company and became a partner with the owners of Hacienda Barú, which was destined, over the coming decades, to evolve from a cattle ranch into Hacienda Barú National Wildlife Refuge.

Whenever I am asked if I came down here on vacation and never left, I always think fondly about that first flight to Costa Rica in a DC-6 full of cattle. 🐾

Southwestern Costa Rica

To view a full map, please visit *www.costa-rica-guide.com*

Part One

1

The Formation of Central America

Bridge Between Continents, Barrier Between Oceans

Prior to the formation of the Central American isthmus, over 15 million years ago, a strong tropical ocean current flowed westward through a two-kilometer deep channel between North and South America, two continents separated by nearly 1,000 kilometers of ocean. The blockage of that flow by the new land mass stimulated profound changes in the dynamics of the planet, possibly triggering the current ice age. It is certainly responsible for the Gulf Stream current which caused a pronounced warming in the northern latitudes of Europe and North America.

Two geological forces were responsible for the appearance of an isthmus where there had previously been deep ocean: plate tectonics and volcanic action. We can generalize and say that northern Central America is mostly old land, formed more than 250 million years ago. It has been pushed around and fitted into its current location by the movement of tectonic plates. As these thick plates move on a sea of molten magma, they collide with each other as one dips underneath the other. These violent interactions result in tremors, earthquakes, the buckling of the earth's surface to form mountains and cliffs, and the leakage of hot magma from the mantle on which the plates rest. When this molten lava breaches the earth's crust and spews forth onto the ocean floor, new land is created where none had previously existed.

Due to drastic and cyclic variations of sea levels, it is difficult to determine when the land bridge finally closed between North and South America. Approximately every 100,000 years a glacial period captured a large portion of the earth's water in glaciers and the polar caps, reducing the amount of water in the oceans and lowering sea levels by 150 meters or more, thus exposing much land previously covered by water. Relatively shallow continental shelves that extend outward from most land masses were exposed during these periods of glaciation, greatly expanding the surface area of dry land. As each ice age passed, a warmer climate melted much of the ice locked up in glaciers and polar caps, causing the seas to rise once again and cover land previously exposed. This glacial cycle, and the rising and falling of sea levels that accompanied it, caused a land bridge to appear for a few tens of millennia only to disappear beneath the sea again.

By ten million years ago the old land forming the northern part of the land bridge moved into its approximate current position, while further south, the same and other forces were bringing new land to the surface. And so an archipelago, or string of islands, was formed.

Around eight million years ago, at a time of lowered sea levels, the first mammals—two species of giant ground sloths—from South America crossed the newly forming isthmus. These sloths were very successful, eventually migrating to every part of North America, as far north as Alaska. No other South American species appeared in Central America until five million years later. Likewise there is no evidence that any North American species migrated to South America until about three million years ago.

Large masses of land dominated the sea between the two continents around three million years ago, completely closing the deep water channel joining the Atlantic and Pacific oceans. During warm interglacial periods with high sea levels, three saltwater passages, none of which was more than about 50 meters deep, were the only connections that remained between the two oceans. Two of these passages were far to the south, near present-day Panama Canal and the Atrato Valley of Colombia. The third passage, which was probably the last to close, separated the areas that later became Costa Rica and Nicaragua.

As plate movements continued and volcanoes spewed molten material, these remaining gaps between the continents finally closed, and the land bridge between North and South America grew steadily, wider and higher.

The South-Central Western Coastline

Spared from most of the volcanic activity, the south-central portion of the western coastline of Costa Rica was formed primarily by the lifting and folding action caused by the tectonic plate slipping underneath it. This new land had been sea floor a few million years earlier.

A mere 100,000 years ago some tectonic event, a slipping or buckling, created a ridge down the western coastline between the present-day Savegre and Grande de Térraba rivers. This ridge is now known as the Coastal Ridge, or the *fila costeña* in Spanish. It juts upward as much as 600 meters near the Pacific shoreline. The strip of lowland between the coastal ridge and the sea averages about one-half kilometer in width and is nowhere more than two kilometers wide. Northwest of the coastal ridge lie vast fertile lowlands created by a steady lifting of the upper plate. To the southeast, but still north of the Osa Peninsula, lies the fertile valley where the Sierpe and Térraba rivers flow.

At approximately the same time the coastal ridge was being formed, a geological force caused the earth's crust to split about 15 kilometers inland from the Pacific coast. The land nearest the ocean dropped 300 meters while the inland side remained at the same altitude as before the split, thus leaving an exposed cliff face. Today this is known as the Tinamastes Ridge.

The generally steep terrain of the Path of the Tapir Biological Corridor is scarred with many short rivers and streams which have carved their winding paths through the sharp ridge lines. Ten rivers originate less than 20 kilometers from the ocean, between the Tinamastes Ridge and the coast.[1] The Savegre and the Grande de Térraba rivers which mark the limits of the corridor, both originate high on the central mountain range many kilometers from the coast.

Along the coastline of the Path of the Tapir Biological Corridor, eight important mangrove forests can be found, including one of the largest in Central America at the combined mouths of the Sierpe and Térraba rivers. The six species of mangrove that dominate these estuaries share a tolerance to salt and an affinity for water.

Mangroves are extremely important ecologically and commercially since they are vital for the propagation of many commercially important species of marine life. Juveniles of many fishes and shrimp require the silty, nutrient rich environment within the tangled mass of mangrove roots for their early development. Unfortunately, many of the mangroves along the Pacific coast have been destroyed.

Ancient Origins of the Fauna

Over 300 million years ago South America split away from Africa and

---

1 Ten rivers: Portalón, Matapalo, Hatillo Nuevo, Hatillo Viejo, Barú, Dominicalito, Morete, Uvita, Ballena, and Ojochal.

steadily moved westward to its present position. Since the separation, its biological isolation from other continents has been nearly total, the few exceptions being life that could arrive by air or by sea. The flora and fauna on each continent have since evolved in their own way and according to their own particular conditions. The lack of any land route over which new species could migrate left the South American fauna relatively secure, with each species safely entrenched in its own niche.

On the other hand, much of the North American fauna migrated from Eurasia across the Bering Strait. You could say that these species were veterans at adaptation, having evolved and adapted to different conditions on several continents. With each new migration these species had fought for a place in the natural order and won, sometimes over existing species that had been well established in their niches. Whether species experience or species wisdom, it served the North American species well when the Central American isthmus finally closed the gap around three million years ago and the faunas of two continents met.

Another important consideration in the development of fauna is that Central America was formed from north to south. The areas we know as Mexico, Belize, Guatemala, El Salvador, Honduras, and Nicaragua were already in place several million years before Costa Rica and Panama were formed and the land bridge completed. North American fauna was well adapted to this semi-tropical and tropical climate well before the majority of the South American fauna had the opportunity to inhabit the temperate climate of North America, giving the northern species a distinct advantage.

Mammal Species Which Crossed the Bridge

It is worth mentioning here that when we talk about a time scale of several million years, the time that it takes for a species of, let's say mice, to disperse over an entire continent is a mere blink of the eye in comparison. Even if it takes a mouse a thousand years to disperse from Panama to Tierra del Fuego, that period is equal to 1/3000th of the amount of time that has elapsed since closing of the gap and the great two-way migration of species.

All species were affected by their encounters with new species whether or not they actually migrated. Those that did not disperse across the land bridge still had to confront all of the new species moving in from another continent, and this involved competition, predation, infection, and parasitization. All species either adapted or failed to establish themselves under the new conditions quite quickly (on a geological time scale)—within a few thousand years. A more recent wave of extinctions, primarily of very large animals, took place 10,000 to 12,000 years ago, leaving a great deal of fossil evidence. It made no difference whether the animals came from North America or South America; nothing weighing over a ton survived to present day.

The two gorilla-sized ground sloths that made that first crossing eight million years ago are now extinct, as are most of their kin that crossed five million years later, including one giant sloth known as *Eremotherium* that stood as tall as a 4½ meters. Certain North American species of trees, such as those of the *Bombacacae* family, are believed to have evolved spines as a deterrent to these leaf-eating creatures. Only two species of tree sloths, the two-toed sloth and the three-toed sloth, have survived to remind us of their giant cousins.

Armadillos from the south also came in both the size we know

Titanis
Illustration: Jarmo Jouha

today and a giant species comparable in size to very large pigs. Toxodonts, which are hoofed animals similar to the rhinoceros, came from the south and established themselves in Central America. One of the few southern carnivores, a giant, flightless bird known as Titanis, stood at

29

2½ meters in height. All of these large species originating in South America are extinct today.

Horses and mastodons originated in North America and migrated to South America. Both became extinct. (The horses found in the New World today were brought by the Spanish in the 1500s.) Mammoths were also found in North America, but apparently never crossed the land bridge. They did, however, become extinct at the end of the last ice age along with most other large mammals.

In general then, surviving mammals were smaller species, including bison, deer, bears, llamas, and tapirs. These North American species, with the sole exception of the bison, established themselves in South America. Some, such as the llama and tapir still survive in the south, but are no longer found in the temperate north. Of the South American species, nothing larger than porcupines, opossums, and armadillos have managed to adapt and defend a niche in the temperate climates of North America.

Other North American mammals that spread as far as temperate South America include shrews, mice, gophers, squirrels, rabbits, skunks, weasels, foxes, raccoons, peccaries, spotted cats, and pumas. The largest of the felines, the saber-toothed cat, evolved in South America from smaller members of the cat family that originated in North America, and then became extinct with other large mammals at the end of the last ice age. The jaguar is the largest surviving feline.

South American mammals have fared better in tropical Central America than in temperate North America. In addition to those already mentioned, spiny rats, agoutis, pacas, anteaters, and many different species of monkeys survive in the tropics. These are species that, for the most part, evolved in the Amazon Basin and migrated north, always remaining within the tropics.

Three million years ago there were fewer forests and more savannas than today. This characteristic favored the incursion of the many species of grazing mammals mentioned above. As tropical forests later developed, other species better adapted to rainforest environments became established and thrived. Nevertheless, much of what is believed about the landscape of the newly formed isthmus is purely speculative, as fossil evidence is sparse. The division of one ocean into two oceans changed wind patterns, ocean currents, and weather, and all of these changes affected the vegetation and the species depending on it.

Extinction of Large Fauna

When attempting to explain the extinction of the large fauna between 10,000 and 12,000 years ago, some scientists have attempted to make a case for a climatic cause associated with the end of the last glacial period about 12,000 years ago. If this theory is correct, why were the giant sloths, toxodonts, mastodons, mammoths, giant bison, horses, and other large mammals able to survive 30 similar periods of glaciation only to perish at the end of the last one? In order to find the answer, we must have a look at an extraneous factor, not directly related to climate change, which nevertheless made a very large difference at the end of the last glacial period. That factor is the arrival of Homo sapiens in the Americas. 🐾

Author's Note: Much of the information regarding the formation of the land bridge was gleaned from the excellent book, *Central America: A Natural and Cultural History*, edited by Anthony G. Coates. Additional sources for this chapter include *The Natural History of Costa Rica*, edited by Daniel Jansen.

2

Hunter Gatherers and Early Agriculturalists

Clovis Hunters and the Region's First Farmers

Scholars disagree as to exactly how and from where Homo sapiens first appeared in the Americas. There are two schools of thought about timing and method of the arrival. One says that the first humans came by boat from different places and at different times, but made their first appearance sometime between 35,000 and 22,000 years ago. The other says they migrated across what is today the Bering Strait, where during the last ice age when sea levels were 150 meters lower than today, a dry land passage existed. Proponents of each theory make valid points, but the general consensus in academic circles and the scientific community is that early humans crossed by way of the Bering land bridge about 14,000 to 12,000 years ago. Nevertheless, the alternate theory has some points worth mentioning.

Arrival by Sea

Foremost in the argument favoring a maritime arrival of the first humans are several archaeological sites where carbon dating suggests that human settlements existed as early as 35,000 years ago. Most of these sites are found in South America. Opponents recognize that there were human settlements at the sites mentioned, but claim that the carbon dating indicates only the presence of dead organic material, such as wood from trees that died that long ago. In other words, carbon-dated material found at the archaeological sites doesn't prove that humans were there at the time the trees died.

Other oft-cited evidence includes the theories of famous Norwegian adventurer and anthropologist Thor Heyerdahl who rode the ocean currents from Egypt to the Caribbean in a reed boat similar to those used by early Egyptians. This adventure was recounted in great detail in the Heyerdahl's bestselling book, *The Ra Expeditions*. Heyerdahl also organized and carried out another expedition in which he and a group of colleagues rode a balsa raft from the western coastline of South America across the Pacific Ocean to Polynesia. This adventure, which took place prior to the Ra Expedition, was described in *The Kontiki Raft*, also by Heyerdahl. These two expeditions were designed to show that it was possible for humans to have reached the Americas by boat, and for their descendants to have later rafted to Polynesia to populate those islands.

Proponents of the seafaring origin of the first Americans are fond of questioning the migration of humans across the Bering land bridge during an ice age. They ask what the migrants ate and how they clothed themselves while trekking many hundreds of miles across Siberia, Alaska, and Canada with temperatures in excess of 80° Celsius below zero (-112°F). One answer put forward is that they ate woolly mammoths, but that brings to mind the question of what these beasts may have eaten when the land masses were covered by a kilometer-thick ice sheet.

Migration Across the Bering Land Bridge

Proponents of the theory of a northern crossing at the end of the last ice age, 12,000 years ago, generally scoff at the possibility of an earlier sea crossing. These investigators have a vast amount of archaeological evidence to support their theory, and have every reason to feel secure in their beliefs. Nevertheless, I believe that it is not only possible, but probable that both theories may be correct. The earlier arrivals by sea were probably very few people and with little experience as hunters. Most likely their impact on the fauna of the Americas was minimal. The major migration which had the violent impact on the Americas' fauna certainly came across the Bering land bridge 14,000 to 12,000 years ago. My reasons for this conclusion revolve around the fact that every species of large animal—those over a metric ton—in both American continents quickly became extinct in the wake of the human migration from the far north to the tip of South America.

Extinctions of Large Game

Once the land bridge was complete large mammals spread in both directions in a great interchange of fauna. Several million years earlier, ice age cycles had begun affecting climate and sea levels on the planet. If we put the date of the final closing of the isthmus at 2.4 million years ago, we can calculate that there have been 24 ice ages which were endured by most of these large species. In actuality, these ice age cycles may have begun as early as 10 million years ago, meaning that these species, while still on their respective continents of origin, may have been subjected to its effects for as many as 70 to 80 times prior to the completion of the Central American land bridge. Then, at the end of the last ice age, about 11,000 years ago, all became extinct in less than 1,000 years. The largest surviving mammals were members of the deer family and the bison. Large mammal extinctions occurred only in the Americas. As renowned anthropologist Richard Leakey writes in *The Sixth Extinction*, 57 species perished at the end of the last ice age, whereas during the previous 20 to 30 ice ages only 50 species perished. What was different about this ice age? The answer seems obvious: human hunters.

Experienced Hunters and Naive Prey

Humans evolved in Africa, expanded into the Fertile Crescent—

between the Tigris and Euphrates Rivers—and from there into Europe and Asia. As their populations grew and competition for food increased, early humans migrated farther and farther from their origins. Those who eventually populated America had to fight their way across Asia and up through Russia and Siberia, enduring very harsh climates and sparse food supplies. These people did not farm, but certainly gathered roots, leaves, fruits, and other plant parts to supplement their diets. They did not domesticate animals, with the possible exception of the dog. Their primary source of sustenance was meat from animals which they hunted and killed. For more than a million years on three different continents, these humans evolved and developed the physical and mental attributes necessary for locating, stalking, and killing large game.

Most of the animals in the Americas, on the other hand, had evolved in the absence of humans. A few animals probably migrated across the Bering land bridge during previous ice ages, but most of those would have continued to evolve for thousands of years in the absence of the threat of human predators and would have lost any instinctive fear of humans. Biologists have long known that fauna which evolves on islands in the absence of humans shows no fear of people when the two eventually come face to face. Darwin remarked on this phenomenon upon his arrival on the Galapagos Islands. This fatal naiveté was certainly characteristic of American game animals at the end of the last ice age.

Some scientists argue that severe climate changes at the onset of the warm interglacial period caused the mass extinctions. In my opinion this assertion borders on the ridiculous if it is proposed as the sole cause of the extinctions. Nevertheless, we can assume that rapid warming at the end of the last ice age certainly did affect the vegetation on which large herbivores subsisted, and this may have weakened populations of these species, making them more vulnerable to other stresses.

We see a scenario emerging. Bands of tough, agile hunters, experienced in the use of sharp, efficient weapons, arrived in North

America about 11,000 years ago to find abundant large, slow-moving game; animals which harbored no instinctive recognition of the much smaller humans as top predators. The resulting slaughter is easy to imagine. Richard Leaky, in *The Sixth Extinction*, quotes paleontologist Paul Martin from the University of Arizona who calculates that within 350 years the first Americans had migrated south to the Gulf of Mexico and had expanded to a population of about 600,000. In less than 1,000 years they had reached the tip of Tierra del Fuego and had a population in the millions. By then all the mastodons, mammoths, toxodonts, giant sloths, giant bison, and saber-toothed cats which had previously preyed on the large herbivores were gone. The largest animals to remain were bison and several large members of the deer family, which seldom reach a metric ton in weight. These species were later arrivals in America, having evolved together with humans in Asia before migrating to the Americas over the Bering land bridge during earlier ice ages. They may have retained a certain degree of instinctive wariness of human predators.

Leakey refers to other mass extinctions at other times and places that also coincided with the arrival of humans. Australia was once home to numerous species of very large animals. Several species of kangaroos, which were the most agile and best able to escape bands of aboriginal hunters, are the largest to survive. This great extinction, which affected 85 percent of Australian large game, took place approximately 60,000 years ago, shortly after the first humans arrived on that continent. The first humans arrived on New Zealand's shores a mere 1,000 years ago. Mammals were absent from the large island, but most of the niches they would normally fill had been occupied by flightless birds, many of which were quite large. In a couple of hundred years all were driven to extinction. Africa, the home of most of the world's truly large game, was also the birth place of humans. There, our distant ancestors evolved together with these beasts, allowing each to develop defenses against the other. For that reason much large game survives in Africa to this day. Sadly the advent of high-caliber weapons is challenging the survivability of many of these large animals.

Clovis People

Discovered at a site near the town of Clovis, New Mexico, the first physical evidence of human presence in North America consisted of finely crafted projectile points chipped from glassy stone. Many sites, dating between 9,500 and 8,000 years ago, with similar points have been found together with bones of mammoths, mastodons, giant ground sloths, and horses in both North and South America. The North American locations tend to be older than the South American ones, indicating that the mass migration of humans moved from north to south. To my knowledge no sites have been dated in Central America, but numerous projectile points similar to Clovis points have been found in many different locations, including Turrialba and Arenal in Costa Rica. They have also been found at Lake La Yeguada in Panama where the following scenes might have taken place about 10,000 years ago in a climate still cool from the receding glaciers. Where today there are tropical rainforests, the vegetation at that time would have more closely resembled a montane forest like those of Cerro de la Muerte, Chirripo, and Monteverde.

❖ ❖ ❖ ❖ ❖

Burikao, leader of the small hunting band, paused in the shade of a gnarled and weathered oak. The rest of the group cautiously emerged from the forest. The men scanned the shoreline, awed by the body of water. A light mist hung over the water, reluctant to dissipate and rise into the soft rays of morning sunlight. They had seen the vast waters of the sea, but this body of water was different. Land was visible in the distance on all sides. "The gods have created this place," declared Burikao. "As surely as the sun crosses the sky, the hunting gods have guided us to this magical place. It is an omen. The hunt will be successful. Of that I am certain."

The hunters stood on a small rise, surveying their surroundings. All were short by modern-day standards, heavy set with thick stout legs and arms. All had coal black hair hanging more or less to their shoulders in ragged, tangled locks which had been hacked off with the sharp fluted edge of a glassy stone. Facial hair was nonexistent, but thick curly hair covered parts of their arms and legs. Hairy chests were covered with apron-like furs bound on the sides with strips of leather. Burikao stood out from the rest with his magnificent apron fashioned from the skin of *jaguao*, a large spotted cat. The hunters scanned every visible nook of shoreline, searching for game. The people needed meat. Over a week ago, they had finished eating their last kill, a giant ground sloth which they called *cuclao*.

"Koiba," said Burikao simply, nodding at a young man of no more than 14 years. Koiba glanced toward the leader, who pointed upward with his thumb. The boy leapt onto the buttress roots and scampered up the bole of the oak, nearly 15 times his own height and into the orchid-laden crown. From his observation post the young hunter could see much more of the extensive lake shore than his tribesmen. "*Tofanto*," he called after only a moment. Koiba pointed in the direction where he had sighted game and quickly descended to the base of the tree.

"A big one, around the next bend near the mouth of the stream," said Koiba. "One *tofanto* is apart from the group, foraging at the edge of the woods." Koiba related the exact position of the toxodont he called *tofanto*, a large herbivorous mammal weighing well over a ton and reminiscent of the rhinoceros.

Burikao listened carefully, then turned and set out at a fast pace along the shore. Eleven hunters followed in single file. After several hundred paces, the band rounded a bend, and the creature came into view. Standing at the edge of the stream in a mucky cove with mud up to its knees, the *tofanto* was grazing on some grassy plants. Another dozen of the magnificent animals were foraging at least 150 paces

back into the clearing. The Clovis hunters focused their attention on the lone beast. Knowing from experience that *tofanto's* sense of vision was limited, they weren't concerned it would spot them. Burikao wasted few words in explaining the hunt strategy. It was a practiced technique they all knew and had often used successfully on large game. One of the youngsters, a boy of nine, was sent to bring the women, children, and elders who would help butcher *tofanto* once the hunters had killed him. Burikao was confident the hunt would result in a carcass. The hunting gods had guided the band to this place of unparalleled beauty, where game was plentiful and the forest rich in other foods. There was no doubt in his mind that the gods would provide his people with a successful hunt and plenty of meat for all.

The sun was already a quarter of the way into its arc across the sky. The boy wouldn't return with the others until much later in the day. He wouldn't even reach the camp of the previous three days until the sun was directly overhead.

The hunters split into three small groups. Four men carefully skirted the lake shore, passing less than 50 paces from *tofanto*, staying close to the water and crouching low to the ground. A second group entered the forest and maneuvered into a position very close to and in front of *tofanto*. The third group stayed with Burikao and quietly made their way through the forest to a point on one side of their prey. By the time the second two groups were in position the first had made its way around the clearing and into the forest at a point about 15 paces from *tofanto's* tail.

Quiboo, leader of that group of four, gave a shrill whistle characteristic of a common forest bird. Upon hearing the signal the three hunters of the second group emerged from the forest and began to taunt the toxodont, shouting and throwing sticks which bounced harmlessly off its tough hide. *Tofanto* snorted and tossed his head. The distraction gave Quiboo the opportunity he needed to slip unseen into the soggy ground behind the beast and work his way closer. Kamuk followed, three steps behind. Both hefted spears longer than themselves, tipped with sharp, shiny points as large as a man's hand.

Tofanto began pawing the ground with one front foot, splattering mud, while raising and lowering his head and snorting loudly, all of his attention focused on his tormentors. He rubbed his head in the mud, then raised it slightly above a puddle and shook it from side to side, still unaware of the two stalkers behind him.

Although not as close as he would like to be, Quiboo took advantage of *tofanto's* rage, which was focused on the other hunters. The lithe-bodied, spear-toting hunter took four long quick strides through the swamp and drove his spear into the left hock of the toxodont, where it sliced through cartilage and scored the bone, then continued on through into the mud, lodging tightly in the crack of a partially submerged tree. The thrust failed to damage *tofanto's* Achilles tendon, as the hunter had intended. *Tofanto* bellowed with pain and fury as he whirled to attack the hunter, but faltered on the injured leg.

In a vain attempt to escape from the enraged beast, Quiboo dropped the broken spear and ran toward the forest, lifting his feet high in the sticky muck. Quiboo's back foot caught in the mud and down he went. He tried to crawl through the soft wet earth to safety, but *tofanto's* broad feet were better suited for swampy terrain than the man's. *Tofanto* almost reached the scrambling hunter when Kamuk attacked from behind, holding his spear tightly while driving it into *tofanto's* damaged leg just above the hock, completely severing the Achilles tendon. The leg collapsed under *tofanto's* weight. Rage turned to frenzy as the beast awkwardly lurched forward in a three-legged effort to reach Quiboo. Kamuk made a second thrust inflicting a deep wound on the tendon of *tofanto's* good leg. A rapid second jab finished the job. *Tofanto's* momentum carried him one last step forward, far enough to plant a front foot on Quiboo's ankle. The beast's entire hind quarters collapsed into the mud.

While the hunters surrounded the toxodont, Quiboo was dragged from the mud by two of his companions. Burikao gave a nod to Quetzar. The large burly hunter clad in the fur of *ursuk*, the bear, stepped forward carrying a heavier spear than those used by Quiboo and Kamuk. Holding the weapon tightly in both hands with the end clamped firmly under his arm, Quetzar made a short, powerful lunge, driving the sharp point into the base of *tofanto's* neck, rupturing veins and arteries and embedding the spear deeply in the fallen animal's chest. *Tofanto* wagged his head from side to side in one last, futile attempt to inflict damage on his killers. The head, longer than Quetzar's arm, dropped heavily into the mud.

The hunter stepped forward, cupped some of the blood in his hands and brought them to his mouth to drink the warm red liquid. Then he threw his hands into the air and screamed in triumph, proclaiming his superiority to the gods and all of nature. In a few seconds the life-blood of the mighty beast spilled into a muddy pool, filtering through the wet earth and forming a thick reddish-brown paste. The other hunters walked up and placed their hands on the fallen ungulate, basking in the exuberance of the kill. Some turned to help Quiboo, moving him completely out of the swamp and over to the edge of the forest.

The pain in his broken leg was insignificant compared to the realization that he would never hunt again. At best Quiboo's leg would heal well enough that he could still travel and lead the nomadic life of his people while serving them in some other capacity, such as crafting and hafting the stone points so important to their survival. But no longer would he share in the glory of the hunt. At worst, he would be left behind as the tribe moved on, and would perish alone, victim of a large cat or of *tinuu*, the giant carnivorous bird.

When the sun had descended a little more than half its downward arc, the rest of Burikao's people, 28 in all, arrived at the hunt scene. The hunters had already partially dismembered the toxodont, but were unable to work efficiently for they needed the specialized blades, half as long as a man's forearm, that the women brought from the old camp. An older woman went about starting a fire from coals she had carried in an earth lined bag made of animal hide. Others quickly set up crude shelters within the shade of the oak forest at the edge of the swamp, near the scene of the kill.

With most of the people at work, the prey was cut into large pieces and carried to drier ground. Some of the workers stuffed small pieces of raw flesh into their mouths as it was being cut, but most of the meat would be cooked or cut into strips and dried. The hide was scraped clean with stone scrapers and given special treatment to preserve it. Though too heavy for the nomads to carry in one piece, parts of the thick tough skin would be used for bindings, cooking vessels and carrying packs. The thinner, more flexible belly hide was used to make clothing and cut into strips for binding. The round bones were shattered for the marrow inside, and the rest were fashioned into various kinds of tools. Little was wasted.

Krebok, the shaman, an elderly man of 32, examined Quiboo's leg. Fortunately it was a clean break between the ankle and the knee. Working quickly with the confidence that came with experience, Krebok set the break and bound it by wrapping a fresh piece of Tofanto's hide around the lower limb, leaving the knee free to flex. The binding was reinforced with pieces of Tofanto's rib to form a support not unlike a present-day walking cast. As the swelling in Quiboo's leg subsided, the hide dried and shrunk, thus remaining snug around the break. The accident would not result in the hunter being abandoned to the whims of the harsh world. Burikao's people would remain at the present site in makeshift shelters for about a week, or until the meat was gone. Nuts and tubers from the forest would supplement their diet; the climate was too cold for most fruit. Hopefully, more large game would be found around the sacred body of water. By the time they were ready to move, Quiboo would be able to follow. Before too long he would no longer need the cast, but his leg would never serve him as it had prior to his accident.

❖ ❖ ❖ ❖ ❖

The Clovis point of Quiboo's spear remained stuck in the log buried in the sticky muck where it would be discovered more than 10,000 years later by a student of archeology from a place of learning located in a faraway land. No bones or other evidence remained to tell the tale of the hardy people who survived harsh conditions at the end of the ice age by hunting many species of large game.

Changing Climate and Early Agriculture

Paleobotanists are able to identify the different types of pollen deposited in layers of sedimentation of a known age, recreating a picture of how the vegetation at a given location changed over time. One such location that has been studied extensively is Lake La Yeguada in north-central Panama.

The record of pollen grains and other particles in the sediment layers show that about 8,500 years ago, approximately 2,500 years after the Clovis hunters depicted above killed the toxodont, the climate had warmed considerably. The oak forests disappeared and were replaced by tropical forests similar to those of today. By 6,500 years ago, pollen from plants that may have been cultivated for food began to appear in the corresponding sediment layers. A millennium later large carbon particles indicative of burning that would be associated with slash and burn agriculture increased notably. Additionally, certain mineral deposits within the layers of sedimentation indicate increased rainfall and runoff, suggesting an increase in deforestation in the watershed of the lake. We can imagine the following scenes taking place.

* * * * *

The rapidly rising thermal updrafts caused by the warming rays of the midday sun tossed *jarpoa*, the majestic eagle, to and fro as if he were a mere brown and white feather floating on an unsteady breeze. The illusion of fragility cloaked the power within the mighty wings capable of supporting and guiding the large bird in a powerful dive from great heights; vise-like talons with sufficient strength to snatch a treetop prey and pry it from its perch; a sharp, curved beak capable of breaking the creature's neck; and again wings with enough reserve to fly away, lifting a burden greater than the raptor's own weight. The eagle's shadow skimmed the forest canopy, his sharp eyes searching the branches for unsuspecting prey. The mere sight of *jarpoa's* shadow was enough to create panic among sloths and monkeys, driving them from the crowns of colossal rainforest trees to the relative safety of the middle and lower branches.

The scene below, however, offered the eagle little chance of snatching a meal. Humans moved within a clearing, as ribbons of smoke drifted on the breeze, tracing winding trails across a nearby stream. The great bird banked and glided in a wide arc across the stream and out to the place where the bubbling flow mixed with the still waters of the massive lake. More humans moved within another clearing dominated by several large brownish-colored cones and a fire in the center. Puffs of smoke rose and dissipated in the air above the settlement. A line of humans moved down the shore, their heads and backs covered with the leaves of an oily fruited palm. The mighty eagle's shadow crossed the figure of a man standing alone atop a log, surveying the lakeside scene below.

From his position on the fallen trunk, its surface whitened and worn smooth by pounding rain and searing sun, Burkoa's imposing form faced the rising settlement. His shiny black shoulder-length hair enclosed a rounded face with almond-shaped eyes, a small rounded nose, thin lips, and slightly receding chin. His smooth brown skin, broken by an occasional wrinkle, was lighter in shade than the eagle's dark brown feathers and absent of any trace of hair. The man's maturity was obvious, but his tough, muscular body spoke of health and strength, not of age. The beautiful spotted fur of *pardauo*, the ocelot, covered Burkoa's loins. The fangs of *nauyaca*, the bushmaster snake, adorned his ear lobes, and four claws and two fangs from *tigrudo*, the jaguar, were held snugly around his neck by a thin piece of sinew. The rest of his body was bare, including his large calloused feet. He would normally feel contentment watching his tribe erect a new village at this sacred spot, where the forest gods had blessed them with plentiful game and fruit, but an inkling of ill-being pervaded Burkoa's spirit. Later he would consult with Krebao, the shaman.

Burkoa observed his people at work, each doing what he or she did best. Young men filed past him carrying palm leaves to the partially constructed village. Others had scaled the palm trees, cut the leaves with coarse stone hatchets and dropped them to the ground. When Burkoa's father, Burduo, was the headman, perhaps 20 years earlier, his people had planted the palm trees. The distance was considerable, and thatching the large rounded frame shelters took time, as progress was limited by the supply of leaves.

Each shelter was formed by placing 12 to 20 poles in a circle, the ends meeting and crossing in the center at a point twice as high as a man. The cone-shaped frame was then covered with palm leaves. Each boy half dragged and half carried three of the cumbersome leaves, making no more than five trips per day. As many as 40 leaves were needed for each family dwelling. Upon arrival at the site of the new village the boys piled the leaves between several shelters in various stages of construction. The builders, older and more experienced than the leaf carriers, were sitting on logs, waiting for the thatching material.

The two men and their apprentices had built many villages, as the tribe usually moved three to four times each solar cycle, traveling with the seasons, abandoning their palm thatch structures and building new ones at the next location. The seasons dictated where abundant food would be found. Their sustenance, both vegetable and animal, came from the forest. Each four-season cycle—dry, to intermediate, to wet, to intermediate and back to dry—was equal to the time it took the sun to journey from the far south, all the way to the north and return again in a full cycle.

A few older women and young children were gathered near the center of the rising village. The flames of a large cooking fire danced under *tasau*, the wild pig, suspended on a spit. Curitoba tended the fire. The matron of 33 years flexed her nostrils, inhaling the delicious aroma of fat droplets sizzling and spattering on the hot coals of the fire. With her status as mother of Burkoa's oldest children, she could choose the chores that suited her. Cooking was her joy. She selected just the right combination of peppers and herbs to flavor each dish.

Another woman sat nearby grinding the starchy pulp of a small tuber between two flat stones worn smooth by the flow of the stream over many years. Younger women worked outside the village planting gardens of arrowroot, squash and plantain. Others scoured the forest for edible fruits and nuts. Near the end of their stay at the lakeside village the women would plant several different kinds of palms in the garden clearing. These trees would be utilized by their children and grandchildren in future years.

Palm was an important source of both food and building materials. The peach palm with its spiny trunk provided large bunches of starchy fruit as well as a delicious and nutritious palm heart. Very old peach palm trees—more than 50 seasons—provided the hard, long-fibered wood the men used to fashion barbed points for arrows and fishing spears. Other palms provided matting for sleeping pads and fiber for twine used to fashion hammocks and baskets. Still others could be tapped for sap which was fermented into an alcoholic *chicha*. Some of the palms grew wild, but most of the ones used by the tribe had been planted in years past by the mothers and grandmothers of those present now. Women were gatherers, planters, cooks, and also raised the children. Men were hunters and builders.

Kamquok emerged from the forest walking in an odd gait, half saunter, half limp. A ragged, cherry-red cut spanned his right thigh. A dog followed at Kamquok's heels. Over his shoulder hung a large reddish-colored monkey. The tall stout man of 19 approached Curitoba where she stood tending the cooking fire. He tossed the monkey on the ground. The dog made a move toward the dead primate, but Kamquok sent it scurrying away with a swift kick of his calloused foot. His smooth, dark body was naked except for a small loin cloth made from the tough skin of *tamodoa*, the giant anteater. "I bring more food, Mother," he exclaimed proudly. "*Mikotuok* is so foolish. He came trembling into the lower branches of the tree when the shadow of *jarpoa* swept over the canopy. My arrow was waiting for him."

47

Curitoba smiled at her son, and glanced at the cut on his leg. It wasn't deep, but the edges were red and swollen. Seeing his mother's glance Kamquok said simply, "claw vine," referring to a wire-like vine laced with wicked, hooked barbs that could easily rip a person's skin. Untreated claw vine wounds often became infected, a serious problem indeed. With the arrogance typical of a headman's son, Kamquok turned and sauntered off toward the shaman's shelter. He was aware of his value as a skilled hunter, providing much meat for the tribe, but even more important, he would soon be the headman. The people had visited the lake 16 times since Burkoa, Kamquok's father, had become headman. Kamquok knew that Burkoa had been about his own age at the time. Before many more visits to the lake, Burkoa would step down and hand leadership over to his firstborn male child.

Krebao, the shaman, examined the nasty gash which zigzagged across Kamquok's thigh. An oily substance secreted from the claw vine barbs always irritated such cuts, causing discoloration. The medicine man didn't have to ask how Kamquok had received the wound. He grunted and motioned for the hunter to sit. The shaman rummaged around in his things looking for the right substances to treat the wound. Having arrived at the site only three days previous, Krebao's collection of herbs was not yet arranged in any semblance of order, nor had he found time to go collecting in the jungle around the new village site.

Finally he found everything he was looking for. First the shaman flushed the wound with a clear liquid taken from the hollow center of a large palm fruit, and then he sprinkled a brownish-gray powder into the cut. Krebao allowed the corners of his mouth to crack in a devilish grin, knowing how harshly the powder stung, and knowing also that Kamquok would proudly refuse to flinch. Next the shaman filled a wooden bowl with water which he heated by pulling hot stones from the fire, holding them between two sticks and dropping them into the water. Each stone fizzled as it touched the liquid, sending up a short burst of steam. Once the water was hot, Krebao added

several dried leaves from a rubbery plant, each a little smaller than his hand. He then added more hot stones. The shaman told Kamquok to lie on his good side. Again using the sticks, he retrieved the now scalding hot leaves, one at a time, and applied them to Kamquok's gash, covering the wound from end to end. Krebao told the hunter to remain still, then turned and walked out of the hut.

He walked through the village toward the forest edge. A group of children stopped playing and stared as he walked past. Though not the oldest member of the tribe, the medicine man had been to the lake 37 times in as many solar cycles. His mother had been shaman before him and had passed on her knowledge as it had been passed on to her by her uncle. Krebao's woman and children had been killed in a mudslide many solar cycles ago, leaving him without kin to whom he could transmit his knowledge. Instead, Burkoa's daughter, Kamquok's older sister, Curitea, had been the medicine man's apprentice since shortly after the accident. Krebao was content that the sacred knowledge of his craft would be secure and not misused. The girl was serious and talented. Curitea's father, Burkoa, as the headman, had absolute authority over members of the tribe, but that authority did not extend to the shaman. Krebao, as spiritual leader and healer, commanded a mixture of respect, fear and awe that transcended authority. He was like a power unto himself.

Physically unimposing, the shaman moved lightly on a thin frame and limbs. His cocoa-colored skin was accentuated by his black hair and coal black eyes so deep, so vast, that a person could become lost simply by looking into them. His small hands and thin fingers were like those of a young girl. A single feather of *jarpoa*, symbolizing winged power, was fixed snugly into a leather head band. Three streaks of red ocher lined Krebao's cheeks on each side of his nose, which was pierced by a single bushmaster fang. On a leather thong around his neck dangled a small oyster shell, the silvery mother of pearl glimmering as it caught a ray of sunlight. In each ear, dangling on a piece of sinew, were three brilliant red and black seeds. The sleek, deep brownish-black loin cloth, fashioned from the skin of *lontura*, the river otter, and adorned with three bright, green and red tail feathers from *caicota*, a splendid bird of the deep forest, rippled and shimmered with each step as Krebao made his way across the village.

At the edge of the clearing the shaman found the mound of dirt he had seen the day before. A line of red ants carrying crescent-shaped leaf fragments were entering a hole on one side of the mound, while ants without leaves emerged from the same tunnel. The shaman stamped his foot hard on the ground near the opening. A stream of ants, triple the size of the leaf carriers, rushed out waving their long curved pincers. With a practiced hand, Krebao quickly picked up the soldier ants one by one and popped them into a tube made of a hollow cane, which he closed with a wooden plug.

Returning to the hut, the shaman found that Kamquok had not moved. The leafy poultice was still in place. The shaman took one of the soldier ants from the tube and replaced the plug. With the other hand he peeled back a leaf, to uncover the top end of the wound. With his free hand Krebao pulled the two sides of the wound together and holding the soldier ant from the back, he moved its head directly over the line where the two pieces of skin joined. The shaman touched the line with the center of the ant's head. The oversized pincers snapped shut, digging into the skin and clamping both sides of the cut together. The medicine man then broke away the ant's body, leaving only the head with its pincers tightly embedded in the skin.

The shaman repeated the process using all the leaf-cutter soldiers, leaving a string of sutures the entire length of the cut. He wrapped the wound with dry palm matting taken from the fold where the palm leaf meets the trunk. Krebao warned Kamquok to tread lightly on the leg for a couple of days so that the sutures would remain in place. He knew the hunter would obey without question. Both had seen untreated claw vine wounds that slowly rotted and turned green before the people died.

Kamquok walked slowly from the shaman's hut and went in search of his woman, Rinau. He found her with several other women engaged in the initial stages of planting a garden. Always the stealthy hunter, Kamquok appeared like magic at the edge of the clearing. The women and toddlers weren't immediately aware of his presence. He smiled as he espied Rinau. She was still beautiful at 16, though she had borne his two children. She was shorter than Kamquok, who stood at 19 hand-widths. Their younger child had been born during the last dry season, five moons previous. Like everyone in the tribe, Rinau was clothed only in a loin cloth made from the hide of *tepesqoa*, the paca, tan splotched with white. Her two children were playing with others under the watchful eye of a girl of no more than eight.

The women tilled the soil in the forest patch the men had burned three days ago. Nine moons earlier, the last time Burkoa's people had lived by the sacred lake, the men had girdled all the unwanted trees using rough stone hatchets, leaving them to wither. The trees had since died and lost their leaves. Upon the tribe's return three days ago, dry wood was piled at the bases of the tree trunks and fires were lit. In a short time the flaming trees fell to the ground and continued to burn. A few of the trunks were still hot with smoldering coals as the women worked.

The soil was not cleared of vegetation, nor was it turned. Instead, the vines and existing plants were parted and seeds or shoots of the crop plants set in the ground. Plants of the banana family were placed as root nodules, and cuttings of arrowroot stem were stuck into the ground where they would take root, while squash was planted with seeds. Herbs used for flavoring and others for medicinal purposes were planted together with the food plants. One shrub provided greens which could be eaten either raw or cooked. The garden was a harmonious mixture of plants, each of which complemented the others. Almost no weeding was necessary, and insects were not a problem. Most pests are specific to a single species of vegetation, so nothing harmful was able to get a foothold. One camphor-like plant even repelled potential insect pests. Half a dozen fruit-bearing trees had been left standing in the clearing. These were another source of food for the tribe.

Kamquok moved toward his woman. Rinau saw him approaching and smiled. She noticed his slight limp and bandage. "You're hurt," she said simply.

"It's nothing," he boasted. "A small gash from a claw vine. Krebao already treated it." He looked out at the planting. "The garden is coming along nicely. It's too bad we are so far from last season's location. There should be mature yams and plantains in the old garden."

"Yes," she replied, "Morkao and Lenau went there yesterday and brought back some arrowroot and greens, but the plantains had already been taken by the tribe who built their village near where we lived last season."

"I can't stay any longer. I have to go check some traps," he stated flatly. Kamquok smiled at Rinau and walked away, a look of smugness on his face. He knew the garden provided certain tasty foods for the tribe, but felt secure in the knowledge that it was he and the other hunters who provided most of the food. The tribe could survive on the bounty of the rainforest alone, but it could never survive on the meager plantings of women.

Burkoa was still on the shore, now sitting on the log as the sun dropped closer to the surface of the lake. *Jarpoa*, the eagle, no longer soared above. The thermals had dissipated into the cool afternoon air. Several kinds of monkeys foraged and squabbled in the tops of tall trees along the stream. Burkoa nodded but didn't speak as Krebao approached. The two elders sat in silence surveying the activity around the clearing. A long-legged white bird circled once and descended into a swampy area at the far side of the village. The headman turned to look out across the lake. Krebao, the shaman, followed his gaze. Another village was visible in the distance. Burkoa broke the silence with a simple phrase, "Too many people."

The people from the other village had taken advantage of some of the slow maturing food plants from Burkoa's tribe's garden of the previous season. Not only that, but the other tribe had cut thatch from the palms planted by Burkoa's ancestors, and there might not be enough left to finish the huts for this season's village. Burkoa's people might have to search the forest for other palms, an arduous task. But the land here was fertile, and the game plentiful. He felt confident the gods would favor his people. Burkoa was pleased that he had chosen this site nine moons earlier when his people had left this sacred lake and moved to another site at a lower elevation with abundant fruit and seeds for the dry season. An uneasiness stirred in his gut. "Too many people," repeated Burkoa, still looking across the lake. Until now he had never lived within sight of another village.

* * * * *

Harpy eagle. *Photo: Chepe Nicoli*

Over 5,000 years later, an ornithologist discovered the descendants of *jarpoa*, the great eagle, and gave the species the name "harpy" because it reminded him of a Greek mythological monster with the head of a woman and the legs and talons of a bird. Today these magnificent birds are nearing total extinction. 🐛

3

Kobuka

The Seeds of an Idea: Growing Food

As is the case today and all through history, social development does not occur at the same pace everywhere. Throughout Central America we find great disparity in the levels of civilization attained in different regions and different tribal cultures. In some cases this divergence can be attributed to differences in the terrain and available resources, but in most cases the reasons are as obscure as the causes of the extreme difference in wealth and poverty that exist in the world today.

While the pollen record in the layers of sedimentation of Lake La Yeguada tell us that 5,000 years ago people were beginning to utilize simple agriculture in order to supplement their diets, the archaeological record about 500 kilometers farther north, in what is now southern Costa Rica, speaks of a much more primitive culture. Several sites, described as "rocky shelters," in Coto Brus, along the Térraba River and near Buenos Aires, have been studied. Initial investigation has yielded evidence that 5,000 years ago the inhabitants were still living a nomadic life, depending entirely on hunting and gathering for their subsistence. With the demise of large game several thousand years earlier, people were forced to subsist on smaller and more diverse species. Many of the stone tools from this period reflect the change in the source of meat. Some of the scrapers, wedges, and hatchets appear to be designed for woodworking. This seems to indicate that many of the instruments utilized in everyday life were fashioned from wood.

It is important to keep in mind that, to date, little archaeological investigation has been done. Scant physical evidence is available and most of the details of how people of this period actually lived is open to speculation. The following depiction of life in southern Costa Rica five millennia before the present, could have taken place in any one of several different locations in southern Costa Rica.

❖ ❖ ❖ ❖ ❖

Kobuka sat cross-legged on the hard ground near the fire, the light skin of a brocket deer draped over her shoulders. The rocky shelter offered little protection from the chill. She shivered slightly as the dew laden morning air caressed her bare arms. A flat stone lie directly in front of her legs and a small bowl made from the skin of a wild pig in her lap. To her left was a pile of palm fruits. Taking a fruit in her hand and placing it in a slight depression on the stone, the girl separated the fleshy outer layer from the hard nut with several blows from a round stone. Pushing the oil laden pulp to one side Kobuka then cracked open the hard oblong nut with one swift blow, tossed the pieces of shell into the fire, then whisked the starchy center of the nut into the bowl. She repeated the process over and over. Each nut held a small amount of edible meat in the center. Several hundred nuts would barely yield enough to fill the small bowl. The oily husk was not entirely useless. The fleshy part was chewed thoroughly and the oil swallowed, but the coarse fibrous part was spat out and discarded. Everyone used the oil laden pulp to groom their hair and rub on their

skin. It gave protection from the constant washing of rain during the wet season.

Kobuka had gotten into a regular rhythm of her chore, and the palm nut meat was accumulating in the small bowl. The light exercise warmed her body and she shed the deer skin shawl. Still considered a child, Kobuka wore no clothing at all. Sunlight filtered into the rocky crag, lightly warming her smooth coffee-colored skin and glistening off of her coal black hair. Kobuka's plump figure was beginning to reveal the first signs of approaching womanhood. She had already fashioned a loin cloth from the skin of an agouti. It was the only thing in the whole world she could call her own.

Rinoa entered the shelter, a bag with more palm fruits slung over her shoulder and a baby on her arm. The older woman emptied the bag onto the dwindling pile at Kobuka's side. Neither spoke. Toruko, a young child, appeared in her wake with a large oblong pod under each of his tiny arms.

"Kobuka, look." The child held out his hand to show her the treasure, but the cacao pod, too large for his hand, fell to the ground, bounced off the slanted face of a rock at the entrance of the shelter and bounced down the hill, rebounding off each stick and stone in its path, finally hurtling out into the air and crashing, with a resounding thud, into the dry hollow trunk of a dying tree. The seeds and the slimy pulp scattered over the ground.

"Toruko, look what you've done," scolded Rinoa. "I knew I shouldn't have let you carry the cacao pods. Now run down there and pick up those seeds."

"I'll help him," exclaimed Kobuka, leaping to her feet and following on the heels of the youngster before the older woman had a chance to protest. She scampered down the slope, romping, racing and teasing Toruko all the way to the bottom.

Sunlight warmed the open ground around the dead trunk where Kobuka and Toruko searched for the almond-shaped cacao seeds. They quickly scooped up one big clump at the base of the tree, but most of the seeds were scattered. The two scurried around the small clearing, searching and retrieving. They were about ready to return when Kobuka spotted one last seed. As she reached to pick it off the ground, something made her hesitate. The seed was starting to open and tiny folded leaves of a new plant were trying to force their way out. A strange awareness entered her mind, an inkling of an idea.

Though hazy and poorly defined, the young girl attempted to clarify her thought. "If I leave that seed here, next year it will be a tree and someday the tree will have more cacao pods with lots of seeds. But if we take the seed and eat it now, we will only be able to eat one tiny seed." She left the sprouting seed where it lay. Then she noticed half a dozen similar seeds among those they had collected. She quickly separated them from the rest. Making a depression in the topsoil with her toe, she placed a seed in the small hole and shuffled loose soil over the top with her foot. Each of the six cacao seeds Kobuka planted around the small clearing.

"What are you kids doing down there?" came the harsh voice of Rinoa. Quickly they scampered back up the hill.

Kobuka pondered the recent change in Rinoa. In the last two moons the older woman's attitude toward her had changed. The adolescent's mind wandered back to the time when she had lived with her own family. It seemed like a long time, but in reality was only nine moons ago. She remembered the day Chirupu and Quapoo had come into her family's camp while her father and Groto were out hunting. The two strange men had taken Kobuka. Neither she nor her mother resisted. It would accomplish nothing but a hard smack on the side of the head.

When she was very young Kobuka had seen another girl from her family's band taken away by strange men. Nutoa, the woman who slept with her older brother Groto, had been brought into their family camp as a young girl. It was the way things were done. Chirupu and Quapoo had taken her to their shelter. Rinoa had been unfriendly at first, but soon warmed up and the two had become friends. Kobuka worked hard and tried to please. Chirupu always slept with Rinoa and paid little attention to Kobuka, but recently she had noticed the big man looking at her differently. At times his eyes would linger, and the expression on his face reminded her of the way he looked at Rinoa when he wanted to play.

"Maybe that's why Rinoa is mad," thought the girl. "Maybe she thinks Chirupu wants to play with me." Her face flushed at the thought. "But why would that make a difference. Chirupo plays with Cubitira sometimes, and Rinoa doesn't get mad at her."

Kobuka and Toruko reached the top of the hill and stepped under the rocky overhang. "Stupid children," grumbled Rinoa.

The youngsters carried the slimy bunch of cacao seeds mixed with dirt and leaves in their hands. They placed the mess on a flat stone and picked it as clean as they could, before popping the rest into their mouths. The three sucked the slimy, sour-sweet outer coating from the seeds before replacing them on the stone. Using a stick to push the hot end of a large stone out of the fire, Rinoa dropped the cacao seeds into a depression where they sizzled, and for a few minutes, she stirred them with a flat wooden spoon-like tool. Then she scraped the seeds off the hot stone and into a crude wooden bowl. As soon as the cacao seeds cooled, Rinoa took the first one, cracked the now brittle outer shell and popped the light brown center into her mouth. Kobuka helped Toruko with his. Though quite bitter, the flavor had a strange appeal and soon the cacao seeds were gone. Cacao was considered a delicacy. Kobuka moved away from the fire and went back to cracking palm nuts.

The sun had passed the highest point in its arc and begun its descent when Chirupu, Quapoo, and Cubitira returned. As he walked past, Chirupu grabbed a handfull of the nutritious palm nut meat, nearly emptying the bowl Kobuka had worked so hard to fill. Cubitira was carrying the limp body of an iguana. She liked to go hunting with the men, taking the opportunity to scout out new sources of edible fruits and nuts and medicinal herbs. Although she often returned with some special treat, today she carried only the dead reptile.

Cubitira entered the small rock-walled hollow and went to the corner where she and Quapoo slept. Rummaging through a deer skin bag she found a sharp-edged chip fashioned from a piece of turtle shell. Holding it carefully between thumb and index finger she made one long slit along the iguana's soft underside. The plump belly opened to reveal about 20 yellow globs. Shells had not yet formed around the nearly formed iguana eggs. Cubitira held the reptile out to Chirupu who grabbed half of the eggs and scooped them into a leather bowl like the one that held the palm nut meat. Quapoo took a smaller portion and Rinoa and Cubitira shared the rest. The older woman shared her portion with Toruko and the baby. Kobuka continued her rhythmic cracking of palm nuts. She had not expected a share of the iguana eggs, and wasn't overly disappointed. Still, seeing everyone else eat and hearing the enthusiastic sounds of slurping, she could imagine the taste and the slippery feeling of raw eggs sliding down her throat.

Kobuka jumped at the unexpected touch, then quickly turned her head to see Chirupu's outstretched hand with his bowl and the slimy remains of broken yokes covering the bottom of the bowl. So strange was the gesture that, at first, Kobuka couldn't comprehend the offering. She looked up at the big man's smiling face. He nodded toward the bowl, "Here, take it." Still not believing what was happening, Kobuka reached out, zombie-like, and took the bowl. Her eyes looked down as she scooped the remains of the iguana eggs into her mouth. Then she tipped the bowl up and finished the rest. The girl returned to cracking palm nuts, careful not to meet Rinoa's eyes.

Cubitira took the iguana out into the forest to finish cleaning it. If she left the entrails too close to the shelter it would attract scavengers. Returning to the shelter a few minutes later, she used fibrous twine made from *piñuela* leaf to fasten the reptile's head to a stick on one side of the cooling embers and the tail to the other. She added several small pieces of wood to the hearth.

Chiripu told of the tracks they had seen, of *tzmin*, the tapir, a mother with a baby. During the day the pair slept in the forest near a creek. Tomorrow, he explained, they would hunt the baby, which was almost weaning age and bigger than *tayassu*, the wild pig. The plan was for three of them to drive the two tapirs into the creek and downstream into a narrow canyon. This morning they had felled a tree across the stream. The trunk would block the large female's exit from the canyon, but allow the passage of the young. Quapoo, the hunter, would wait at the barrier and spear the young beast as it squeezed under the log. They would allow the mother to escape. Attempting to kill a full-grown tapir was risky. Rinoa turned her head to face Chirupu, with a look of puzzlement. "Four people?" she asked. Chiripu turned and smiled at Kobuka. "Yes, four," he stated flatly. "Kobuka will be going too." Rinoa's face dropped in a sad look of understanding. She turned and left the shelter.

Upon hearing Chirupu's words, a flush of excitement tinged with fear penetrated to Kobuka's very core. Things were changing much too fast for her to comprehend. She didn't know what would be expected of her or how to act. This was all new ground and she had no one in whom she could confide. Chiripu stood up and stretched, then moved over to his leafy sleeping mat and lay down. Soon he was snoring. Kobuka went back to her palm nuts.

Quapoo, who had returned from the morning hunt with a piece of a peach palm trunk, retrieved three stone chisels and a couple of wedges from the same bag where Cubitira had found the turtle shell chip. He moved out of the shelter into the shade of some overhanging branches. Kobuka could see him from where she sat. A jagged scar marred the smooth brown skin of his left shoulder. A wider, uglier scar broke the smooth muscular lines of his lower thigh on the same side. Cubitira had told her it had been made by the sharp tusk of *tayassu*.

The young man laid the piece of wood, as wide as his hand, lengthwise on a fallen log. He called to Cubitira to help him. Kobuka watch the couple work together. The woman had a slightly lighter complexion, more of a cocoa-brown. She squatted on slim, muscular legs and held the piece of peach palm wood. Quapoo studied the stick for a moment and placed his first wedge near one end and whacked it solidly with a rounded stone. A second wedge was placed in the split, about two hand-widths away. Again he drove it in with the stone hammer. He retrieved the first wedge, moved it forward into the split and repeated the process. This time the stick split all the way to the end. Quapoo repeated the whole routine on the remaining part of the stick until he had three wooden shafts, each as long as his arm and thicker than his big toe. He examined them carefully and seemed satisfied. Using the larger of two stone chisels, he went to work on the shafts, smoothing the rough edges and shaping them into the points he expected to drive into *tzmin* tomorrow.

Cubitira sat on the log and watched Quapoo work, sometimes helping hold a stick or reach for a tool. Kobuka watched the couple work together. The two were close to the same age. Cubitira had confided in her that they had met on the beach two turtle seasons ago. Her family band had been camped near Chiripu's band. Cubitira had just begun wearing her loin cloth. When Chiripu's band left the seashore camp, Cubitira went with them. Quapoo didn't have a woman of his own and she started sleeping with him from the first day. Kobuka didn't have words to describe the relationship between the couple. She only knew that they seemed to belong together and worked together almost as one person. Pensively, the early adolescent contemplated a foggy and poorly understood vision of her own future. ꙮ

4

Petroglyphs, Headhunters, Grave Robbers

Indigenous Occupants of Southwestern Costa Rica

Quite a few years ago someone wrote a short article for the local Dominical newsletter in which they stated that at the beginning of the twentieth century the area around Dominical was covered with forests and inhabited by indigenous people who lived at peace with each other and in harmony with nature. The person who wrote those words obviously hadn't studied any of the available evidence about indigenous people in this part of Costa Rica and was writing straight from his imagination. The part about the area being covered with forests is true, but at the beginning of the last century, there were no Indians here at all, and hadn't been any for at least 400 years. Far from living in peace with their fellow man, the last Indians to inhabit this region were headhunters who practiced slavery and human sacrifice, and constantly warred with each other. Whether or not they lived in harmony with nature is a matter of debate, but they were fairly advanced agriculturalists and must have done a lot of deforestation in order to grow the corn that was the basis of their diet. Nevertheless, they probably didn't do as much damage to their environment as we have.

I first visited the National Museum in San Jose in 1971. At the time I was familiar with both Guanacaste and the Caribbean zones, but had never been to the southern Pacific part of the country. One of the things about the museum that stuck in my mind was a map of Costa Rica containing information about the pre-Columbian cultures. Curious about the people who had once inhabited the areas where I worked, and knowing there was a richness of artifacts and grave sites in both places, I studied the map with great interest. Most of the country was colored and covered with drawings and notations, but there was one large blank area located on the southern Pacific coast with only a notation saying there had been no indigenous peoples in that particular area. I remember thinking how strange that the whole country had been rich in pre-Columbian culture, but one area apparently had no indigenous people at all. The blank area was centered around what is today known as the village of Dominical.

The following year I visited Hacienda Barú for the first time, and later came to work and live here. On my very first trip to the hacienda I learned there were a great many pre-Columbian grave sites on the property, many of which had been dug up by grave robbers. Rumors abounded of elaborate gold ornaments that had supposedly been found in these graves. I later learned there was much more here than cemeteries. Artifacts of all kinds were found on the property and in the surrounding area. Additionally there were petroglyphs (figures etched on rocks) and a little to the south of Dominical some strange stone spheres were found. These spheres have been found only in the southern Pacific region of Costa Rica and have puzzled archaeologists for years. I remember thinking about the blank white area on that map and wondering why the people at the museum thought this region had been devoid of Indians. When I visited the museum 10 years later, the map had been changed. The once white area now had some coloring, and the notation read that nothing was known about the indigenous peoples who once inhabited this area.

There has never been a formal archaeological study of the area between the Savegre and Uvita rivers, though there have been some extensive studies in other parts of the southern zone, such as Quebradas, Rey Curre, and the Diquis Valley. There have also been several informal visits to Hacienda Barú by museum personnel. From these and other sources we can glean certain information and draw some tentative conclusions about the cultures that once thrived in the area. In reality though, there are more questions than answers.

If we take a map of Central and South America and draw boundaries between the different indigenous cultures, the Central American civilizations of the Aztec and Maya would be found to the north and the Inca empire to the south. In between these two is an intermediate area where no great civilization existed and the indigenous people were considerably more primitive. There were no cities, pyramids or great temples, and the people lived in tribal fashion. This area includes the eastern half of Nicaragua, all of Costa Rica except Guanacaste, all of Panama, Venezuela, and Colombia, and the northern part of Ecuador.

Archeologists and anthropologists have classified the pre-Columbian inhabitants of this intermediate area in three different categories which correspond to three different chronological phases. The first archaeological record of nomadic bands of hunter-gatherers in Costa Rica and Panama dates to about 8000 BC, but this doesn't rule out that they may have been here earlier. The first evidence of village dwellers in southern Costa Rica—people who practiced an agriculture based primarily on roots and tubers—appears in the record around 1000 BC. That phase, called Aguas Buenas, lasted until about 700 AD when the record shows a sudden jump to a higher level of social organization, and an agriculture based primarily on corn. Far more evidence exists about this Chiriquí phase. In addition to the archaeological record we have a great deal of information about the Chiriquí people from the records of the Spaniards who lived with them and observed them at the time of first contact and in the years that followed.

The first Spaniards to explore the Pacific coastal lands of Costa Rica were led by a man named Gil González Dávila. When their ship was damaged they were forced to abandon it near present-day Golfito. From there the group consisting of sailors, soldiers, and priests walked northwest up the coastline for three years until they were picked up by another Spanish ship in what today is known as Guanacaste. There was little information in their log about the area around Dominical, but they did mention that no indigenous peoples inhabited the area between the Barú and Savegre rivers. This is surprising because those of us who live here today know from an abundance of evidence that there must have been a sizable population here at one time. So what happened to them?

According to archaeologist Dr. Francisco Corrales, the petroglyphs and most of the grave sites on Hacienda Barú belong to the Chiriqui phase, meaning they are between 500 and 1,300 years old. There may be some evidence of the Aguas Buenas phase as well, but Dr. Corrales didn't find any of it on his two brief visits here. We have counted 268 open grave sites on Hacienda Barú; open because they had been excavated by grave robbers prior to my arrival. There is a similar density of pre-Columbian cemeteries on all of the neighboring properties. Yet when González Dávila came through here in 1522, there were no people in this area, an observation reflected in the old museum map.

One theory as to why no one was here in 1522 is that the Quepo and Boruca tribes were constantly at war, and the area between the Barú and Savegre rivers was kind of a no-man's land. A second theory is that small pox had killed a large portion of the population prior to 1522, and the few survivors returned to tribal centers such as Quepo or Boruca. Though no Spaniards had yet visited the area, diseases may have preceded them. The first case of small pox was recorded in Mexico in 1508, and according to Inca records, the first case appeared in Peru in 1518, four years prior to the arrival of the Spaniards. I find this theory the most plausible.

So what were the Chiriqui people like, and how did they live?

The late Chiriqui were organized into chiefdoms each of which consisted of several tribes. In most cases a tribe was one village, but sometimes large villages or population centers were shared by more than one tribe. The Quepo, near present-day Quepos, were a chiefdom and the Coctú in the Diquís Valley were another. In other cases one tribe might occupy several villages. Each tribe had its own chief, but several tribes would unite to form one chiefdom. Each chief would still reign over his own tribe, but only one chief presided over the chiefdom. The chiefs controlled the distribution of food and other goods produced by the tribe, like pottery, textiles, tools, adornments, or weapons. Their agriculture was productive enough so not everyone in the tribe had to work at growing food, which in turn allowed people to specialize.

Tribe members lived in thatch-roofed structures, some of them large enough to house over 400 people. These structures were heavily fortified for protection against attacks by enemy tribes.

The family structure was complex, but was definitely matrilineal. People didn't marry within the same family. The female members of the family all stayed together in the same village and the men came from other villages and tribes. If a man was injured or fell ill, he convalesced with his own family rather than staying with his wife's people. Chiefs inherited their authority from the maternal side of the family.

Each tribe had a shaman who was both religious leader and medicine man. The shaman could be either a woman or a man. In some cases the shaman and the chief were the same person. Most of what we know about the everyday life of the Indians comes from the writings of Jesuits. Very little is known about the religious beliefs and practices of the Indians, however, since these priests did everything possible to suppress the tribal religions and replace them with Christianity. It is known that like many tribal religions they had many different gods. It is also known that some religious rituals required human sacrifice.

The sacrifice victims were prisoners of war, and it appears that the main purpose of tribal wars was to acquire prisoners who could be enslaved and later sacrificed. Only the women and children were kept for such purposes. The men were beheaded and the heads kept as trophies by the victors. It was believed that if a warrior killed and beheaded an enemy and kept the head as a trophy, he would acquire the power that had once belonged to the slain warrior.

The petroglyphs found throughout this region have always been a mystery. Though most anthropologists believe that they have something to do with religion, nobody knows for sure. Theories abound. Some people think they are star maps done by extraterrestrials. Others think they are village maps. It has been noted that petroglyphs are surprisingly similar regardless of where on the planet they are found. This has given rise to the theory that designs etched in the stones were inspired by psychedelic experiences. Apparently many of the shapes found on the petroglyphs are similar to the shapes that are formed on the human retina during a psychedelic experience, and all of the disparate cultures where petroglyphs are found were known to have used psychedelics.

Today at Hacienda Barú people often take a tour called the Pre-Columbian Rainforest Experience which allows people to see Indian cemeteries, artifacts, and petroglyphs firsthand. They see a sample of the archaeological evidence, hear the story of what we know about the pre-Columbians who once lived here, and glimpse how they probably lived.

I find the history of these first Costa Ricans fascinating. Perhaps someday funds will be available for the national museum to do a formal study of the area around Dominical and fill in some of the blank space on Costa Rica's pre-Columbian map. 𝒞

5

A Place Where Nobody Wanted to Live

How Geology Shapes the Earth and Our Lives

I used to think of geology as the study of rocks and geologists as scientists who sit in laboratories looking at rocks with magnifying glasses. Then I discovered how geological events have influenced my life and how certain geological features of the region around Dominical have affected the way in which the area developed. I am referring primarily to the coastal ridge, that small mountain range that parallels the coast from the Savegre River to the Térraba River, and the Tinamastes Ridge. Let's look at how the geology has affected the people, communities, and governments here ever since the area was first inhabited by humans about 5,000 years ago.

The first humans to inhabit the region were hunter-gatherers who lived a nomadic life and took refuge from their environment under rocky outcrops and in other natural shelters. These people didn't form settlements, but moved from one place to another depending on the season and the abundance of food in different localities. By about 1000 BC early agriculturists began migrating into the area from the south. Though the earlier ones probably hunted and fished to supplement their diets, these people acquired most of their sustenance by cultivating crops such as cassava and corn. The most attractive areas and the first to be settled in what is now southern Costa Rica were the fertile lowlands of the Diquis Valley around present-day Palmar, the Valley of the General around present-day San Isidro, and the lowlands that extend north and west from the Savegre River around present-day Quepos, Parrita, and Jaco. These were the three areas where people congregated, eventually forming villages and what could be called tribal centers. Each area developed into chiefdoms which later became known as Brunka, Boruca, and Quepo.

Early settlements expanded and more land was cleared. Eventually the cultivated land stretched far from the tribal center, reaching all the way to the mountains. Though farming was possible in mountainous areas, the land was less productive and harder to work. As populations grew, these agriculturists did eventually move into the mountainous areas to grow their crops, but the hilly land was marginal at best and the most prized land was still to be found in the valleys and alluvial plains.

At first nobody paid much attention to the strip of lowland between the coastal ridge and the sea, stretching from the tribal center in Palmar to the one in Quepos. It was narrow, swampy, bisected by many rivers and interspersed with estuaries and mangroves. The soil was either very sandy or made up of heavy red clay with little fertile loam. The ridge that rose up a short distance from the coast was steep and broken and offered little to farmers. But as populations expanded, people did settle and farm the narrow strip of flat land and eventually even the coastal ridge and the hilly land farther inland. The Brunka people moved northwest and the Quepo southeast along the coast. The Borucas moved out to the coast and probably occupied the land between present-day Ballena and Dominical.

By the time the first Spaniards arrived in Costa Rica, the coastal lowlands and much of the coastal ridge had probably been deforested. Abundant evidence tells us that there were a lot of people here, probably more than today. They were agriculturists who grew food to survive, but they couldn't do that in the forest, so they must have destroyed it. Unfortunately the official Spanish journal, where the events of the first expedition to this coast in 1522 were recorded, didn't mention anything about the vegetation of the coastal ridge or whether or not it had been deforested. As mentioned in chapter 4, the first Spanish expedition found no people at all between Barú River and Savegre River. My personal opinion is that the population was devastated by diseases, especially small pox transported overland by the indigenous people. The few survivors probably migrated back to the tribal centers, which would also have been greatly reduced in population, leaving plenty of fertile agricultural land for those remaining. The coastal ridge would no longer have had anything to offer the Indians and it remained uninhabited for 400 years.

It had nothing to offer the Spanish either. A colonial government was established and all of Central America became part of the Kingdom of Guatemala. Costa Rica was a marginal territory within that kingdom, and the southern part was a marginal region within the territory. The coastal ridge wasn't even worth mentioning. Nobody had the slightest interest in it.

In 1821, when Costa Rica, along with the rest of Central America, gained its independence from Spain and became the Republic of Costa Rica, the coastal ridge area was still unpopulated. Don Hipolito Villegas, who was born in Uvita in 1910, says that when he was a child no other people lived in the area. He remembers that a couple of times a year a lone Indian would visit the family, and just as often his father would walk for a full day to El Pozo, a small village which would later become known as Puerto Cortés. Other than that, the family had no contact with other people. Not until about 1918 would people begin filtering into the region along the coastal ridge.

A cantón is a Costa Rican territorial and political division similar to a county in the United States. The cantón of Osa was named after the last chief of the Brunkas. It became a cantón in the year 1915, with the first municipality, or seat of local government, in Buenos

Aires (later moved to Puerto Cortés). Pérez Zeledón was to become a cantón in 1931, with San Isidro as the seat of government. Aguirre, with the municipality located in Quepos, didn't become a cantón until 1948.

It is worth noting that the seat of each of these three local governments is a great distance from Dominical. We started out as a marginal region for early indigenous agriculturists. We later became a totally ignored area in a marginal region of a marginal territory in the Kingdom of Guatemala. Next we were to become a largely ignored part of three *cantones* that correspond to roughly the same areas once occupied by the Brunkas, Borucas, and Quepó. In other words, we were the last place anybody wanted to live, mainly because of that steep coastal ridge so close to the sea.

Naturally, living at the far end of three cantones involves certain hardships. The sparse population means few voters, so the municipality has little incentive to spend money on infrastructure or solve the area's problems. Chronically bad roads and bridges were perpetual problems. Dominical is in Osa cantón; Hacienda Barú, where I live, is in Aguirre; and the upper half of the village of Barú is in Pérez Zeledón and the lower half in Aguirre. If you own land in more than one cantón you have to go to more than one municipality to pay taxes or get permits. There are, of course, certain advantages, the main one being infrequent visits by municipal inspectors and tax collectors. Another big advantage is that it has been one of the last areas of interest to developers and one of the last to suffer the environmental and social impacts of rapid development. Up until now the area has remained relatively undeveloped compared to places like Manuel Antonio and Jacó.

Beginning in about 1920 the area was exploited and deforested for farming and cattle ranching. As machinery became available, deforestation increased and the devastation became severe. By 1985 most of the steep hillsides had been cleared and were barren and eroded, and all of the arable land in the lowlands was being exploited.

Prior to that time nobody had attached any particular value to the fantastic ocean views from the coastal ridge.

Today this geological attribute is the primary factor in determining land values. For the first time in history, the coastal ridge, with only a narrow strip of land separating it from the sea, is a place where everybody wants to live, and this has brought a rapid influx of people into the zone, people who have no interest in farming and ranching, but who like seeing monkeys, toucans, and the tropical forest. The forests have been recovering since 1985, and, at the same time, roads and bridges have been built, basic services are improving, and the population is growing. My hope is that it doesn't grow so much that recent environmental gains are lost to rampant development. That is the biggest challenge the residents of the coastal ridge face today.

Just imagine, all of this because of the collision of a couple of tectonic plates about 100,000 years ago. Who says geology is a boring subject? 🐾

Part Two

6

Carmelita and El Tigre

A Grand Journey

"Baarooom" resounded the hollow buttress-root of the *chilamate* tree with each blow of the thick branch. Carmelita wasn't sure which was louder, the "baarooom" of wood against wood or her pounding heart. Again she struck the hollow root. "Baarooom."

"Carmela, honey," her father's voice penetrated the darkness before his silhouette came into view. "What's wrong? What's all the noise?"

"Oh, Daddy," she cried, "thank God you've come. It's *el tigre* come to eat our pigs, and probably me too. It was my turn to guard them. I tried to scare him away, but he keeps coming closer."

The elder Morales took the club from her hand and struck the root, "baarooom…baarooom…baarooom." He paused to listen. Nothing. "Baaroooom…baarooom…baarooom." Another pause. Again he hefted the stout stick, but before he could swing, the jaguar's snarl ripped from within the jungle through the coal black night, close-by, too close. He began shouting, "Go away, devil cat. Leave our pigs alone."

Carmela saw the torches first. "Daddy, everyone's coming,

look!" Her uncle was in the lead followed by a cousin, her mother, and aunt. Flames danced off the ends of their short torches, tufted with dry, frazzled pulp from the *chonta* palm and dipped in fat. They surrounded the pigs, singing and shouting at *el tigre*. Again her father struck the root. "Barooom…barooom." Time passed; the small group continued their vigil. Finally came the mighty roar of *el tigre*, this time from faraway. *There'll be another time*, it seemed to bellow. Carmelita's father patted her head. "You've done your job well, honey. Go get some sleep now."

Nine-year-old Carmela Morales was traveling with her father, two uncles, an aunt, and three cousins. They were herding 19 pigs from their home in Boruca to the market town of San Marcos de Tarrazu, near Cartago. The incident described above took place in Barú, where two rivers meet, in the year 1909. It wasn't the only occasion the jaguar tormented their camp. In fact, before the trip was over, *el tigre* would pick-off, one by one, eight of the pigs, including the only two belonging to Carmela's family.

Carmelita's size belied her strength. She left Boruca bearing half a *quintal* (50 lbs) of corn to feed the family's pigs during the journey. Each day, as the grain was consumed, her burden lessened slightly. The mud was sometimes so deep and Carmela's load so heavy that she sank to mid-thigh in the mire, yet she never dropped the corn and never complained.

From Barú they walked inland and upward to the Valley of the General (current day San Isidro) and from there over the Cerro de la Muerte. One of Carmela's uncles was bitten by a *lora*, a poisonous snake, near a place called División, and died two days later. Ironically, his death marked the beginning of the worst part of their journey, the six-day trek over a high mountain peak.

Carmelita had never imagined that such bitter cold and freezing rain existed. The coldest nights in Boruca were nothing like this. Even though everyone slept huddled together to conserve body heat, Carmela still shivered all night and slept little. Keeping dry was the worst problem. One night they stayed at a house built by the government for use by travelers. The house was packed with people going both directions, and there was a fire. That was the only night she slept soundly, curled up on the floor. The next morning the sun was shining. Carmelita helped gather firewood to replace what they had burned the night before. Another night they found a small rocky cave, in which they would barely fit, and were able to keep out of the rain and wind, but most nights they just slept under the dense forest cover in the highest, driest places they could find.

Three weeks later the tired and bedraggled bunch of Borucans arrived at the bustling market town of San Marcos with 11 pigs. All that remained for Carmelita to sell was a quarter of a *quintal* of corn, and only because of the loss of the two pigs that would have eaten it.

Carmela received five *centimos* for her corn, one-twentieth of a colon. Her father let her spend it all. "You carried the corn, the money's yours." San Marcos was a fascinating place with so much to see and buy. Finally she decided to spend her money on two kilos of salt and some candies for her mother and a necklace of pretty stones for herself. The group of Boruca Indians left San Marcos three days later, loaded with merchandise. They had driven a hard bargain on the pigs and finally settled on a price of 1.25 colones for each one. Salt, machetes, and other iron tools were their primary purchases.

Carmela Morales reached home again 47 days from the day she had left Boruca on that grand adventure. She passed away in Boruca 84 years later in 1993. None of her friends or family can remember ever hearing her complain about anything during the entire 93 years of her life. 🐢

Note: Recounted by Marina and Margarita Morales, granddaughters of the late Carmela Morales.

7

The Coming of the Bongos

Early Settlement of the Coastal Area

On the Pacific coast of Costa Rica, about 65 kilometers south of Quepos, lies the thriving little town of La Uvita and the Ballena Marine National Park. Anyone who has ever flown over La Uvita in an airplane will probably agree that the most striking feature of the area today is Uvita Point, more commonly known as the "whale's tail." The resemblance to the tail of one of these great cetaceans is remarkable and quite appropriate as the Ballena Marine National Park acquired its name because it is often frequented by humpbacked whales.

Seen from the air at low tide Uvita Point might also remind you of the letter T, the base of which is attached to the shore and juts out into the sea. The line across the top of the T could be thought of as a 300-meter wall that holds back the waves. That wall, referred to locally as *el tombolo,* is actually a rocky reef, and the stem or base that connects it to the shore is a sandbar. Only when the tides and swell are large do the waves wash over the top of the reef. The waves breaking around of the ends of the reef create a gentle swirling action that carries sand inward. Over time this sand has accumulated to form the sandbar and the curve on the inside of the whale's tail. At high tide the sandbar is usually covered with water, and with very high tides the cross on the "T" will be submerged as well. Even when below the surface of the water, both are visible from the air.

At the beginning of the last century, Uvita Point had a much different appearance. The entire structure was considerably higher, and the cross on the T, rather than looking like a whale's tail, was more like an island connected to shore by a straight stretch of sand. Even the highest tides of the year did not wash over the reef and the sandbar was almost always passable. In fact people referred to the reef at the end of the sandbar as "the island." At that time it was comprised of about one hectare (2.5 acres) of land with a diversity of vegetation including white cane, Indian almonds, coconut palms, gourd trees called *jícaro,* and the notoriously poisonous *manzanillo* tree. Right in the middle of the island, near the point where it connected to the sandbar, stood the most prominent feature of the area, a giant fig tree of a type known locally as *chilamate.*

Although the exact year is not known, we can estimate that José María Villegas was born sometime between 1880 and 1890. We do know that his birth took place in a small shack on the island near the

Uvita Point is often referred to as the Whale's Tail.

chilamate tree. No information is available regarding his parents or when and how they came to live in the area. In all likelihood, José María's birth was not recorded, nor was he issued a birth certificate. We do know that his son, Hipolito Villegas Escalante, was born in 1910 in a shack on the shore. At that time there were no other inhabitants in the area. The closest thing to a neighbor was a lone Boruca Indian who visited the Villegas family about twice each year. A rudimentary horse trail to San Isidro was barely passable, but very seldom did anyone from there venture as far as La Uvita. Hipolito, later known fondly as Don Polo by friends and family, remembers that he was seven or eight years old when several other families moved into the area and became the Villegas's first neighbors.

Everyone in the Villegas family worked hard to eke out subsistence from the land. Their methods were much the same as those of the indigenous inhabitants 400 years before. The forest was cut, burned and planted to cassava (a starchy tuber), bananas, plantains, corn, beans and rice. Additionally there were two milk cows, five to ten pigs, and a flock of chickens. After several years of farming the same patch of land, soil fertility dropped, resulting in lower crop yields. At that time the land was abandoned and another agricultural patch was cleared and burned. The previous clearing was used for pasture for the cows until the secondary forest growth completely took it over. The pigs were usually kept in a nearby pen and fed bananas. Free roaming pigs soon became dinner for jaguars and pumas. The big cats were even known to take the pigs right out of the pen, even though it was located only a few meters from the house. The chickens roosted under the same roof as the people.

Each time an agricultural plot was abandoned, so was the home. This meant the Villegas family had to build a new one- or two-room shack every three to four years with materials provided entirely by Mother Nature. The basic frame structure was fashioned with poles cut from any one of several different readily available tree species. Fibrous bark, stripped from the trunks of other species of trees, was twisted and used as twine to tie the poles together and form the framework of the house. Other plants with fibrous vines, leaves and stems were used as well. Once the frame was complete the roof was thatched with the most readily available thatching material, usually the leaves, of either the native royal palm or the *suita* palm (sometimes called rooster tail palm). Then the walls were fashioned with any one of several different materials: white cane, *viscoyol* cane, and *chonta* palm were the most common. Availability was the important thing as all material had to be carried on the men's backs. Dried fibrous canes were tied into place both vertically and horizontally to form a lattice work. Then the lattice was lined with *chonta* palm trunk. The soft, pulpy trunk of this versatile palm tree was flattened by blows from a heavy stick, then dried and tied to the canes to form a crude wall board.

An open cooking area was constructed outside of the house, but still attached to it. Cooking was done over an open hearth called a *fogón*. Being roofed but open allowed smoke from the cooking fire to escape and lessened the danger of a serious fire. Family members slept on the floor on sleeping mats made from the same soft *chonta* palm trunk used on the walls. Durability was not a consideration when building a home, as a new structure would be erected the next time a new agricultural plot was cleared.

Location was an important consideration when building a house. Not only did it need to be near the agricultural plot, but also near a stream or river. Cooking and drinking water had to be carried to the house and clothing and kitchen utensils were carried to the stream for washing. All nine family members went to the stream to bathe. In addition to Hipolito's parents, there were five boys and two girls in the family.

The food grown in the agricultural plot and the pigs that were fattened with bananas formed a large part of the Villegas family's diet, but, like the indigenous peoples before them, the rainforest was also an important source of sustenance. The *chonta* palm, in addition to the uses mentioned above, also provided a delicious and nutritious palm heart. The *ojoche* tree provided nuts, and numerous other trees provided edible fruit at certain times of year. But the most important food provided by the jungle was meat, and the animals that provided it were abundant. Among the favorite sources of bush meat were two wild pig species: the white-lipped peccary and the collared peccary. Tapir, the largest game animals, were abundant, especially in and around water. The fruit-eating spider monkey was hunted for meat as were two raccoon-sized rodents, the paca and agouti. Hunting was not only important as a source of food, but fun and exciting and was one of young Hipolito's favorite activities. He claims to have killed three jaguars in his lifetime, the last in 1943. All three jaguar kills were accomplished with the help of hunting dogs.

El Pozo, the nearest village to the Villegas household, was a two-day walk down the coast to the south. At least once, and sometimes twice each year, José María and his older sons would herd a small group of pigs to El Pozo to be sold. With the money, they purchased the basic necessities that the jungle didn't provide. Their purchases, which were limited to items they could pack on their backs, included tools such as machetes, axes and shovels, cooking and eating utensils, materials such as cloth, thread and needles for making clothes, and bullets for the family's .22 caliber rifle, which was referred to as the *bala U*. The name comes from the cartridges which always had the letter U stamped on the bottom. The Spanish word *bala* means bullet.

The Villegas' first neighbors were three families of Panamanian origin who moved into the Uvita area when Hipolito was still very young. The Nicodemo López, Eucedio Centeno, and Andres Morales families settled in the fertile lowlands of La Uvita around 1918.

The Bongo Captains

Shortly after these three families arrived in La Uvita, another family sailed into Bahía in a long dugout sailboat called a bongo. Doña Antonia Rios Rios and her sons Daniel and Cristino settled in La Uvita around 1920. Cristino was less than a year old at the time. Both of the boys were sons of the legendary bongo captain, Simón Arzu.

While Simón sailed the coastline between El Pozo and Puntarenas, trading and transporting products of all kinds, Doña Antonia set about raising her family. This was the beginning of a new era for the region. With an outlet for the products that the pioneers produced on their small plots, and a source of the basic products that these families needed, isolated areas such as Uvita and Dominical became more attractive to settlers.

The boats that brought this progress to the region were made of very large tree trunks from the *jabillo, ceiba,* and *espavel* trees, all of which have straight, tall trunks that are nearly perfectly round. From 15 to 20 meters in length, 3 meters in width, and rigged with up to three sail-bearing masts, the bongos stopped at every suitable anchorage where there were inhabitants. With a favorable wind, the trip from Uvita to Puntarenas took only about 12 hours. The daring bongo captains made a business of transporting any product that the settlers produced and wanted to sell to the market in Puntarenas. There, the bongo captain sold the agricultural products the settlers had entrusted to him and purchased the items they couldn't acquire locally. These he carried back on the return trip. This advent of commerce into the region radically transformed the lives of the settlers from one small step above hunter-gatherers to that of producers, traders, and merchants, albeit on a very basic level.

So important was the service provided by the bongo captains that it attracted commerce from as far away as San Isidro in the Valley of the General. While the inhabitants of Uvita produced corn, beans, and rice to trade in Puntarenas, the farmers of San Isidro produced much more valuable products such as sugar, coffee, and tobacco. The high value of these products made it feasible to transport them on pack horses from San Isidro to Uvita, a two-day trip. Later, as the trails were widened and improved, much of the merchandise was carried in ox carts rather than pack horses. Although it took an extra day or two, the increased carrying capacity was sufficient to warrant the trip. Time was not a major factor.

Indeed, time wasn't really a factor at all, as the bongos didn't sail on any kind of a schedule. This lack of regularity created an opportunity for the inhabitants of the coast, many of whom went into the business of storing and handling other people's products. A farmer from San Isidro with a quarter ton of coffee for sale could transport his product to La Uvita by pack horse or ox cart, but then he might have to wait a long time for a bongo to sail into port. Not wanting to wait in Uvita for the next bongo, which might come by tomorrow or next week or next month, the coffee farmer would entrust his product to one of the local residents. Taking advantage of the situation, some of the Uvita residents built thatch-roofed storage houses where they received the merchandise from the highlands and held it until a vessel going to Puntarenas passed by. Usually the farmer would have a list of merchandise he needed from Puntarenas, and the intermediary would handle this merchandise as well. The Uvita residents charged for this service and, in so doing, moved up one more step in status. They began as hunter-gatherers, then became cash farmers, and now had become middlemen.

Bongos were able to load merchandise at several locations along the coast. Any semi-protected cove would work. El Pozo—today known as Puerto Cortez—and Puntarenas were the main ports, but Punta Piñuela, Punta Uvita, Puerto Nuevo, and Dominical—called Dominicalito today—were all places where merchandise was loaded and unloaded. Of these, La Uvita and Dominical were the most important. The next stop, 50 kilometers up the coast to the northwest of Dominical was Quepos, as there was no suitable anchorage in between. Quepos was destined to become a larger, more economically important port than any of the others, mainly due to the acquisition of large tracts of land by the United Fruit Company for the production of bananas. But that is another story outside the scope of this book. ❦

8

A Bad Day Fishing

Dealing with Life-Threatening Situations in Times Past

The excitement welled up in his chest from the moment young Nitos Gómez blinked the sleepiness from his eyes. He and his dad were going fishing. The youngster leaped out of bed, pulled on his clothes, and wolfed down his breakfast. "Slow down," reprimanded his mother. "You'll choke on your food eating so fast. Your daddy still has to milk the cows. You aren't going fishing for a while yet."

It seemed like forever, but in reality it was less than an hour when Nitos and Don Miguel Gómez started off for the Barú River where they would try their luck. Several of the fishing methods commonly used in the 1940s would today be considered unorthodox and in some cases downright illegal. Conventional fish hooks with bait were sometimes used, but more often than not, nets were extended across the river, poison was used to kill the fish, or dynamite was exploded in the water to stun them. The latter was the method that Nitos and Miguel would use today.

Twelve-year-old Nitos wasn't allowed to touch the homemade bombs, but he nearly shouted with joy to see the sparks fly when his father lit the fuse and heaved the baseball-like bomb in a long arc into a pool in the river. The seconds seemed like minutes until a muffled "bar...rooom" erupted, producing a spout of water that shot out of the pool like a geyser. Then he raced down to the edge of the Barú, dove into the water all the way to the bottom of the pool where the stunned and dead fish had sunk. He grabbed a fish in each hand, returned to the surface, threw the fish up on the bank and returned for more. On the second dive he found a lobster-sized crayfish and on the third a three-pound croaker. Most of the fish were croakers and snappers, but there were always a few of the big red crayfish. Once he had gathered all the dead fish, more than 20, Nitos and his father moved upstream to another pool.

The second pool was Nitos' favorite, as it always yielded something special. Last time they went fishing he scooped a five-pound croaker off the bottom, the biggest he had ever seen. Don Miguel and Nitos got everything ready. The boy waited excitedly as his father lit the fuse. But the sparks flew only for a second and then fizzled out. Don Miguel looked at the stubby fuse, but it showed no signs of life. "Must be bad," he grumbled. "I'll light another." Nitos relaxed as Don Miguel turned away and reached out to set the bomb with the bad fuse on a rock.

The sound of the explosion was deafening. Nitos felt the concussion from the blast, but was mostly shielded by his father. A pang of fear shot through his body followed by an intense desire to lunge into the protective arms of his parent, but at that moment Don Miguel turned around. Where seconds earlier there had been a wrist and hand, there remained only a blackened stump, ragged with burned and mutilated flesh, oozing with blood. Don Miguel's face was blackened and blistered and his clothing charred. Nitos' fear turned to anguish at the thought that his father might be snatched from his life by a cruel twist of fate. In a surge of comprehension, Nitos realized he had to take charge of the situation and get his father home. His father's life was in his hands. The boy swallowed his fear, bravely took the elder Gómez by his good hand, and began walking slowly toward the rancho where they lived.

Nitos wanted to run for help, but he didn't want to leave Don Miguel alone, so he stayed with his father and helped him slowly up the hill. They walked in silence. The courageous boy and the injured man, in a state of excruciating pain and on the verge of shock, took more than half an hour to traverse the 200 meters to their house. Once the rancho came into view Nitos began shouting. "Mami, come! Daddy's been hurt real bad! Come and help!" He was on the verge of tears, afraid she wouldn't hear his cries. But his mother did hear and came running.

They got Don Miguel to the rancho and made him as comfortable as possible. The heat from the blast had cauterized the stump, so blood loss was not a problem, but the elder Gomez' condition was still extremely serious. Nobody expected him to live until nightfall. Nitos ran out and found his brothers, Chuta and Evangelista, and the boys ran out to all the neighbors and spread the news. People came from miles around to say their final good-byes to Don Miguel Gomez, one of the first pioneers to homestead Barú and carve a farm out of the jungle. But he refused to die.

By noon the next day the family allowed themselves to hope. They talked of ways to deal with the situation. Don Miguel's condition was very serious, and they ruled out carrying him 35 kilometers to San Isidro on a stretcher. But he needed medical treatment soon. Finally it was decided that Fermin Mora, Don Miguel's son-in-law, would ride to San Isidro on horseback and try to get help. He left at four o'clock that afternoon and returned at seven the following morning. "Is he still alive?" was Fermin's first question.

"Thanks to God, he is still with us," said Doña Peregrina softly, "but he is weak and his arm is worse. I think the gangrene has gotten into it. But tell me please, were you able to get help?"

Everyone gathered around as Fermin explained the solution that he and the doctors at the hospital in San Isidro had come up with. "There is only one chance to save Don Miguel's life," he began. "They didn't have a doctor in San Isidro who could come with me, and besides, Don Miguel needs to be in a hospital. We called San Jose and hired a plane. Low tide is about 10:30 a.m., and that is the only time the plane can land. We need to get Don Miguel to the beach. We'd better get started…time is ticking away. Oh, I almost forgot. I promised we would pay the plane 100 colones as soon as it lands."

"We'll get it. I don't know where. God will help us. We'll come up with the money somewhere," said Doña Peregrina.

"We've got to get moving. The plane will be here in three hours," reminded Fermin.

Nitos and Chuta ran out and cut a couple of stout, straight sticks. They tied the sticks to both sides of a hammock. There was plenty of help from family and friends, and they took turns carrying a nearly comatose Don Miguel three kilometers from the rancho in Barú to Dominical beach. Neighbor and friend Eliecer Sibaja, who owned all of the land that is now Dominical, gladly loaned them 100 colones to pay the pilot. The plane landed on the beach that morning, loaded Don Miguel and took him to San Jose where he was transferred to San Juan de Dios hospital. The doctors amputated what was left of his right arm just below the elbow that same afternoon. He remained in the hospital for three weeks before he was released, but he still needed to get home. The Pan-American Highway was being built at the time, and he was able to hitch rides in several different construction company vehicles which took him as far as San Isidro. From there he walked the last 35 kilometers to his home in Barú where he lived for many years.

Don Miguel Gómez Chinchilla died in San Isidro de el General in 1995 at the age of 99. Neither he nor anyone else in the family ever again fished with explosives. 🐾

Note: Recounted by José María Gómez Adanís, known to his friends as Nitos, son of the late Miguel Gómez and Peregrina Adanís.

9

Stub-Tail

The Day the Crocodile Lost His Tail

The three friends had been fishing in the Los Burros pool on the Barú River since yesterday morning and had caught more fish than they could carry, mostly croaker. "My god, it's hot today," sighed Vicente. "I think I'll go for a dip." Stripping down to his jockey shorts, Vicente waded in thigh deep, pushed off the bottom and glided out into the pool.

The water looked so refreshing that Guido too began undressing. Joaquin just kept on fishing. "Hey, you guys," he groaned, "you're gonna scare away all the fish."

Suddenly something big broke the water and Vicente disappeared in a swirl. But before the turbulence subsided he surfaced and swam desperately toward his friends. Again the monster broke the surface, caught Vicente's legs, rolled and waggled in the water, and dragged him down, but again Vicente broke free, surfaced, and struggled toward the edge. Half-dressed and barefoot at the river's edge, Guido stared in horror at his friend's blood tainting the clear blue surface of the pool. Joaquin, fully clothed, rushed head-on toward the pool, raised machete in hand, while at the same time the monster again grabbed Vicente and began to roll and submerge. With adrenaline-charged courage and strength he didn't know he had, Joaquin lunged into the water and swung his long knife at the rolling beast. The blade penetrated the soft underside of the thick armored tail, severing more than half a meter. Vicente, traumatized and exhausted, surfaced once again. Joaquin stepped chest deep into the water, stretched a helping hand to his friend and pulled him safely to the edge of the pool. The crocodile headed downstream, oozing blood from the stub of its severed tail. Vicente was more frightened than hurt. His two friends helped him to his home two kilometers away. There his mother washed his wound and disinfected it with alcohol. He healed up just fine in a couple of weeks and was ready to go fishing again.

Don Nitos Gómez (who, as told in chapter 8, saved his father's life when the elder Gómez blew his hand off with a homemade bomb while fishing) remembers that it was about a year after Vicente's encounter with the crocodile that he and his brother Chuta were tending their banana plantation at the edge of the Barú, slightly up river from present-day Rio Mar, five kilometers downstream from Los Burros pool. Hearing a loud splashing in the river they went to investigate. No sooner had they reached the edge when Stub-tail attacked, leaping out of the water and falling against the sharply inclined bank, unable to reach the two men. Don Nitos remembers the crocodile being well over four meters long. Confident that Stub-tail couldn't reach them, the two brothers threw sticks and stones at the infuriated beast which eventually retired to a deeper part of the river and disappeared.

But everyone knew that Stub-tail was always lurking there. The crocodile is said to have attacked Juan Bautista Santa María as he crossed the Barú River on horseback, knocking the horse from beneath him. Both horse and rider managed to escape.

At some point in the 1960s Stub-tail left the Barú and appeared in the mouth of the Morete River, 20 kilometers down the coast to the southeast. He is reputed to have killed a man there, but considerable doubt surrounds the story. Some say that the man was murdered and the rap pinned on Stub-tail. The large American crocodile (*Crocodylus acutus*) with the stubby tail hasn't been seen for years. No one knows if it died of old age or migrated along the coast to another river, but regardless of its fate, Stub-tail will always be remembered in these parts and its descendants are certainly found here still. 🐊

Note: The attack on Vicente took place in the late 1940s. He lived to tell the story and eventually died in San Isidro at a ripe old age.

This crocodile, about 3 meters long, was seen along a Hacienda Baru trail.
Photo: Pamela Bergman

10

Markets and Wars

Big Incentives for Roads and Bridges

A round the turn of the last century, when people from the Valley of the General—present-day San Isidro—began exploring the coastal region around Dominical, they hacked a crude horse trail through the jungle to La Esperanza, and San Josecito, and finally arrived at the coast near present-day Uvita. From there another trail was blazed to Dominical, mostly down the beach. Juan Bautista Ceciliano was ten years old the first time he rode to the coast with his brother Otoniel and their friend Nosario Segura. The year was 1915. The trail was almost nonexistent in places, and they often had to get off their horses and chop their way through the jungle with machetes.

In the 1920s, as mentioned earlier, the sailing vessels known as bongos began transporting merchandise to and from the area. The existence of transport for products such as coffee, sugar, and tobacco to the market in the large port of Puntarenas provided a big incentive to farmers to widen and improve the horse trails so they would accommodate ox carts, which could carry more cargo than a pack horse.

War was another incentive to improve the roads. In times of war, roads become strategic even if they don't happen to be in the war zone. A road far from the fighting can be strategic if it is a supply route or part of some contingency plan. During World War II the United States government was concerned about defending the Panama Canal from the Axis forces, a difficult proposition without a land route from the US to the canal. At the time many regions in Central America lacked adequate roads. Completing the Pan-American Highway became a priority.

By 1940 a reasonably good road traversed the northern part of Costa Rica as far as the central plateau, and a narrow-gauge railroad connected the Caribbean coast with the capital, San Jose. But the southern part of the country was not accessible to motorized vehicles. Something had to be done.

In 1941 the Charles E. Mills Construction Company landed a great deal of heavy equipment on the beach in present-day Dominicalito and began building a road to San Isidro over which they could move more men and equipment.[2] Once in San Isidro, the company organized itself into two construction teams. One started building a road toward Cartago over the Cerro de la Muerte mountains, while another team started working toward Puerto Cortes, to the south. While all this was going on, a third crew had landed machinery in Puerto Cortes and split into two groups with one working toward San Isidro and the other toward Panama. By the time all of these crews met, the road would be complete.

The objective was to finish the Pan-American Highway (now called the Inter-American Highway). The road from Dominicalito to San Isidro was only a means of getting men and equipment from the coast to San Isidro. Once that highway was completed, the road to Dominical was more or less forgotten by everyone except the people of Dominical and San Isidro who used it. They repaired the road and kept it maintained, with only sporadic help from the government. Though the original road was rudimentary and the passage difficult, it nevertheless made possible the influx of a great many settlers into

---

2   Remnants of the steel girders from the temporary pier built for unloading the machinery were still visible up until about 1990.

the zone. It marked the beginning of the massive deforestation of the region by the people who moved there to farm and raise cattle. It also marked the beginning of the local eradication of several species of wildlife such as the brocket deer, white-lipped peccary, jaguar, and tapir.

That first crude road was very steep in several places, the worst places being Las Farallas between Barú and Platanillo, and El Alto de San Juan between Tinamastes and La Palma. On my first visit to Dominical in February 1972, the Las Farallas route had already been altered to avoid the steep hill, but we still had to deal with the incline at El Alto de San Juan. On a later trip, the first time I brought my wife, Diane, to see Hacienda Barú, the back door of our Land Rover popped open going up that steep hill, and our supplies fell out in the dusty road. Over the next three years, the road was rerouted around that steep part.

In 1972 there were only two bridges, one over the river at La Palma and another over the Guabo River at Barú. I'm not sure when the bridge in La Palma was built, but the bridge over the Guabo

Road building equipment working in the jungle between Dominical and San Isidro. *Photo courtesy of Evelyn King.*

River, just above its junction with the Barú, was constructed in 1956 and 1957. Prior to that time there was a cable car—like a box on a zip line—that allowed people to cross the river. Few other bridges were built until 1986, and until then most of the streams had to be forded. The only way to drive from Barú to Dominical was across a narrow suspension bridge over the Barú River.

In the year 1986, the road from San Isidro was paved and the remaining bridges were built. This brought more hunters into the region as well as an entirely new threat to wildlife: roadkill. With the old bumpy gravel road there weren't very many vehicles and they traveled slowly. The new paved road meant more people traveling a lot faster. The mutilated bodies of coatis, iguanas, anteaters, and sloths on the pavement became a common sight.

The large bridge over the Barú River at Dominical was built the same year, 1986. Prior to that time we could cross the river at a point about 300 meters upstream from the present highway bridge. The crossing was known as "El Paso del Guanacaste" because numerous guanacaste trees, with their enormous trunks and branches bigger in diameter than the trunks of most other trees, adorned the banks on the Dominical side of the river. This crossing was possible only at low tide and only during the driest times of the year.

Diesel vehicles were better than gasoline for crossing rivers, mainly because they don't have a distributor or spark plugs to get wet. But people with gasoline vehicles still needed to cross rivers and everybody had their own favorite technique for keeping the ignition system dry. Entering the stream on the run caused a big splash, and the spark plugs were almost certain to get wet. The first rule of crossing a river is to enter the water slowly and drive steadily to the other side, not too fast and not too slow. In high water, some people remove the fan belt so the fan won't splash water all over the engine. Another method is to put the vehicle in reverse and back through the water. Of course, it is always better to have four-wheel-drive, but not everybody did. Needless to say, getting stuck in the middle of a river or stream was a fairly common experience. People who owned farm tractors and lived near rivers made lots of extra money pulling stalled cars out of the water. Once in a while a vehicle would even get carried downstream.

In 1982 there was a very crude road going south to Uvita, and no bridges at all. That was the year the government began building the coastal highway from Dominical to Piñuela, about 15 kilometers south of Uvita. It took many years to finish the project, but by the middle of the decade there was reasonably good passage all the way to Puerto Cortes with bridges across most of the rivers. Going the other way, from Dominical to Quepos, the road had been passable for many years, but the only rivers with bridges were the Savegre and Naranjo. Those who lived near Dominical and needed to go to Quepos could only do so in the dry season, as it was necessary to ford 13 rivers and streams. This situation also had its advantages, mainly that municipal officials had a hard time getting to Hatillo and Barú to collect taxes and business license fees.

Again, it was the military that worked to improve the roads in rural Costa Rica. The 1980s were times of turmoil in Central America with civil wars raging in El Salvador and Nicaragua, and another on the verge of erupting in Panama. The US government was concerned about an alternate route through Costa Rica and decided to promote the building of bridges on the coastal route of the Pan-American Highway between the Savegre and Barú rivers. In 1986 we got word that the US Army Corps of Engineers would be coming to build the bridges.

Though Costa Rica was not directly involved in any of the civil wars plaguing the rest of the isthmus, public opinion was polarized regarding who were the good guys and who were the bad guys. In El Salvador, the Soviet Union supported the rebels and the United States backed the government. In Nicaragua the situation was reversed. Costa Rica was officially neutral, but everyone in the country had an opinion. As you might imagine, news that the US Army was coming to build bridges precipitated a tremendous amount of commentary and gave rise to numerous rumors. Those on the political left claimed that the soldiers who were coming were drug addicted, disease ridden, insane Vietnam Veterans who would wreak havoc in our communities, rape our women, and corrupt our youth. It was even claimed that most of them had AIDS. Those on the other end of the political spectrum claimed that the engineers were the salvation of Costa Rica. There were few opinions between these two extremes.

Soon after the engineers arrived, it became apparent there was nothing to worry about. Most of the men and women were much too young to have been in Vietnam. In addition to building bridges, they carried out community assistance programs. Medical teams visited each village and attended to a diversity of ailments and emergencies. A crew of engineers built much-needed infrastructure for schools and churches. On Sundays, the soldiers played soccer with the local teams. And, of course, they really did build bridges.

During construction a group of 30 engineers from the Costa Rican Ministry of Transport and Public Works (MOPT) worked with the US Army Corps of Engineers. The objective was to learn

Engineer for the Charles E. Mills Construction with his family, 1944. *Photo courtesy of Evelyn King.*

how to erect Bailey bridges; prefabricated bridges made from steel girders that connect to one another and can easily be adapted to many situations.

That first year soldiers camped out at a farm belonging to Don Carlos Rojas, located between La Guapil and Hatillo. The largest bridge built that year was over the Hatillo Viejo River. Five smaller bridges were erected over smaller streams. When the work was completed, Costa Rican President Luis Alberto Monge came to Hatillo for the inauguration of the bridge. It was a great honor for the small town to receive a visit from the national president.

The following year, 1987, the army engineers returned. They camped at the farm of Don Eliecer Castro, near Matapalo. That year they brought more men and more machinery and built the big bridges over the Hatillo Nuevo River and the Portalón River as well as another five bridges that hadn't been completed the previous year.

The torrential rains that came with Hurricane Caesar in 1996

Suspension bridge of Hatillo River, 1980. *Photo: Eddie Ramsey.*

took out the bridge over the Hatillo Nuevo River. The engineers from MOPT, who had worked with the US Army Corps of Engineers, erected a new Bailey bridge in less than a month. In 2005 when heavy rains washed out the bridge over the Portalon River, it took a little longer, but within a year a new Bailey bridge was erected.

The final major road project for the southern zone was the highway called the Costanera Sur. The section between Dominical and Palmar was begun in 1982, but wasn't completely finished until 1996. The road was passable within four years, and the bridge over the Barú River was completed in 1986. The final section of the highway, between Quepos and Dominical, was finished in February 2010.

The completion of the Costanera Sur greatly facilitated travel to Quepos and San Jose. The airport in Quepos is now only 30 minutes from Dominical, as is the hospital. The airport in San Jose is about three hours away. To the south the hospital in Puerto Cortes is an hour, the airport in Palmar Sur an hour and a half, and the Osa Peninsula is three hours. In the 1970s it was an all-day trip to reach any of these locations.

This ease of travel is all very convenient for the people of the region, but it is taking a tremendous toll on the wildlife. With the higher speed limits of 80 kph it is much more difficult for animals to evade the speeding vehicles. 🐾

11

Getting to the Other Side of the Road

Building Wildlife Bridges and Tunnels

When preparations for the construction of the highway between Dominical and Quepos began, the engineers in charge of the project came to see me at Hacienda Barú, which by that time was an officially recognized nature reserve called Barú National Wildlife Refuge. "As you know the highway passes right through the middle of the reserve," they told me. "We know you are concerned, and we want you to know that we are concerned as well. We are willing to work with you to lessen the impact of the highway on the reserve."

The engineer from MOPT put us in contact with the biologist who was working with other professionals to elaborate the environmental impact study for the highway. We determined that our best options were wildlife bridges suspended above the highway and tunnels or underpasses crossing beneath. By locating and marking the routes of animal trails we were able to determine where wildlife had traditionally crossed the existing road, and decided there needed to be 21 square tunnels, approximately one every hundred meters. Other places in the world had experimented with underpasses and found that animals tend to shy away from round tunnels, but don't have much of a problem passing through square ones.

We also decided that suspension bridges were needed for the monkeys. The most important sites were two locations on the existing gravel road where tree branches from both sides overlapped, and the monkeys were already using them to cross from one side to the other. Being much wider, the new highway would take out those trees and eliminate the natural crossings. The people in charge of the environmental impact study consulted with biologists from the University of Costa Rica to determine the best design for the bridges. They decided that two cables with space bars between them and netting wrapped around them would be best. When it came time to build the bridges we suggested putting a cable above the netting so the monkeys would have something to grab on to with their tails. The highway department (MOPT) agreed to this modification.

In 2010 the project was completed and we were anxious to see how the crossings would work. There was still a lot of roadkill at first, but within a month we started finding animal tracks at the entrance to the tunnels, and it appeared that the number of animals running across the surface of the highway had diminished. Though most of the tunnels were located in places where water wasn't a problem, heavy rains tended to wash mud and gravel into them. Fortunately, it simply made the floor look more like the ground outside. For us it was easier to see the tracks, and we were delighted to learn that many different species were using these underpasses.

In 2013 we put a trail camera at the end of one tunnel. I normally leave my trail cameras out a couple of weeks before checking the memory cards, but I was so anxious to see what kind of wildlife might be using the tunnel that I retrieved the card after only five days. In that short time the camera had recorded a total 33 videos of three different species—collared peccary, pacas, and coatis—walking through the underpass in both directions. We were all elated.

As of this writing we have had the camera at the same tunnel for five months and have recorded 10 different species. In addition to the three mentioned above we have videos of white-faced capuchin monkeys, tamanduas (anteaters), armadillos, common opossums, raccoons, ocelots, and several unidentified species of bats. On two occasions, we have found puma tracks. Needless to say we are delighted with the success of these tunnels, but we never imagined the impact they might have on the rest of the country.

In June of 2013 we posted an excellent quality video of a herd of peccary crossing the highway through one of the underpasses on the Hacienda Barú Facebook and YouTube pages. The video was viewed by more than 4,000 people and drew comments from all over the country. We started receiving invitations to seminars that discussed methods for reducing the impact of highways on the environment, and were asked to show videos of animals using the underpasses. The environmental division of MOPT brought a group of visiting engineers from Argentina to Hacienda Barú to see the videos and listen to our experience. Environmentalist organizations in several locations petitioned MOPT to build animal crossings over and under highways in their areas. National environmental groups started pressuring the legislature for a law that required MOPT to build animal crossings into all new highways. This reaction to a single video that appeared on Facebook left us utterly astounded. When I first brought the memory card back from the camera and started watching the videos, I couldn't wait to show it to the guides, park guards, and other personnel. I never imagined it would snowball and become an issue that would attract national attention.

The impact of the bridges was less dramatic, but just as satisfying. The main problem with the bridges was their length, the longest being 63 meters and the shortest 26 meters. From our own experience and the experience of environmental groups at Manuel Antonio National Park we knew that monkeys, opossums, raccoons, kinkajous, olingos, and anteaters will use a bridge, but we weren't sure they would use one that long. A year went by and nobody reported seeing an animal on a bridge. Monkeys were occasionally seen crossing the road on foot, and at least two had been hit by cars and killed. A year and seven months after the completion of bridges an employee

White-faced capuchin monkey crossing the highway. *Photo: Ronald Villalobos*

of Hacienda Barú watched and photographed a troop of monkeys crossing the highway on the shortest bridge. Curiously they did a tight rope act on the single cable above the main bridge. Later they were seen on the bridge itself. Soon thereafter they started using a second, 43-meter bridge located nearby. Since that time many sightings have been reported and many photographs have been taken. Tourists become quite emotional when seeing the monkeys. One ecological tourist commented how nice it was to be in a country where the Highway Department cared enough to provide animal crossings. "This is a wonderful example for the rest of the world," she said.

By March of 2014 we had seen two different species on the bridges, white-fronted capuchin monkeys and kinkajous. It appears only two different troops of monkeys are using the bridges, although there are seven troops of monkeys on the lowlands of Hacienda Barú that have access to them. We are curious to see how long it will take the other troops to learn. Occasionally a monkey will move from one troop to another. For example, a young male that is expelled from his troop by a dominant male may later be accepted into another troop, and it is probable that he will teach his new troop mates to cross the bridges, possibly the longer ones. Only time will tell. 🐾

12

Law and Lawlessness in Rural Costa Rica

The Evolution of a Police Force in Dominical

Prior to the early 1980s, the Osa Peninsula was a wild and lawless place, a land of exiles. Any criminal wanting to escape the authorities and willing to endure the hardships of the jungle, fled to the Osa. Most panned gold for a living. They earned enough to buy food and lots of drink and carry on their daily routines, but none got rich.

I first visited the Osa Peninsula in 1972. We landed on the small air field in Puerto Jiménez in a single engine Cessna and were met by a man named Sanitago. Driving through Puerto Jiménez I noticed several bars, a small hardware store and even a gas station, but no police station. We stopped at a general store to buy some snacks and drinks. From there we drove over a rough jeep trail to look at a farm, and several hours later returned to Puerto Jiménez where we caught the afternoon passenger boat to Golfito. There were only five passengers that afternoon, and Ignacio, the boat driver, was in a talkative mood. He explained that about 90 percent of the population was wanted by the law for one thing or another. As long as they stayed in the Osa, there was nothing to worry about, but sooner or later most would delude themselves into thinking that the police had forgotten about them. They would board one of the two passenger boats that made regular runs to Golfito with the idea of slipping back into society unnoticed. What they didn't know was that the police had a pretty complete list with photos and descriptions of every criminal who lived on the Osa Peninsula. Two or three policemen waited for every boat and arrested every "wanted" person who stepped off.

My good friend Patrick lived in Osa for 26 years from the early 1960s to the late 1980s. He walked over every inch of the peninsula with a small scale in his pack and a big wad of cash in his pocket, buying gold from the miners. He always paid a fair price for the gold and never cheated anyone. "Nobody ever bothered me," he said. "I started buying about the time that the price of gold started to climb, and everyone thought I was the one who made the price go up. Nobody wanted anything to happen to me. They were afraid that if I left, the price would fall." When Pat started buying, the price of gold was less than $100 per ounce; when he moved away it was around $800 per ounce.

According to Patrick, no occurrence was serious enough to bring the police to the Osa. On two occasions he saw people killed in bar-room brawls. They just dragged the dead men out front, and everyone went back to drinking. The next day someone would bury the body. Everyone carried a hand gun. It was a real Wild West scenario. The 1980s brought roads to the peninsula, and with the roads came the police. The area is still far from being a prime example of law and order, but at least nobody gets away with killing people in public bars.

Prior to 1940, the area around Dominical was also without law and order. The nearest police office was in San Isidro de El General and was called the Agencia Principal de Policía; the police chief was the Agente Principal de Policía. I believe the first Agente Prinipial in San Isidro was Juvenal Venegas Garcia from 1914 until his death in 1928. Later his son-in-law, Trino Montero Rodriguez, took over the job.

Though there was no police presence in Dominical or Uvita, the people living there were mostly hard working farmers and ranchers, much different from the residents of the Osa Peninsula. Homemade liquor was the main illegal activity, but I doubt if the people who lived here thought it was much of a problem; only the government didn't like it because they couldn't collect tax on the moonshine. That didn't mean there weren't thefts, disputes between neighbors, and even killings, but the area didn't boast the type of lawlessness so characteristic of Osa.

During a brief but bloody interlude of the 1948 civil war, local police agents took up arms on both sides of the conflict. The revolutionary troops of Jose "Don Pepe" Figueres Ferrer arrived in San Isidro by way of the Cerro de la Muerte and set up a stronghold. On March 16, 1948, government troops under the command of General Tijerino arrived by sea and landed in Dominicalito. They marched to San Isidro where they clashed with the revolutionaries in a fierce battle lasting 36 hours. General Tijerino was defeated and fled south. The rebels caught up to him in Palmares where he was killed in a short skirmish.

After the victory, Don Pepe returned to Cartago, from where he took San Jose and ended the war. On April 20, however, a second detachment of government troops landed in Dominicalito and marched to San Isidro, digging in on the hill where today we find the installations of the Ministry of Transport. Either they didn't know the civil war was over, or just didn't want to give up, but when the rebel victors returned to San Isidro, what ensued was more of a slaughter than a battle. There were so many casualties that the people of San Isidro had to build a make-shift crematorium to dispose of the corpses.

Shortly after the war, Don Pepe abolished the army, and Costa Rica became the only country in Latin America without a military. The men who had previously been Agentes de Policía were replaced with those who had demonstrated absolute loyalty to Don Pepe. For many years thereafter, every time a new president came into office the entire police force was dismissed and a new one hired. The job of local policeman was like a reward to supporters. It insured loyalty to the new president, but did little to promote professionalism in police work.

When I first came to Dominical in 1972 Don Pepe was serving his third term as President of Costa Rica, and a loyal supporter of his, Don Antonio Chacón, was Agente Principal de Policia in Dominical. His job was to keep order in the community, but he also had the authority to issue citations and levy fines. If the offender was not in agreement with the fine, the case moved to the next level which, at that time, was called the Alcaldía, the equivalent of a Justice of the Peace in the United States. The Alcaldía was located in the seat of the cantón.

But Don Antonio Chacón was much more than a policeman. I used to say that having Don Antonio as the Agente Principal de Policía was like having a lawyer in Dominical. When I first came to Hacienda Barú a squatter had slashed and burned about seven hectares of rainforest, and one of my first tasks was to evict him. Don Antonio suggested a meeting with the squatter, a man named Memo, and recommended that I offer to buy his shack and corn field, which were the only two things of any value he had on the land. Don Antonio sent a summons to Memo requiring his presence at the Agencia Principal de Policia, at three o'clock the next day.

In those days the Agencia was a shack built on a rock near present-day Roca Verde. At the meeting Don Antonio explained to Memo that if I took the case to the Alcaldía in Quepos, he would be evicted and probably end up in jail. He agreed to sell me his shack and corn field for 700 colones, $81 at the time. Don Antonio drew up a contract on legal paper with official seals and stamps. We both signed, I paid Memo 700 colones, and he voluntarily left the land. A small corner of the parcel he had slashed and burned is today Hacienda Barú's campground in the rainforest where we do the Night in the Jungle tour. The rest is the oldest secondary forest on the reserve.

At that time there was another police force active in the country called the Resguardo Fiscal. Their job was to go after people involved in activities that would cheat the government out of tax revenues, things like contraband cigarettes and liquor, and moonshine stills. This police force had a reputation of being rough and tough and not at all friendly to the community, so much so that they earned themselves the nickname of "gorillas." During the time that Don Antonio Chacón was the Agente Principal de Policía in Dominical, Don Pepe decided to combine the Resguardo Fiscal and the Agencia Principal into a single police force called the Guardia de Asistencia Rural (GAR).

Don Antonio became the first delegate of the GAR, but was dismissed in 1974 at the end of Don Pepe's term as president when the incoming president, Daniel Oduber, gave the post to Don Emilio "Millo" Vargas. "The GAR was more than just a police force," says Millo. "Just like the name implies, it gave assistance to rural areas." GAR officials were always involved in community development, serving on committees and school boards and helping in any way they could. "Sure we were policemen, but we were there to serve the people as well."

During his 20 years as a GAR delegate, Don Emilio never had to fire his gun. He once disarmed a drunk who was shooting a pistol into the air at the Miramar Bar (now Roca Verde) on New Year's Eve, but he did it without drawing his own revolver. He served in both Uvita and Dominical. "Dominical was always an easy-going place," he reminisced. "Uvita was where all the problems were." He had to deal with two homicides while he was there, and a lot of minor crime. In Dominical there was some minor crime and cattle rustling. The most exciting thing that ever happened was Hurricane Joan, during which Don Millo worked tirelessly to help the community, which was totally isolated from the outside world for six days.

During the time that the GAR existed, its urban counterpart was called the Guardia Civil. In the late 1990s the government decided to combine these two police forces into one. The new service, the

Fuerza Pública, is today in charge of maintaining law and order in the entire country. It is much more professional than the GAR and better prepared to deal with modern crime, but like the Guardia Civil, it lacks that wonderful element of community service so characteristic of the GAR. This is not to say they haven't done their job; they have worked diligently to maintain law and order with the limited resources available to them. But the Fuerza Pública has been represented by a steady stream of nameless policemen who have passed through Dominical, done their job, and been transferred somewhere else, never to be remembered.

Recently a new police force has come into being, one that appears to be quite professional yet very attentive to the needs of the community. The Policía Turística was organized with the objective of making the country safe for tourism, and attends directly to crimes against tourists. In so doing the officers are involving themselves in the communities they serve, bringing back memories of the Guardia Asistencia Rural. 🐾

13

Lencho's War

The Hunting Trip

The year of the revolution, 1948, is a special year in Costa Rican history, but its significance was perceived differently by different people. If you were on the winning side you would remember it as a heroic revolution. The losers would call it a power grab. Most outside observers saw it as a bloody civil war, and none of the participants will ever deny that it was bloody. Today everyone recognizes that the single most important result of the war was the abolition of the Costa Rican armed forces six months after its conclusion.

The war of 1948 had been brewing for some time, but the incident that triggered the eruption of violence was alleged election fraud in the presidential elections of 1948. The people who lived in Hatillo de Aguirre knew that there was an election, but didn't care who was running. Had there been a place to vote, no one was eligible, as all were Panamanian citizens. The government barely knew that Hatillo existed, so the people weren't at all concerned with who ran the government. Likewise the war wasn't of any special importance to them. It wasn't their war. For that reason, when word arrived the soldiers were coming, Marvin Espinosa called a family meeting. It

112

wasn't very democratic because Marvin made all of the decisions. But everyone, the men at least, had their say.

The Espinosas were the first pioneers to settle the area around Hatillo. Fabio came in 1925 and carved out a homestead in the fertile rainforest soils along the Hatillo Viejo River. Marvin and Carmen later followed. Young Florencio, more commonly known as "Lencho," arrived in Boca Barú (present-day Dominical) in 1934, at the age of two, with his mother, Magdalena Espinosa. They moved to Hatillo in 1939, by which time Magdalena's brothers Marvin and Carmen possessed most of the land between there and Hacienda Barú. By 1948 young Lencho was 16 years old, a perfect age for cannon fodder, and cannon fodder is what the soldiers were after.

When the Espinosas met, they agreed that the rumors about the soldiers were probably true. They didn't know for sure which side the soldiers were on, only they were coming. They also knew that all of the men and boys would be forced into the war at gun point, so they decided to head for the hills. It wasn't their war.

"But, what about the women?" cried Magdalena.

"You'll get by," replied Marvin gruffly. "Better to do without your men for a few weeks. If we're here when the soldiers come, you may have to get along without us forever. We're heading into the jungle. Tell them some soldiers came from Quepos and took us with them. They'll believe that and can't verify it."

Deep into the rainforest they went, traveling two days on foot to a place called Dos Bocas. The group was comprised of Lencho, his brothers Gustavo, Primo and Pablo, his cousin Serafin, and his uncles Marvin and Carmen. They took rice, beans, sugar and lots of salt. They set up a camp—a crude thatched shelter and a cooking fire— near the headwaters of the Hatillo Nuevo River. Occasionally one of the men would cut a *chonta* palm for the palm heart, but mostly they lived on wild meat. The meat they didn't eat was salted and dried, and would be taken with them when they returned to Hatillo.

The Espinosa men loved to hunt, and hunt they did, to their heart's content. There was plenty of wildlife around Dos Bocas, a

Illustration: Georgie Wingfield

hunter's dream come true. Lencho recalls they always went in pairs, and he usually accompanied his uncle Marvin.

One day they headed up toward a place called Las Nubes to try their luck. Thirty minutes out of camp they came across a white-lipped peccary (wild pig) trail. The spoor looked fresh and the pungent odor of peccary was strong. "Whew, smell them pigs. We ain't far behind 'em," exclaimed Marvin excitedly. "There must be a whole mess of 'em, look at all them tracks." With the breeze in their faces as they followed, the pigs wouldn't catch their scent. It didn't take much tracking skill to follow a herd that size. After an hour they began to catch glimpses of a straggler here and there and were able to calculate where the main group was headed. "Let's go up on that ridge and get around 'em. Then we can drop down by the creek and surprise 'em."

The two men moved up to the ridge line and skirted the peccary herd. After about 30 minutes they worked their way back down where the pigs would probably be. They weren't disappointed. Coming around a big tree next to the creek they found the herd of around 150 peccaries. Lencho scampered up a tree for safety. Marvin held his ground, raised his 28-gauge shotgun, fired, and hit a big boar broadside with a full load of buckshot. The boar dropped to its knees momentarily, but quickly regained its feet and bolted off with the fleeing herd. "He won't get far," shouted Marvin. "Get your butt down out'ta that tree and let's go."

They followed the blood trail for a ways, but never spotted the boar. Suddenly there was the big sow. Marvin fired head on at close range. She dropped near the large trunk of a fallen kapok tree, and lay on her side kicking and twitching. Marvin nodded at the dying sow. "I don't wanna waste no buckshot on her. Bleed her out and gut her. I'm gonna go after the herd an' see if I can get us another one."

Lencho didn't have a gun. He didn't even have a real machete, only a broken hand-me-down about a foot long. It would do to remove a pig's entrails. Lencho cut her throat and watched the blood pour out on the ground.

Suddenly from behind him Lencho heard a loud "thump, thump" of something striking the hollow kapok trunk. He whirled around to find himself face to face with a jaguar, the mighty claws of both paws gripping the trunk, its enormous head and chest at eye level. The boy leaped over the sow to put her between him and *el tigre*, as the big cat eyed him. Lencho whacked a limb of the fallen trunk with his knife, hoping to scare it away. Instead, it flattened its ears and crouched, its eyes narrowing to form small black beads. The sow kicked a leg and shuddered a dying spasm. Lencho slapped her belly with the flat side of his knife, "whap." Again, "whap." The jaguar raised up slightly, thumped the trunk again with its paws and looked at the sow. Then its tail began to wag, the last thing a jaguar does before attacking. It occurred to Lencho that *el tigre* was more interested in the pig than

in him, and also that it had probably taken the wounded boar. Then he remembered his uncle Marvin.

"*Tio, tio,*" he shouted, for all he was worth. "It's *el tigre* come to eat our pig."

"I'm on the way," echoed the distant shout.

The jaguar perked up its ears and snapped its head toward Marvin's voice. Then, like magic, it disappeared. Lencho heaved a sigh of relief. Thinking back on the incident he doesn't recall being afraid, but was certainly impressed by the power and magnificence of the big cat.

After about three weeks, Pablo sneaked back to La Casona in La Guapil, where the women were staying. He received the news that the soldiers had come and left. They had apparently believed the story about the men being in Quepos. Also there were rumors the war was over. Pablo returned to the hunting camp in Dos Bocas with the news. The weary hunters headed home. It had been an unforgettable hunting trip, and they brought home enough dried and salted meat to last the clan for a long time.

When they returned to Hatillo they found that the women had gotten along just fine without them. 🐾

Note: This history was recounted to me by Florencio "Lencho" Espinosa.

14

Seafood and Sailors

Marine Transport in the Early Days

I didn't know any better at the time, and I thought it must be okay if it were for sale at the Automercado in San Jose, so I bought the frozen turtle meat. According to the package it came from a turtle meat processing plant in Limon. That was in 1972. I found out later that the people from the Caribbean coast had always been allowed to harvest a limited number of marine turtles each year and sell the meat. About a year later a lot of controversy erupted over the harvesting of the endangered green turtles and eventually the decision was made to stop issuing permits. The slaughter continued illegally for several more years, but was eventually ended and the slaughterhouse closed.

We were newly arrived in Costa Rica, and several different friends from San Jose had been emphatic in their warnings not to eat seafood unless it comes from the very best establishments. I was told that many people get sick from eating fish. Later I discovered the reasons for this were that many places bought their fish at the Central Market, where there was little control over freshness and handling. Over time, methods of transportation and distribution of seafood were improved, with special attention to sanitation, and for many years now everyone in the country has been able to enjoy a fish dinner with few worries about food poisoning.

According to Don Benjamin Dario Cedeño, long-time mariner, fisherman, and fish dealer, commercial fishing was almost nonexistent until the 1960s. In the coastal towns people caught and ate fish, but there was so much seafood, and it was so easy to acquire, that it had no value. People went fishing, caught fish, ate some, and gave the rest away. People farther inland had no tradition of fish in their diets and there was very little tourism in Costa Rica. And with no way to ship seafood from the coast to the larger cities of the central plateau, it all added up to very few fish buyers.

According to Don Benjamin the first fresh fish sent to the market in San Jose traveled on the train in wooden boxes full of ice. With frequent delays and the uncertainty of rail travel in those days, it is understandable the fish often arrived at the market in bad condition. It wasn't until around 1965 that Johnny González began shipping fish to San Jose in refrigerated trucks. When I arrived in Costa Rica five years later, good fresh fish was available at the better restaurants and later at the supermarkets, but most people had yet to accept that seafood was safe to eat.

Though fishing as an occupation in Costa Rica was almost unknown prior to 1960, sea-going vessels had long been an important form of transport in the region we now call Costa Ballena. As mentioned earlier, in about 1920 the legendary sea captain, Simón Arzu, sailed into Bahía and anchored in what is now the Ballena Marine National Park. With their bongos, Simón, and later his sons, made their living sailing the coastline between El Pozo (present-day Puerto Cortes) and Puntarenas, trading and transporting products of all kinds. With an outlet for the products the few pioneers produced on their small slash-and-burn plots, and a source for receiving the basic products families needed for their daily lives, isolated areas such as Uvita and Dominical became more attractive to settlers.

In the late 1930s the first cargo boats built with sawed planks began visiting the same small ports visited by the bongos. One of the best known captains was a man known as "El Turco." An acquaintance of his told me El Turco's real name was David Naja and he was from Turkey. His two ships with diesel engines, La Sara and La Neme, carried passengers, cargo and even live pigs, and worked the same route as the bongos: Puerto Cortes, Piñuela, Uvita, Puerto Nuevo, Dominicalito, Quepos, and Puntarenas.

Benjamin Dario Cedeño became a sea captain in 1955 at the age of 25. He worked with a shipping company called Edete, and his first ship was the La Santa Rosa. They sailed between Puntarenas and Puerto Cortes carrying passengers and cargo; the fare was 15 colones one way. At that time, Puerto Cortes was an active port, mainly due to the proximity of the large banana plantations around Palmar.

The year 1955 brought the worst torrential rains and flooding anyone can remember. Benjamin navigated the La Santa Rosa into the middle of Puerto Cortes and rescued over 50 people from the second story of the Municipal Building, the only two-story building in town. La Santa Rosa drew about eight feet of water, and Benjamin estimates the water in the middle of Puerto Cortes was 13 feet deep. "There was never another flood like that one," says Don Benjamin. "There wasn't any road to evacuate the people, so we had to do it by boat."

Benjamin later captained a boat called La Santa Fe, previously known as La HG. In 1949, before Benjamin began working with Edete, the La HG had a tragic accident. He knew about the accident, but didn't learn the details until he came to work for the company. Several surviving crew members and passengers told him the story.

La HG was a big beautiful passenger and cargo boat that ran the route between Puerto Cortes and Puntarenas. Some say the captain had been drinking that night and had a woman in his cabin, leaving a young, inexperienced sailor at the wheel. One sailor said he noticed they were much too close to shore when they sailed past Dominicalito. A few minutes later La HG collided with a submerged rock near the large protruding landmark rock called La Viuda. The damaged hull slipped back off the rock into the sea, but the sailor at the helm hadn't cut the power, and the propeller drove the boat forward against the rock again and up onto it. There she stuck, tilted steeply to one side. The boat, heavily loaded with cargo, carried about 80 passengers, most of whom jumped into the water. About half drowned.

Don Tino and Don Lencho Rios, both bongo captains and sons of Simón Arzu, were on shore in Uvita at the time of the accident. Being agile swimmers, they swam out to the boat and helped all of those that they could. Later people from Puerto Cortes came to help, but most ended up looting personal items from the dead passengers and cargo from the boat. Part of the cargo was liquor which the people readily consumed and the whole affair turned into a great drunken brawl. The bodies were buried in a common grave. Many of the victims were Nicaraguans traveling to the banana plantations in search of work.

The Edete company sent another boat to pull the La HG off the rock and tow her into the mouth of the Térraba River to a place called Boca Zacate, where she could be patched up. Later they took her back to Puntarenas and refurbished her completely. They renamed her La Santa Fe and one day Don Benjamin Dario Cedeño became the captain.

Once adequate roads were built into the southern zone, the importance of marine transport diminished. But at the same time, Costa Ricans were learning to eat fish and new markets were opening up. Many of the vessels once used for transport, including the bongos, were converted into fishing vessels and the mariners who sailed them learned a new trade. Don Benjamin was one of them. Today he and his wife, Doña Alicia, own and operate a retail fish business in San Isidro de el General. They own a truck with a large ice chest on the back big enough to hold half a ton of seafood. They buy fish from the fishermen at Dominicalito and transport it to San Isidro where they sell it in their own business located in the Central Market, and also to other retailers. 🦐

15

When There Is No Doctor

Dealing with Tragedy

A *trapiche* is an oxen-powered sugar mill. It consists of a mechanical press with a long pole extending out from the center shaft, about two meters above the ground. Two oxen, yoked to the pole, walk around the mill and turn the shaft, which drives two wide, corrugated wheels; the sugarcane is rolled between them, squeezing out all the sugar laden juice. This sweet liquid flows into a bucket placed beneath the mill. The remains of the cane, *bagaso*, now nothing more than shredded and broken fiber, is discarded. The person who feeds cane into the mill steps aside each time the oxen come around. Usually there are several helpers; one to hand sugarcane to the operator and another to retrieve the juice. Off to the side, the juice is cooked in a large, dome shaped bowl called a *paela*, which is heated over a big wood-burning hearth.

The hot juice, *caldo*, must be stirred constantly with a large wooden paddle. As the ever hotter liquid thickens, a foamy film called *cachasa*, which contains most of the impurities, is skimmed off the top and used as pig feed. Just before the boiling point is reached, some of the juice is scooped out and poured into shallow molds where it cools and forms *sobrado,* a soft candy-like substance. As the cane juice begins to boil, most of the liquid is poured into round molds where it quickly hardens into brown sugar cakes called *tapas.* The final product is *tapa dulce,* or sweet tapa. Cutting and milling the cane and making the *tapa dulce* often becomes a family affair. Even the children help with minor chores like stirring the *caldo,* pouring it into molds, and handing the sugarcane to the mill operator.

The day Don Moncho Rodriguez got his hand caught in the press, he had only one helper, his hired hand Pepe. It took Pepe a second or two from the moment he heard Moncho's ungodly scream to figure out what had happened and stop the oxen. By then Moncho's hand, wrist, and lower forearm had been crushed beyond recognition. Blood mixed with small globs of flesh dripped into the bucket and mixed with the cane juice. Struggling to remain on his feet, Moncho held the trapped arm with his good hand. His screams could be heard as Pepe backed up the oxen, putting the mill in reverse and allowing what was left of his mangled limb to fall free.

Moncho dropped to the ground. From mid forearm down was bloody flesh and crushed bone. His screams dwindled to a whimper and finally silence. He had reached a point where the pain no longer had meaning. Pepe made him as comfortable as possible. Moncho's wife, Milena, having heard the screams, came running from the house while Pepe ran to get help.

Word spread quickly. Within a couple of hours a group of neighbors had arrived to offer their support to Moncho. There were no doctors or anyone who had any formal medical experience.

"We've gotta get him to a doctor," offered someone from the crowd.

"That's ridiculous," commented another. "La Cocaleta[3] is broke down and won't be running again till next week. It'll take two days to get him to San Isidro in an ox cart. He'll have gangrene by then. There's no way he can ride a horse. We're gonna have to deal with it here."

3   La Cocaleta was an old 4-WD truck that made regular trips between Dominical and San Isidro.

Moncho, though weak and on the verge of going into shock, recognized the seriousness of his situation. He was still able to speak. "Listen to me." Everyone quieted down and strained to hear the weak voice. "I know what you gotta do. Cut my arm off…that's my only hope. Get me some *guaro contrabando*. I wanna be good and drunk when you start cuttin'."

Rigo, a rancher from Barú, rode up, dismounted, and summed up the situation. Everyone was talking at once. Rigo took control. "Okay, everyone. I once saw an amputation out in the jungle in Guanacaste. We can do it, but we need to get to work. The sooner we get it done, the better. He's right about the *guaro*; Arnoldo get him some from your still. The drunker he is the less he's gonna feel. Pepe, find me a couple of small machetes, and make sure they're good and sharp. You got a saw in that shed over there?"

Moncho didn't own a saw, but one of the neighbors went to get one. The women started boiling water in a large kettle over the hearth. Someone else moved a table out to the dirt-floored porch. Soon everything was ready, and Moncho, still lying on his back near the *trapiche*, was so drunk that he was feeling no pain.

Rigo was firmly in charge now. "Pepe, is that machete sharp yet?"

Pepe handed him a machete. Before anyone had figured out what was happening, Rigo cut off the mangled piece of arm, wrist, and hand. It held only small pieces of bone, and the machete met no resistance. One quick swipe and off came the whole bloody mess. A piece of splintered bone was still protruding from the stump of Moncho's arm.

"Alright everyone, I need a little help here. Let's get him over to the house and onto that table. Somebody take that mess and bury it," nodding toward the part he had just severed.

Rigo wrapped a clean cloth around the bloody stump. Four men, two on each side, picked Moncho up, moved him over to the porch and onto the table. The women washed his arm from the shoulder down with homemade soap and warm water. One of the neighbors offered a bottle of rubbing alcohol, a treasure from a meager medicine chest. They used it to disinfect the area of his arm where the cut would be made. Moncho was barely conscious. The *guaro* had done its work. Pepe brought the sharp machetes, a couple of kitchen knives and the saw. Rigo told the women to heat them in the hearth. "I want them almost red hot," he called.

Fourteen-year-old Braulio "Lulu" Jiménez had heard about the accident and came to see all the excitement. He was repulsed by the blood and gore, but at the same time it held a strange fascination for him. His eyes remained glued to the scene. He stared at the disfigured pieces of Moncho's arm behind the *trapiche*, and imagined that only a few hours ago it had been a functioning part of his neighbor's body. He helped a man named Carlos from Platanillo unyoke the oxen and turn them out in a small pasture near the house. But he turned away with a queasy feeling in his stomach when Carlos gathered together the mutilated remains, took them over to the same pasture to bury them.

"We're ready to go. I need some strong men to hold him down. He looks helpless now, but that's gonna change when I start cutting. Juan, Manuel, Memo, come on over here. Tie his feet and legs to the table, and you three hold his upper body. Tie that free hand to something. Make sure it won't come loose."

Soon everything was ready. Rigo tied a piece of twine made from *cabulla* fiber tightly around Moncho's wounded arm just below the elbow and above the protruding bone. He took a not-quite red-hot machete in his right hand, peeled the skin back from the bone and flesh, and cut through the flesh on the underside and back of the forearm. Moncho screamed and struggled to break free, but the three men held him tight. Rigo pulled the machete back and waited for Moncho to settle down. He exchanged the machete for a hotter one, nodded to the men to hold tight again, and cut all the way to the bone on the top side of the arm. Again Moncho screamed and struggled. Then he passed out. Rigo breathed a sigh of relief and finished cutting all the way down to the two bones. He held the incision open with the machete, took a hot kitchen knife and cauterized a few blood vessels that hadn't completely closed. "Hand me the saw," he said solemnly.

Young Lulu had found a place to stand at the edge of the porch a little ways from the table. The queasiness returned to his stomach when the horrible smell of burning flesh reached his nostrils, and Moncho's screams sent shivers down his spine, but he was unable to tear his eyes away. Lulu had seen death, but never in his life had he witnessed anything as gruesome as this crude surgery. The impression left on his young mind by the experience was to stay with him the rest of his life. Though he hadn't known Moncho well, Lulu could feel his suffering, as if it were his own. But the worst was yet to come.

Rigo quickly began sawing through the bones. It only took a minute, but for Lulu it seemed much longer. The sound of the saw teeth grating on the bone was worse than anything yet. Lulu could see the clean-cut bone on the stump of Moncho's arm and the discarded piece on the table. Rigo checked for bleeding vessels, splashed alcohol on the open wound, pulled the flaps of skin over the exposed flesh. "One of you women will have to sew the skin together," he said, walking away.

"You'll need to get him to San Isidro to a doctor," said Rigo to Milena. "I don't know how you're going to do it without la Cocaleta, but you need to try. He's strong and healthy, but something like this is a tremendous shock."

They never did take Moncho to a doctor. Doña Paula, an Indian lady, sewed the flaps of skin over the stump and treated it with herbal remedies. His arm eventually healed. For the rest of his life everyone would call him "*Pituco*," a rather crude reference to his stub arm.

Young Lulu was deeply affected by the tragedy and the medical procedure he had witnessed. When I interviewed him 60 years later, he still didn't like to talk about the amputation. It may have affected him even more than his own father's death a few years earlier.

✳　✳　✳　✳　✳

125

Braulio "Lulu" Jiménez arrived in Dominical in 1945 at seven years of age. What he remembers most about his arrival was the vomiting and sea sickness. The whole family floated in on a barge loaded with people, oxen, pigs, cattle, chickens, and all of their earthly belongings. As the barge came into the port at Dominicalito, someone paddled out in a small boat and tied a line to it. Then the tugboat cast it loose. A diesel-powered winch, anchored to three huge concrete blocks, pulled the barge to shore. The winch and crude docking facilities were brought to Dominicalito a few years earlier by the road builders from the Charles E. Mills Construction Company.

The Jiménez family homesteaded some land in the area between Barú and Platanillo where they farmed and raised livestock. Lulu grew up in a thatched-roof house with a dirt floor and never wore shoes until he was 15. His early years were spent milking cows, taking care of the animals, and raising fruit to sell to the road crews.

The main source of trade came from boats and barges that stopped often in Dominicalito, taking the *campesino's* livestock and farm products to the market in Puntarenas and returning with much-needed supplies, such as salt, cloth and sewing materials, soap, kerosene, candles, and metal tools. There was no soccer field or other social gathering place. Social life consisted of visits to other families.

Water was carried from the stream in buckets or, in some places, was channeled to the house in open gutters made from *chonta* palm. There were no sanitary facilities of any kind. Everyone just went out into the jungle when nature called. After a few years the health department taught people to dig holes and build outhouses. Both internal and external parasites were the predominant health problem, but accidents were frequent and medical care scarce. Doña Paula always seemed to have a special herbal remedy, regardless of the ailment.

Lulu showed me a *papalomoyo* (leischmonaisis) scar on his ankle. If you go to a doctor with a *papalomoyo* today, you will receive painful injections of heavy metals directly into the wound. Doña Paula told Lulu to thoroughly chew a leaf from the *anisillo* plant, pack the moist glob over the lesion and tie it in place with another leaf, keep it wrapped for 24 hours, and repeat the process the next day. In three weeks, Lulu's *papalomoyo* was cured. In fact, he cured two more of them in his lifetime using the same remedy.

A couple of years after the Jiménez family settled near Platanillo, Lulu's father, Santana, was driving a bunch of fat cattle to the barge in Dominicalito with his brother, Sen, and a couple of *peones*. They stopped at a cantina owned by "El Negro Grafil," located where today stands Villas Rio Mar. They had a bite to eat and a couple of drinks. When they finished, Sen and the *peones* went ahead while Santana paid the owner. There were a couple of shady-looking characters in the cantina who spoke with a Nicaraguan accent. As Santana was on his way out the door one of them made a vulgar remark about his daughter, Lulu's sister. Santana took offense and in the fight that ensued was hit straight across the forehead with a machete. It penetrated his skull and embedded part of his straw hat in the wound. He received another deep cut on his waist. Someone called out to Sen who returned and took up the fight, eventually severely cutting one of the assailants and chasing them off. They later heard that the two Nicaraguans had fled as far as Parrita where the wounded one died.

Sen managed to get Santana home, but the machete cut was serious. Later someone took him to San Isidro in la Cocaleta. The next day the doctors at the hospital sent him to San Jose in a small plane. Santana Jiménez lived for ten days, but the wounds had become seriously infected. He died leaving nine-year-old Lulu and his older brother Nardo to fend for the family, a job which they did admirably. The area around Dominical was a wild place back in those days, and only the hardy survived to a ripe old age. Lulu Jiménez is one of those who did.

Years later, around 1990, Don Lulu and his family began taking foreign visitors to a beautiful waterfall that borders their property on the Barú River. They have since developed the famous "Don Lulu's

Nauyaca Waterfall Tour." Every year they take thousands of visitors on horseback to view these spectacular falls and swim in the pool at their base.

Don Lulu has the distinction of having survived the hard times of the past while learning to adapt and prosper in the world of today. 🐚

Note: In about 1952, a man named Moncho did get his hand caught in a *trapiche* and had his arm amputated just below the elbow. The surgery was done by a group of friends at his home near Platanillo. Fourteen-year-old Lulu Jiménez witnessed the amputation. Nevertheless the passing of 60 years and the traumatic impression left by the experience have clouded his memory.

16

A Small Golden Eagle for Juanito

Excavating the Chief's Tomb

In 1957 Juanito was 12 years old, the youngest member of a group of six who left San Isidro early one morning on an adventure they would all remember for the rest of their lives. Rodolfo's 4x4 pickup was loaded to the brim with supplies, including enough rice and beans for two weeks, shovels, picks, bars for digging and prying, machetes, and a few other basic items. Juanito rode in the back of the pickup with Ignacio's son, Jorge, and a man named Luis. Rodolfo drove and the other two men, Ignacio and Quincho, rode up front. The Pan-American Highway was rough and full of holes, but after nearly four hours they pulled into Buenos Aires and stopped for a bite to eat. There the group was joined by Porfirio, an Indian who would serve as their guide for the rest of the trip. Porfirio rode with those in the back of the heavily loaded pickup. They drove out of Buenos Aires and again headed south on the Pan-American Highway.

Though the construction of the road had begun 16 years earlier, much of it was yet unpaved and several bridges were still under construction. They worked their way south through Palmar, across the Térraba River, and about halfway to Rio Claro to a village called

Coquito. After parking at the home of an acquaintance, Porfirio pointed to a ridge line in the distance. "That's where we're going," he informed the men.

Porfirio led the way, machete in hand, clearing vines and fallen branches from the path. They walked single file for an hour and a half, arriving at the location that would be their home for the next two weeks. Juanito stood in an open area and looked back down in the valley where Coquito was barely visible.

"Juanito, come lend a hand," called Rodolfo. "We need a roof over our heads before dark." Three of the men returned to Coquito for the rest of the supplies while Juanito helped cut and carry poles to make a frame for their temporary home. Several nearby palm trees provided leaves for thatching the roof. By the time the others returned with supplies, a crude open-sided shelter had been constructed. It wasn't much, but would provide protection in case of an unseasonable rain. A cooking fire was located at one end with the food stacked nearby. After a dinner of rice and beans, and a few pieces of meat from a toucan that one of the men had shot, everyone dozed off early. It had been a long day. Tomorrow they would begin the job they came to do: the excavation of a large indigenous cemetery.

Porfirio not only served as a guide to the treasure hunters, he was their advisor on all things indigenous. He had discovered the cemetery where he believed the chief's tomb to be located and had led the group here to excavate it. In return for his services he would receive a portion of the gold. Porfirio repeatedly poked a pointed piece of construction rod into the ground until he found an area that was completely covered with flat river rocks. There was no river nearby, so those stones must have been carried at least 500 meters. The men began digging and prying up the smooth, flat stones and laying them off to the side. Juanito piled the stones and carried water for the thirsty diggers. The men kept removing the stones until they had uncovered a 6-meter square, an enormous area for a tomb. Porfirio had obviously led them to something bigger than any of them had imagined. That night the men stayed up late, speculating on what they would find over the next few days. Juanito finally fell asleep as the flames of the cooking fire dwindled to a few glowing coals.

It was still dark when Juanito awoke the next day, but Ignacio was already fixing coffee and the others were in various stages of waking and getting up. Everyone was anxious to get on with the day's work. Now that the stones had been removed, the serious work of digging would begin. They started in the corners and dug a trench around the perimeter of the tomb. Half a meter down, in each corner, they found a cylindrical stone with monkey faces carved around the edge. The digging continued with a heightened level of expectation. That first day, the men removed almost a meter of soil, a tremendous amount considering the large surface area of the tomb. By dark everyone was exhausted, but in good spirits, and no one complained about the work, even though nothing was found, other than the monkey stones and a few shards of pottery.

By the end of the second day, it became obvious that it would be necessary to move the excavated soil farther from the edge of the pit. Porfirio explained that an Indian chief would have been buried at least 4 meters deep and maybe as much as 6 meters. They calculated that the amount of soil would be such that it would be necessary to shovel it several meters back from the edge of the site. Part of this work fell to Juanito in addition to his water-carrying duties.

On the fourth day when one of the men threw a shovelful out of the tomb, Juanito noticed a slight glitter. He picked up what appeared to be dirt clod and, scratching away the red clay, he realized that the center was metallic. "Hey, is this gold?" He held the partially cleaned piece between thumb and forefinger. Quincho was out of the hole and by his side in an instant. Grabbing the piece from the boy, he rubbed off some more dirt. "That's what it is, a golden eagle." He happily slapped Juanito on the back. "Good work, boy, our first piece of gold." The decision was made to dig slower and sift through the soil more carefully. By the end of the day the hole was two meters deep.

Over the next week the treasure hunters removed another two

meters of soil from the tomb. The work grew harder as the hole got deeper, as they could no longer throw dirt out of the deep hole. Instead it was necessary to shovel it into sacks which were hoisted up with ropes. They found no more gold, only pottery decorated with drawings of monkeys and iguanas, and figurines of clay, some of which were very elaborate. Most had been broken by the shovels. As these pieces had little resale value, the men threw them aside. Gold was what they were after.

One day, while digging in one of the corners, Rodolfo's shovel struck something hard with a dull metallic clang. "Hey guys, I think I've got something here." Quickly clearing away the dirt he exposed a golden plate just a bit bigger than his hand. Digging deeper they found seven plates stacked on top of a stone cylinder. According to Porfirio, this was typical of a chief's tomb, and there were probably similar stone cylinders and golden plates in the other three corners as well. One man moved to each corner and began to dig. Again Porfirio was right. They found seven golden plates in each corner. Ignacio calculated that altogether the plates weighed about six kilos. They were probably nearing the bottom of the tomb, the layer where they would hopefully find the big payoff: the Indian chief with all of his belongings.

That night the group sat around a kerosene lantern and discussed what to do next. After nearly two weeks of excruciatingly hard work, they finally had something of real value. Protecting that investment was now a concern. They were especially worried because Luis and Jorge had walked to Coquito two days earlier for supplies, and had mentioned the tomb to several of the villagers, who seemed overly interested. Nobody blamed Luis and Jorge, but all agreed there was a real danger of losing their treasure, either to thieves or the police. By law, all Indian artifacts were the property of the government, but they all knew if the police "confiscated" their gold, it would never make it to the National Museum. The decision was made to post a guard at all hours and hide the golden plates.

The next morning Rodolfo and Ignacio took the gold and walked to a creek they had crossed on the way in. A little ways upstream they hid two sacks containing the golden plates in a small cave and leaned a rock over the opening.

It was now necessary to sift every shovel of dirt, as gold pieces were appearing frequently. Golden eagles, kings, bells, and simple cylinders were the most common. Late in the afternoon of the thirteenth day of digging Quincho's startled voice echoed out from the hole. "Oh, my God! I think I've got some bones here." A few seconds later Rodolfo, Ignacio, and Porfirio were at his side. Juanito peered down from above. The four men began moving dirt away from the skeleton. Near the skull appeared the feet and ankle bones of another skeleton. Working until dark the men uncovered three skeletons in a row, head to toe. The next morning they found five more. The skeletons were perfectly preserved, even the teeth. Juanito was visibly shaken. Seeing the bones and knowing that they had once belonged to a living person was really spooky. The men tried to act like they weren't bothered by the find, but Juanito noticed that everyone was quieter and more subdued than normal. They all turned in early that night, but most tossed and turned and got little rest.

At 4:00 a.m., Rodolfo, who had been on guard duty, aroused his sleeping companions. "Hurry, we've gotta get moving. Somebody's coming. I can see their flashlights. We've got less than an hour." The group abandoned the site as a yellowish hint of daylight was peeking over the horizon. Leaving all of the tools and heavy items behind, they circled down and behind the uninvited visitors. They recovered the two bags of golden plates, then continued on to Coquito with another bag of golden trinkets weighing about a kilo.

Arriving in Coquito, it took less than five minutes to load their meager cargo in the truck. Porfirio's friend told them that it was the police from Buenos Aires who had gone to raid their dig. On the way out of town they saw two police pickups at the local guard station where normally there were none. They drove straight on past.

On the way to Buenos Aires, Porfirio told those in the back of the pickup that he believed the chief's chamber was even deeper, and the discoveries up to that point were only his loyal servants and maybe some family. Rodolfo didn't drive all the way into Buenos Aires, but pulled up at the edge of town. He left the motor running while Porfirio climbed down and waved goodbye. He had received a golden eagle, a king and two small bells for his help.

Shortly after two o'clock in the afternoon the weary travelers rolled to a stop in front of Ignacio's house in San Isidro. Over a cold beer, they divided the gold into four equal portions. Rodolfo figured that each man's share was worth more than $5,000 on the open market, although the archaeological value would be much more. The two boys, Juanito and Jorge, each received a small golden eagle for their help.

As the sun descended in the western sky, Rodolfo and Juanito set out for Dominical. They rode in silence, pondering the events of the past couple of weeks, an experience neither would forget for the rest of his life. 🐾

Note: The basic facts of the story related above, including dates, places, and the items found in the tomb, are true and were recounted to me by one of the participants. Names of the people have been changed.

17

There's More To It Than Just a Name

How Our Towns and Villages Got Their Names

Whether obvious or obscure, the stories of how places in the south-central coastal region of Costa Rica got their names are quite interesting and can tell us something about the area.

Quepos, the seat of the cantón of Aguirre, for instance, was named after the indigenous tribe that once inhabited the area. Puerto Cortés, the seat of the cantón of Osa, was originally called El Pozo; the current name, given to it in the 1920s, honors former President of Costa Rica, Leon Cortes.

Many places in Costa Rica were named by the Catholic church and our region is no exception. Examples of these are San Isidro, San Juan de Dios, and San Josecito. A few villages already had local names when the church decided to give them the names of Christian saints, but the inhabitants didn't always embrace the new name.

Tinamastes is an example of a place where both the church name and the traditional name are used. The early settlers to the region cooked over an open fire, or in a fire box called a *fogón*. Much of the cooking was done either in a large pot or in a *comal*, a rounded cast iron platter. Rather than setting the pot or *comal* directly in the fire, three stones were placed in a triangular arrangement and the utensil was placed over the fire with the edges resting on the stones. These stones were called *tinamastes*. On a hilltop near the present-day village of Tinamastes were three enormous boulders placed by nature in the same pattern as three *tinamastes* in a cooking fire. People began referring to the place as Los Tinamastes, and the name has remained to the present day. At a later date the church decided to change the name of the village to San Cristobal with limited success. Today both names are used by the residents of the town. Tinamastes is the seat of the District of Barú in the cantón of Pérez Zeledón.

On the other hand, the town of Matapalo, which was named after a parasitic vine, is an example of a place where the church name never took hold. In tropical climates parasitic plants abound. One such plant is a vine with thick round leaves which completely covers the crowns of trees, eventually capturing most of the sunlight and killing the tree. The vine is referred to locally as the *matapalo*, meaning "kill tree." The first settler to the area, Juan Bautista Santa María Concepción, arrived along the beach, having walked northwest from the mouth of the Hatillo Nuevo River. Upon discovering a flat fertile area that appeared to be a promising site for agriculture, he carved out a section of jungle and made his farm there. The most prominent feature seen from the beach was an enormous strangler fig tree with its crown completely covered with a *matapalo* vine, its tendrils drooping all the way to the ground. In describing how to get to his farm, Juan Bautista would tell people: "Walk down the beach until you get to the *matapalo*." Although the tree with the vine eventually died and fell over, the name stuck. At a later date the church tried to change the name of the community to San Pablo, but the members of the community refused to use the new name. Matapalo is the seat of the District of Savegre in the cantón of Aguirre.

I used to assume that a military general had once ruled San Isidro and the Valley of the General, but delving into the history of the city we find there never was a general or a military presence of any kind. The name probably came from the General River which had already been named when the town of San Isidro was founded. The source of the name of the river is not entirely clear, but some historians believe that since the river is the central waterway in the valley, and all other rivers and streams flow into it, the first adventurers to explore the region began calling it the General River, and hence, the Valley of the General. There are many places in Costa Rica called San Isidro, so the words "of the General" were added for clarification. San Isidro de El General is the seat of the cantón of Pérez Zeledón.

Like Matapolo, many other places are named after plants. Though plants are not permanent fixtures, they often last long enough to become landmarks and end up lending their names to the place where they once stood. The Valley of the Guabo, Platanillo, Playa Guapil, Uvita, and Dominical are prime examples. Some of these have interesting stories behind them.

In Spanish a double-barreled shotgun is called a *guapil,* but the word can apply to anything that has two side-by-side cylinders. At the entrance to what is today called Playa Guapil, there once stood a coconut palm that was really two trees with the trunks stuck together like Siamese twins or like a double-barreled shotgun. People started calling it *palma guapil* and later Playa Guapil. I once had a nursery of coconut palms. Out of about 1,000 palm trees, three turned out with double trunks. Since the original double-trunked palm had long since perished, I thought it'd be nice to plant one of them on Playa Guapil, but within a week, someone dug it up. I planted each of the other two, but both suffered the same fate shortly after planting.

Viscoyol is a sturdy cane-like plant with leaves similar to those of a palm, and a tough, straight stem lined with long, sharp spines. Commonly found in humid soil throughout the coastal region, this plant produces bunches of small, round, purple fruits resembling grapes. Grape in Spanish is *uva; uvita* is the diminutive form and means "little grape." When people first began exploring the area around present-day Uvita, the humid lowlands were covered with thick stands of *viscoyol,* and so they referred to the location as *La Uvita.* Hipolito Villegas, who was born in Uvita in 1909, says that it was called that when his father was born around 1890. La Uvita is the seat of the District of Bahía-Ballena in the cantón of Osa.

There is a well-known local story of how Dominical got its name. In Costa Rica we have many different types of bananas, including plantains, cuadrados, guineos, and dominícos. In Spanish a field of bananas is called a *bananal*; of plantains, a *platanal*; of cudrados, a *cuadradal*; of guineos, a *guineal*; and of dominicos, a *dominical*. Before the appearance of roads, everyone walked down the beach to get from one place to another. In the lowlands near the beach of present-day Dominicalito, one of the original pioneers of the area, Victor Sibaja—usually known by his nickname, Chucuyo—had a plantation of dominicos. When people walked down the beach and arrived at that point, they would say: "There is Chucuyo's *dominical*." For many years I believed this story, and it is certainly possible that Chucuyo did have a plantation of dominicos in present-day Dominicalito. However I recently came across an 1868 map of Costa Rica that shows the stream today known as Pozo Azul, as the Dominical River. Also Punta Dominical is likewise labeled P. Dominical. The name probably did come from the dominico, but it existed long before Chucuyo was born. The place we know as Dominical today was formerly known as Barú or Boca Barú. As late as 1958 the place known today as Dominicalito was called Dominical. It is shown as such on a 1958 map of Costa Rica published by the Costa Rican Tourist Bureau (ICT).

Another story about a place name that was put to rest by the appearance of the 1868 map is that of Portalón. According to old-time residents of Portalón, the first settler to establish a large farm along the river, Leitano Céspedes, had the custom of building beautifully decorated archways and gates at the entrances to his properties. This type of gateway is called a *portal* in Spanish, and a very large one would be called a *portalón*. As more settlers moved into the area they referred to his farm by this outstanding feature. However, Leitano Céspedes didn't come to Portalón until the early 1900s, and there is a place called Portalón on the 1868 map. It is located near the estuary of the present-day Savegre River. The Portalón River isn't shown on the map. We may never know the real story behind the name. People get old and die, and local knowledge passes away with them.

Present-day Barú is located about three kilometers upstream from the mouth of the Barú River, at the point where it joins the Guabo River. Barú appears to be a name of indigenous origin. For over 2,000 years people have migrated to this region from the Chiriqui province of Panama, the home of the Barú volcano. These people probably brought the name when they came to settle in this region.

According to the linguistics department of the University of Costa Rica, the word "barú" comes from the indigenous language Guaymi. I once spoke with two native Guaymi speakers, neither of whom spoke more than rudimentary market Spanish and asked them about the meaning of the word "barú." They knew what it meant, but had great difficulty explaining it to me. Although their explanation wasn't very clear, it appears the word means "river basin" or "watershed." Also, you may remember in chapter 6 in the story about Carmelita Morales, the group of Boruca Indians camped near Barú. Carmelita told her two granddaughters, Marina and Margarita, that it was called Barú because it is a place where two rivers meet.

The village of Hatillo is situated between two rivers, the Hatillo Nuevo and the Hatillo Viejo. The derivation comes from the Spanish word *hato* meaning herd. Some of the pioneers of the area around present-day Hatillo believe that a rancher from the Valle del Guabo, when looking for new land on which to expand his herd, cleared an area near the edge of the smaller of the two rivers between which we today find the small town of Hatillo. Once the rainforest was cut, sunlight flooded the area, and several species of grass began to grow. The rancher returned to the area every six months or so to hack away the reemerging jungle. After a couple of years the natural pasture was well established and the cattleman drove a small herd of cattle from his main ranch about 20 kilometers away, leaving them in the new pasture. He and his cowboys visited the site periodically to check on the small herd. In Spanish the diminutive of most nouns is produced by adding the letters "ito" or "illo" to the end. Therefore, if a regular herd is an *hato*, a small herd is an *hatillo*. The rancher and his men referred to the small herd as *el hatillo*. The new pasture was so successful that the unnamed rancher repeated the process nearby, close to the banks of the larger river and brought more cattle to begin grazing that pasture. He and his cowboys began referring to the first small herd as the Hatillo Viejo (old little herd) and the second group as the Hatillo Nuevo (new little herd.) Thus the two rivers came to be known as the Hatillo Viejo and Hatillo Nuevo. Later when the coastal region became inhabited by settlers, the community that developed between the two rivers retained the name Hatillo. If this story about the origin of the name is true, it had to have taken place prior to 1868, since both rivers appear on the old map. The one which is today called the Hatillo Nuevo, was labeled as Hatillo V., and the river we now call the Hatillo Viejo, was labeled as Hatillon.

The coastal village of Bahía was named after a large ranch called Hacienda Bahía that once existed near Uvita. In the 1950s the ranch was sold to the Alcoa Aluminum Company, which had hopes of mining bauxite. The mining venture faltered and the land was abandoned. In the mid-1960s, ITCO (the land and colonization institute) took title to the land, subdivided the ranch, and distributed the parcels to landless peasants. The new settlement was called Bahía, after the ranch. It is located on the coast in front of the bay where Ballena Island is located, just to the southeast of Punta Uvita.

The name Lagunas, meaning lakes or lagoons, is ironic because the area has never had an abundance of water. Nevertheless, about two kilometers above present-day Barú, on the left side of the road is a small lake. Prior to the deforestation of the area, there were several lakes. Since lakes are a rarity in Central America, these small bodies of water were a notable landmark. The first pioneers to work the land in this area were Don Miguel Gómez and his sons. His eldest, Evangelista Gómez, felled the rainforest and made his ranch in the area around the lakes. He and other settlers began referring to the area as Las Lagunas, which was later shortened to Lagunas.

Somebody once gave me a book entitled *The Mother Tongue* about the history of the English language. As the book was a gift I felt obliged to read it. To my surprise and delight, it turned out to be one of the most interesting books I have ever read. I especially enjoyed the chapter on the origins of people's names. Later I was to discover that the ways in which places acquire their names are no less fascinating. Since the names of the places in this region are relatively new, most having been acquired in the last 100 years, researching them is a matter of talking with the oldest members of the communities. As new information, such as old maps, comes to my attention, I have had to modify or discard several old ideas. This has brought me to the realization that as colorful as the old-timers' tales may be, they come from people's memories, and may not be entirely accurate. That doesn't, however, make them any less fun to learn about. ẽ

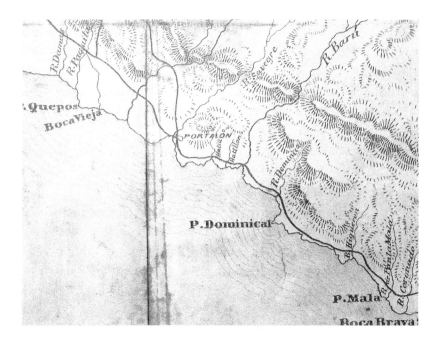

18

The Last Tapir

An Incredible Journey

The sun poked its brilliant face through the clouds to shimmer lightly on the shallow waves, the glassy sheen broken only by a bulky form rising slightly off the sand with each withering swell. Manuel Angel marveled at the bright rays, the first he had seen in over a week. After six days of torrential rain it was nice to be out of the house flexing his taut muscles and nicer still to feel the sun's rays warming his back. But the object on the beach remained a mystery. The sun slipped back into hiding behind the clouds as another wave rolled in and slid under the form. *"It flexes like a body,"* his heart quickened a beat. *"But no, it's too big to be human; a cow maybe."* Earlier Manuel Angel had seen a dead paca and a puma cub washed up on the beach. He continued walking toward it.

A few minutes later he stared down at the bloated form of an adult male tapir, the first he had seen in half a decade. *"It must've got caught in that horrible current in the Barú and washed out to sea. I thought they were all gone,* he mused. *Maybe this is the last one."* The lifeless tapir was the size of a small cow and shaped like a pig with a short trunk for a nose.

The year was 1955, the month October. For the last week Dominical had endured the worst flood in history. The water rose slowly but steadily, and the rain kept coming, day and night. It rained until people began to wonder if Noah's flood was happening all over again. Water reached within a half meter of Manuel Angel's house, occasionally sloshing against the pilings. The home was located near the Guanacaste crossing four meters above the normal level of the Barú. At no time in the memory of those still living had the Barú reached such heights, and on top of everything else, the October tides were exceptionally high.

Manuel Angel looked up from the dead tapir and gazed down the beach. *"There it is,"* he thought. *"There's my boat. Thank God!"* He let out a whoop and hurried across the wet sand, breaking into a run when it looked like a wave might pull the boat back out to the sea. Rushing waist deep into the surf, Manuel lunged forward and grabbed the edge of the dugout, just before it slipped down the backside of a small, receding wave. The paddle was missing, but he had a spare at home. He tied a rope to the bow and began the long walk, half dragging, half tugging the boat to the mouth of the Barú River and then a thousand meters upstream to his house.

"I wonder if the Red Cross launch will come today," thought Manuel Angel hopefully, tugging on the rope. His wife Blanca, seven months pregnant, had a severe infection in her right foot and, on top of everything else, had suffered a relapse of malaria beginning on the second day of the unrelenting rain. He had no other choice but to sit helpless and watch her suffer through fever and chills, first soaking the bed clothes with sweat, followed by chattering teeth under layers of blankets. This morning, when the downpour waned to a drizzle, Manuel Angel left Blanca with the kids and went in search of the small craft that he was now towing home. Two days previous the dugout had been ripped from its moorings by the raging waters and carried out to sea. Now there was hope.

The house came into sight. "Manuel, Manuel," came the excited voice of his brother-in-law, 12-year-old Daniel. "The Red Cross is waiting. We gotta take Sis now." Manuel didn't waste time asking questions. The tide was rising and would staunch the river's powerful surge. He carried Blanca's limp form, wrapped in a blanket, to the dugout, laid her carefully in the bottom, climbed in himself and paddled the small, unsteady craft across the treacherous river, ever fearful of capsizing in the tumultuous water.

They were met on the other bank by two Red Cross workers and a small group of villagers from Dominical. Everyone took turns carrying Blanca in a stretcher for two kilometers to Dominicalito and the waiting motor launch. The Red Cross boat had arrived a couple of hours earlier with food for the stranded village. Friend and neighbor, Consuelo Agüero, insisted on accompanying Blanca on her journey to the hospital in Puntarenas.

Manuel Angel and Consuelo's husband, Mr. Tommy, bid them farewell and headed back toward the Barú. A light but steady rain began to fall. "Plenty of work ahead cleanin' up the mess," remarked Mr. Tommy.

"You got that right," agreed Manuel, surveying the aftermath of the flood. The forest along the river bank protected the village from the full fury of the current, but not from the water. The town was flooded for three days. Mr. Tommy's two-story, 16-room Hotel Dominical had suffered extensive damage, and the main floor was covered with knee-deep mud.

After a nine-hour boat ride on rough seas, in and out of rain, the two women arrived in Puntarenas where a debilitated and fever-ridden Blanca was admitted to the hospital and kept under observation for one night. The next day Consuelo tended to her friend through a five-hour bus ride to San Jose where Blanca would spend the next three weeks in the hospital. After her release she stayed with an uncle in Escazú for another three weeks until bus service to San Isidro de El General was finally resumed.

Blanca was on the first bus since the hurricane to make it from San Jose to San Isidro. During the seven-hour journey she worried about Manuel and the kids. *"I hope someone came to help with the cleaning and cooking. Manuel can't do woman's work. How on earth did he manage with the two kids?"* Arriving in San Isidro, Blanca learned that it would be six months before the jeep trail to Dominical was passable. Manuel Angel's employer, Rafael Cruz, advanced her 25 colones, more than a month's wages, for a flight to Dominical in a light plane. Two weeks after her homecoming, Blanca gave birth to a strong healthy boy, Rigoberto, her third child. Her friend Consuelo was the midwife.

The dead tapir that Manuel Angel found on Barú Beach was not the last he would ever see. Two years later, in 1957, he shot and killed a tapir in the highland rainforest of Hacienda Barú. At the time he didn't think anything about the possibility that he was killing the last one. Manuel was a hardworking, hard-drinking macho man, and he was also a hunter. He killed almost any wild

A 3-year-old Baird's Tapir.

animal he saw. To him the last one was no different than the first. Years later he grudgingly admitted that he probably should have let it live, but showed no signs of remorse.

Today people's attitudes have changed considerably. Not all of the old-time hunters are like Manuel Angel. Many have seen species they once killed such as tapir, jaguar, and white-lipped peccary disappear from the rainforests. They realize that entire species can become locally extinct, and many now support environmental protection movements. Since the advent of environmental education in the schools in the year 1990, ASANA has been teaching our youth the value of natural systems. Today many of the first children to hear presentations about nature have grown up and now find themselves in decision-making positions in their communities.

The advent of ecological tourism in this area has also been a decisive factor in altering public opinion about hunting. Hacienda Barú employs between 34 and 45 people, depending on the season. These people all know that the tourists who visit the hacienda and other places in the zone come here to see birds and animals. Hundreds of people who work directly or indirectly with tourism owe their living to the wildlife and natural beauty of the region.

A hunter once threatened me with a machete for confiscating his hunting dog. Today that man's son owns and drives a taxi. One day he brought some people to Hacienda Barú for a bird watching tour. I asked him how he was and we got to talking. "Years ago when you and my dad were having problems, I couldn't understand why you didn't want people to kill the animals," he remarked. "But now I understand. Most of the people who ride my taxi want to see our birds and animals. If we lose the rainforest and the wildlife, we lose our way of making a living. My dad will never understand, but I sure do." 🐾

Note: Recounted to me by Manuel Angel Sánchez and his wife Blanca Valverde.

19

A Real-Life Superwoman

The Hardships, Tragedies and Challenges of a Pioneer Woman

How many women do you know in their early 60s who have given birth to 13 children, most of them at home, and without the assistance of a mid-wife? Eleven of this woman's children are still living and have, up until March 2014, given her 16 grandsons and 11 granddaughters, who in turn, have given her two great-grand-daughters. In spite of having lived through years of hardship that most women can barely imagine, Doña Porfiria Gómez carries her 64 years well. My impression was that of a self-confident woman who looks upon her family as her reward for a lifetime of sacrifice and perseverance.

Her humble home is located in San Miguel de Aguirre, seven kilometers from the nearest place where a person can buy a bag of rice or a bar of soap. For the last 15 years she has lived in a real house with a tin roof and wooden floors, where previously she had known only thatch-roofed structures with dirt floors. Her husband, Don José, with the help of some neighbors, built the house. The only power equipment used in its construction was a chainsaw to mill the boards. Everything else was done with hand tools.

She proudly showed me their solar electrical system which generates enough electricity during the day to power three light bulbs at night and enough energy left over to charge her cell phone. The Costa Rican Electrical Institute (ICE) installed this system about ten years ago, and charges only 1,000 colones ($2) a month. ICE had promised them a regular electrical hook-up within a year. "It's now been two years," she said. "When they told us a year, we figured it would be three."

"We've always been poor," she told me, with no trace of regret or complaint. "I was born in Guanacaste. My mother wasn't married, and we didn't have a house of our own. A man let us stay in a *rancho* on the condition that my mother took care of his pigs." She agreed to the deal, but told the *señor* that if *el tigre* (jaguar) came to eat the pigs, she wasn't going to defend them. "That *rancho* had a thatched roof and walls made from the bark of a soft-wooded tree. At night we slept in a loft and locked up the pigs in a pen under the house. After we climbed the ladder to the loft, we could pull the steps up after us. That way *el tigre* couldn't climb up and get us. We were lucky. He never came."

Doña Porfiria continues, "I never had a chance to go to school or learn to read or do numbers. All I ever did was work. We had to go to the creek to wash clothes and bathe, and carry water for the house in buckets. There was no place to buy detergent and even if there had been, we had no money to pay for it. We used crushed papaya leaves for soap. When you soak the leaves in water and rub the clothes with them they foam." Doña Porfiria went on to explain that they made their own tableware from clay, molding the wet clay with their hands into the shape of a bowl, setting it in the fire, and covering it with coals. More than half of the bowls broke. The ones that endured the fire they kept or sold.

One month after her fourteenth birthday in 1963 Porfiria Margarita Gómez married José Artávia Jiménez, nine years her senior. There was no work where they lived in Guanacaste so the newly-wed couple decided to move away and start a new life somewhere else. José's brother-in-law owned some land in San Miguel, south of Quepos, so they set off with the few items they could call their own, all of which they carried on their backs. It took three hours to walk to Jicarál where they boarded a wooden boat made from a hollowed-out tree trunk. The boat ride took them to Puntarenas where they stayed the night, though they weren't able to sleep much. Very early the next morning they boarded another boat for an eight-hour ride to Quepos, and from there went by bus as far as the Savegre River. They walked across the suspension bridge, which was limited to light vehicles and foot traffic. There was no public transportation for the next 12 kilometers, so they walked and caught rides as best they could on the rough and rutted road from Savegre to Hatillo. The two weary travelers walked the last seven kilometers on a horse trail that led to San Miguel. They had reached the place where they would live to this day.

To appreciate the enormity of this trip, consider the psychological trauma young Porfiria must have endured. Here was an adolescent girl, recently married, who said good-bye to the only family she had ever known, not knowing if she would ever see them again. Leaving with her new husband, the couple walked and rode for two days to a strange place in hopes of finding a better life. And they both made the entire trip barefoot.

Thinking back on that fateful journey Doña Porfiria remembers she didn't really feel sad about leaving her home and family. She was young and full of dreams. Life in Guanacaste was difficult, to say the least, and she and José had high hopes of finding something better in San Miguel.

Though the young couple had arrived at the place where they would make their home, the challenge ahead of them seemed insurmountable. They had no place to live, no place to build a hut, and no money. They moved into a small *rancho* with José's brother-in-law, Eladio Céspedes and his family. José was a good, strong worker and found occasional work with several different landowners around San Miguel, all of whom had come from elsewhere in years past and

had experienced difficulties similar to his own. He helped Eladio
plant corn, beans, and plantains. The young couple got to know
their neighbors and came to like the area. One day a neighbor named
Rafael Céspedes offered to sell José seven manzanas (12 acres) of land
for 300 colones (less than a dollar at today's exchange rate.)

"I'd love to own the land Don Raphael, but where am I going to
get 300 colones," shrugged José.

"Don't worry about the money," replied Raphael. "Pay me when
you can." They shook hands on the deal, and, after that, whenever
José had 5 colones to spare he made a payment.

With Eladio's help, José began their first home, a one-room pole
structure with an earthen floor. The walls were made from bal-
sa-wood boards and milled with a two-handed saw that took two
men to push and pull the long blade. The roof was made with the
broad leaves of the salt plant. It wasn't much, but it was theirs.

I asked about mattresses.

"Mattresses? The only mattresses we knew for years were nothing more than a couple of balsa boards shoved together. If we were
lucky we had a piece of cloth to put over the boards so we wouldn't
get splinters."

"What about clothes?" I asked.

"I've never had a sewing machine," replied Doña Porfiria. "I
made all of our clothes by hand with a needle and thread. We bought
cloth in Quepos or San Isidro and I made everything we wore."

She showed me the iron that she still uses to iron clothes. It is
shaped like an electrical iron but bigger and has a lid. Coals from the
cooking fire go inside. She sprinkles the clothes with a little water,
passes the iron over them, and shirts, trousers, and undergarments
come out as if ironed with a modern-day steam iron.

Before they had electrical lights from the solar panel their only
lighting came from kerosene lamps they made at home with a glass
jar, a cotton wick, and a spout. It burned with a small flame at the
top of the spout, much like that of a candle. Their "flashlight" is a

shiny sardine can with a candle inside. They still use these sources of light when the solar system isn't working.

Bowls and spoons were the only eating utensils. Today they have ceramic bowls and metal spoons, but up until recently they used the hard shells of the *jícaro* fruit, a gourd that grows on a tree, for both. Though she now has a store-bought broom, Doña Porfiria still keeps a broom like the ones she used for years, made from brushy plants. In the past she used the seeds from the Guanacaste tree as detergent. Clorox, disinfectant, and scrub pads were things she had heard of but never used until recently.

Doña Porfiria served us home-grown coffee from some coffee trees she grows near the house. "First you pick the coffee," she explained. "Then you have to dry it in the sun and shell it in the *pilón*." She showed me how they put the coffee beans in the *pilón* (a wooden bowl carved into a trunk of wood) and pounded them with a big blunt piece of wood called a *mano*. The beans were then toasted and ground. The ground coffee was placed in a tightly woven cloth bag and hot water poured over it drips into coffee pot placed beneath. The coffee was delicious.

"For years we cooked with a *fogón*, but now I have a nice wood-burning stove." She proudly showed me the cast iron stove located in a corner of the kitchen with a pipe extending up through the roof, carrying the smoke out of the house.

There is a high incidence of lung cancer among rural women in Costa Rica from years of inhaling smoke from the *fogón*, an open fire built in an elevated wooden box filled with earth, sand, or concrete. However, Doña Porfiria assured me that she doesn't have any lung problems.

Doña Porfiria's first child was born in their first home several months after they moved in. When the labor pains began, she wasn't sure what was happening, but as the pains got stronger, and her water broke, it became obvious that the baby was coming. They sent word to the nearest mid-wife, a woman named María who lived a good distance away and had to travel on horseback. By the time María arrived she was almost too late. She took one look at the expectant mother, smiled, placed her hand on Porfiria's swollen belly, and the baby was born, a healthy young boy. They named him Jose. Three months and eleven days later José died at home from gastrointestinal problems. They buried him in the cemetery in Hatillo. The young couple was heart-broken, but before long Porfiria became pregnant with their second child, another boy. This time they didn't bother to call the mid-wife. María had explained what needed to be done, and José did it. Porfiria, of course, did most of the work.

By the time she had five children running around the house, the Health Ministry opened a basic rural clinic in Matapalo. Doña Porfiria had managed to get herself and her children to the clinic on the rare occasion of a doctor's visit. The doctor told her she shouldn't be having her babies at home, that this posed a grave danger to her health and she could die during childbirth. She took the doctor's words seriously and after completing the eighth month of her seventh pregnancy, went to stay with friends near Matapalo. Several people in Matapalo had cars and there was a good possibility of finding a ride to the hospital in Quepos.

When Doña Porfiria felt the first labor pains she told her friend that she wanted to bathe. "I'm all sweaty, and I don't want to go to the hospital like this." After showering she told her friend, "I don't think I have time to go to the hospital. I need to lie down." She did, and the baby was born. "After that," she told me, "I figured doctor didn't know what he was talking about." Her next four children were born at home. But as the roads and availability of transportation improved, she and José finally decided that maybe it was time that she should have medical assistance with her births. Her last three children were born in the hospital in Quepos.

Living as they did, far from the comforts and conveniences enjoyed by most Costa Ricans, Doña Porfiria learned a great deal about the use of natural remedies for common ailments. The nearest doctors or medicines were at the hospital in Quepos, although a handful of over-the-counter medicines like aspirin and eyedrops were available at the small general store in Hatillo. The most common health problem with the children was internal parasites like worms and amoebas. This has always been the primary cause of infant mortality in Costa Rica, and, though considerable improvements have been made, continues to be so today. Learning how to deal with intestinal problems and parasites was an absolute necessity for women living in San Miguel.

Once a year a representative from the health department visited the family, vaccinated the children for childhood diseases, and distributed medicine for dysentery and parasites. "That worm medicine from the health department never worked," she told me. "I always gave the kids a tea I made from the stem of the *estrella* plant. Make sure you cut only stem, no knots," she emphasized. "I chopped it up and boiled it in water. You couldn't believe the rolls of worms

153

that came out of those kids." She went on to explain she used bark from the *nance* tree cooked with avocado to treat gastritis. Another remedy that continues to be popular in rural Costa Rica is what is called the *sobada* or deep massage of the lymph nodes. This is used to treat what is called *el empacho*, a term used to describe uneasiness in the stomach that persists for days and won't go away.

In March of 2013 Doña Porfiria and Don Jose celebrated their 50th wedding anniversary. In this day and age, many people would be horrified at the thought of a 14-year-old girl marrying a 23-year-old man. Yet in the rural Costa Rica of 1963 their marriage was not considered unusual. When I was with them they laughed and teased each other and were obviously a happy couple.

Today many things have changed in the nearby communities, but life is much the same for Doña Porfiria and Don José. In spite of all the hardship life has brought them I never detected the slightest indication that they considered themselves to be victims of poverty or that life had dealt them a bad hand; rather they were thankful for their good health, the roof over their heads, the food in their stomachs, and above all, the health and prosperity of their extensive family.

The most amazing thing about this story is that only the details are unique. Many rural Costa Rican women have lived equally difficult lives, fraught with hardships, tragedies, and challenges. 🦥

20

From Destroyer to Protector

Learning New Ways of Making a Living

As countries and regions develop, the way people use the land changes, forcing many to learn new ways to make a living. Since the mid-1980s, the land usage and economy in the Path of the Tapir Biological Corridor have undergone a transformation from farming and ranching to tourism and real estate development. People whose families have for generations cut down the rainforest, grown crops, and raised cattle were forced to learn how to deal with changing conditions. In most cases, this meant learning a new trade. Children who were born in rural environments and grew up assuming that they would either farm or marry farmers, today find themselves working as construction workers, taxi drivers, cooks, waiters, bartenders, receptionists, and bookkeepers. Most have also learned the importance of protecting nature, because that is why tourists come here. This is the story of one rural Costa Rican family and how they have adapted in a changing world.

Three Generations of Seguras

As young man of 17 years Ramón Segura Barrantes came to San

Isidro de El General. The year was 1948, and he came with the troops of José "Don Pepe" Figueres to battle the forces of ex-president Dr. Rafael Calderón. Following Figueres' victory, young Ramón decided to settle near Pacuarito where his grandfather had homesteaded and cleared about 100 hectares of jungle. Later he inherited his grandfather's farm.

In the late 1950s Ramón married Irma Lidia Picado Méndez from Bijaguales, near Pacuarito. On February 28, 1959 their first child, Juan Ramón, was born in the hospital in San Isidro de El General. The couple would later have four more sons and two daughters.

Ramón was one of the first settlers to move into the area around what is today known as Lagunas, near Dominical. In 1949 he began clearing land to plant corn, beans, rice, and pasture. The Lagunas farm, also about 100 hectares, was the maximum area to which one person could acquire title under the same homestead program utilized by his grandfather. It was on these two farms that his firstborn son, Juan Ramón, was to spend his childhood and early adulthood.

Juan Ramón's early memories are primarily of his life on the two farms. He attended the local school at Pacuarito for six years where, under very restricted classroom conditions, he more or less learned to read, write, and do basic arithmetic. That's where his formal schooling ended and after graduating from the sixth grade, he went to work with his father and uncle.

The Pacuarito farm had pasture and grew coffee; the Lagunas farm grew corn, rice, and beans, and also had cattle pasture and forest. Each year Juan Ramón helped his father and uncle fell and burn a little jungle and kept on doing so until there was virtually none left. The homestead law requires that the land be worked and developed as a condition for issuing the title. This was considered progress. Conservation was a totally foreign concept to the pioneers of that era. The procedure followed by the Segura family was to clear the rainforest, plant two or three crops, and then plant pasture. The trees used for building houses, barns, corrals, and fence posts were extracted before the forest was clear cut and all of the undergrowth cleared away with a machete. Juan Ramón says that the actual felling of the rainforest was hard work, but he enjoyed it. He loved everything about it: the dull clang of metal against wood, blow after blow of the finely honed axe head biting into the trunk, chips flying from the mighty tree, and the anticipation of the moment when the once mighty lord of the forest would finally yield and break with a resounding *caaarraack!* followed a moment later by a *whish* and a deafening *whump!* as the falling giant hit the ground.

But as much as he enjoyed felling trees, the part he loved most about clearing land was the burning; it held a strange fascination for him. In the 1970s the practice of burning the aftermath of felled rainforest and certain types of pasture grasses was so widespread that at times great clouds of smoke shrouded the entire countryside and visibility was so bad that small planes couldn't fly. All during the dry season the smell of smoke filled the air and over-shadowed all other odors. Most people, Juan included, didn't see anything wrong with the burning and smoke. It was simply a side effect of progress.

Juan's uncle, Wilson Segura, who lived on the Lagunas farm, taught ten-year-old Juan to hunt paca, agouti, and iguana. To his credit he instilled in his nephew a respect for the rest of the animals. They never hunted white-collared peccary, coati mundi, or fowl of any kind. They ate what they hunted and when the hunt was very successful they salted and smoked the meat over the open hearth. In this manner it could be kept for several months without spoiling. Wilson was a veteran hunter and taught Juan all of the tricks. He even taught him how unscrupulous hunters poached on properties where the owners didn't allow hunting. He made sure, however, that Juan understood that the Seguras were honest people and never infringed on other landowners' property rights. The main precaution poachers took, said Wilson, was not hunting with dogs. Their baying can be heard for a great distance. However, if you set a trap, or bait the prey, the property owner is unlikely to find it and a poacher can still get a paca once in a while.

The most effective type of trap was made with an empty 55-gallon drum buried in the ground near a fruit tree where pacas feed during the fruiting season, often at one of several types of palm that drop ripe fruits to the ground. The open top of the barrel was covered with flimsy palm leaves, and palm fruits were scattered around the opening. If a paca came to eat the palm fruits and fell into the empty drum it couldn't climb out.

Another way to hunt without dogs was to place bananas or plantains near a tree that had a sturdy, low hanging branch to sit on. Every few days the poacher returned with more bait and checked the ground for tracks. Some hunters built small platforms in suitable trees. Once the pacas were coming regularly to the bait the hunter would wait for an evening when the moon set early, then climb up, sit on the branch or platform, and wait with a .22 caliber rifle with a flashlight tied to it. Upon hearing the prey eating the bait, the hunter would turn on the flashlight, illuminate the paca, and shoot it.

Juan always hunted with dogs, and craved the excitement when the dogs came across a hot trail and started baying. This marked the beginning of the chase. The paca usually ran to its den, a tunnel that led to a chamber deep in the ground. If the dogs found the tunnel, the paca would leave by the rear exit, and the chase was on again. The trick was to catch the paca before it got to the tunnel, or find both the entrance and the exit, and dig it out.

When in his early 20s Juan Ramón often went to Playa Barú, the beach in front of what was later to become Hacienda Barú National Wildlife Refuge, to hunt for turtle eggs. It was on one of these expeditions that he met Didilia Cascante Hernandez whose family owned a farm adjoining the hacienda. Didilia worked in our household. The young couple was married in 1982 when Juan Ramón was 23 years old and Didilia was 21.

The newlyweds moved to Lagunas to work the farm. Scratching out a living raising cattle and growing corn and beans wasn't easy, but neither of the pair was a stranger to hard work, and they were able to make a reasonable living. Their first two children, Shirley and Jason, were born during the seven years they lived there. When

Shirley reached six years of age, Didilia and her children moved to Pacuarito where she lived with her in-laws so Shirley could enter primary school. Not long after the move she gave birth to their third child, Mauren.

Juan Ramón remained behind in Lagunas where he continued to work the farm and earn a living for the growing family, which he visited from time to time. This type of double life, separated from his wife and children, didn't go well. The worry of being apart from his family, combined with cooking for himself and too much *guaro*, the local hard liquor distilled from sugarcane, led to major health problems. The once strong, healthy, hardworking father developed a bleeding ulcer. In 1991 the whole family moved to Didilia's parent's home near Hacienda Barú. Juan Ramón had deteriorated to such a delicate state of health that the doctors wouldn't perform surgery on his stomach ulcer until he had rested and built up some strength. They even warned the family of the possibility that he might not live.

When he first came to see me about a job at our nature reserve he was thin and frail. His eyes were sunken back into his head and his skin had an ashy, pallid tint that hinted of anemia. I remember thinking he should be home in bed not out looking for work. We talked for a while and I began to get a glimpse of the man behind the physical appearance. I had known him casually when he was courting Didilia and when they came to visit her parents, but this was the first time I had a chance to really sit down and converse with him. I liked what I saw.

We agreed that he would begin working three half-days per week as a forest guard. His job was to walk through the rainforest of Hacienda Barú and look for signs of poachers. As he got stronger we gradually began increasing his hours. At that time the wildlife refuge was already doing some hiking tours, but that concept was totally foreign to Juan Ramón. He couldn't fathom why anyone would pay hard cash to be guided down a jungle trail.

During those weeks that he wandered through the rainforest alone, a change came over Juan Ramón. Cast in the role of protector of the jungle rather than destroyer, he had the opportunity to rethink many of his earlier beliefs from a new point of view. He saw a beauty and power in the inner workings of ecosystems that he hadn't seen before. He began an ongoing experience with nature which he describes as spiritual. Rather than looking at the forest as something to be exploited and destroyed, he came to see it as a giver of life, a force that produces a multitude of life-forms and promotes well-being. His health improved rapidly, so much so that the planned surgery was no longer necessary.

Within a month he was working three full days per week, then five, and later six. He began guiding. At first he accompanied groups that Diane or I were guiding, but he learned quickly, and soon he was taking groups on his own. His extroverted personality and reverence for the rainforest made him popular with the visitors. It was the only work he knew where he enjoyed providing the service as much as the tourists who were paying him to guide them.

Like many Costa Ricans Juan believed that all of the important things in the world came from other countries. Though he enjoyed and revered the rainforest, he couldn't imagine what someone from North America or Europe would find interesting about it. He knew people liked monkeys and toucans, but he couldn't understand why they would enjoy seeing a sloth or an armadillo. One day he was guiding some people from the United States when they came across a three-toed sloth very near the ground and moving along a branch. The guests got very emotional about the sloth, took lots of photos, and congratulated Juan. One man reached in his pocket, pulled out a $10 bill and handed it to him. This was Juan Ramón's first tip, and it was a tremendous incentive for him to do even better to find more animals and share even more of his knowledge about the rainforest. I believe it wasn't so much the money, but rather the idea that the things many *ticos* take for granted, have real value for people from other countries.

Juan Ramón and I noticed that monkeys, toucans, and sloths were the animals Hacienda Barú's guests most wanted to see. Many of them had already seen monkeys or toucans, which were easier to find, but sloths were dull colored, didn't move much, and often slept shrouded in leaves. So we set about looking for ways to spot more sloths. The combination of Juan's eagle-eye and natural instinct about the jungle soon had him finding more of both the two-toed and three-toed varieties than anyone had previously believed possible. This talent earned him the nickname of Hacienda Barú's resident "slothologist." His record to date is seventeen of these charismatic mammals on a five-hour hike.

The more he guided, the more hungry he became for knowledge about nature. Hacienda Barú sponsored several seminars for nature guides, inviting employees from other nature tour providers in the area as well as our own. We usually brought in a nationally known guide to conduct the

Juan Ramon Segura bird watching.

seminar. In spite of his meager formal education Juan Ramón was always seriously involved in these short courses. In 1994 Hacienda Barú made it possible for him to attend a guiding seminar sponsored by Costa Rica Expeditions held at Monteverde Lodge near the Monteverde cloud forest. The speakers were internationally known experts on ecological tourism, and he counts the experience as one of the highlights of his guiding education.

About the same time as the Monteverde seminar Juan became good friends with an ornithologist named Jim Zook and developed an interest in birds. Jim was a former Peace Corps Volunteer who had married a Costa Rican girl and made Costa Rica his home. He worked for about a year as a guide at Hacienda Barú and accompanied Juan to the seminar at Monteverde. Because of his newfound interest Juan decided to learn everything he could about birds and quickly became proficient in spotting and identifying all kinds of avian life, both visually and audibly. He soon learned to identify most of the 368 species found at Hacienda Barú by their songs as well as their markings. Like all bird watchers, it is difficult to find Juan Ramón without a pair of binoculars dangling from his neck.

In rural Costa Rica, people tend to jealously guard any knowledge or special talent they have acquired and never teach it to anyone outside of the immediate family. This attitude is commonly explained as necessary to protect yourself from unscrupulous coworkers who might have ideas of stealing your job. Juan Ramón did not agree; he always shared his knowledge freely, earning him the respect and friendship of his colleagues and securing his position as leader amongst the Hacienda Barú employees. In his early years of guiding he was extremely influential in training. He has instilled a profound respect for the rainforest in his coworkers, particularly Pedro Porras, who has become an outstanding birder and naturalist guide, and Deiner Cascante, who was born on Hacienda Barú and now has his own business driving tourists to their destinations in his large van. Juan Ramón has unselfishly shared his knowledge with all of the guides who work here now and have worked here in the past.

Another of his character traits that has helped make him an outstanding nature guide is his ability to communicate with non-Spanish speaking people, regardless of which language they speak. He always carries English language copies of *Birds of Costa Rica* and *Mammals of Costa Rica*. Upon spotting some interesting wildlife he first points it out to the visitors and then quickly finds its picture in the book, where they can read more about the bird or mammal if they wish. But his ability to communicate goes far beyond merely pointing to a picture in a book; he seems to communicate with his whole being. I have had people who were dubious about going out with a non-English speaking guide return from the tour and correctly describe complicated interrelationships between living things in the rainforest that Juan had explained to them. When I ask how he communicated such a complicated idea, no one can explain it.

As part of his work with ASANA in their environmental education program, Juan Ramón gives talks to school children about different aspects of ecology, the environment, and the need to protect it. Juan has organized field trips for local school children to visit Hacienda Barú's marine turtle project. I once heard him remark, "We may not be able to get their parents to change, but we can educate the future community leaders while they are still young and open to new ideas."

As of this writing he is president of the Hacienda Barú Solidarity Association, President of the Association for the Administration of the Hatillo Community Aqueduct, and has served four years as a councilman on the Quepos municipal council. I don't know where he finds time for all of these activities, but he manages to do a good job at all of them and never lets his job at Hacienda Barú suffer. Juan Ramón still does some guiding, but spends most of his time managing the Hacienda Barú operation. He is the man in the field making things happen when and how they should.

The preservation of the rainforest is Juan Ramón Segura's top priority in life. He explained to me that he feels a close affinity with the jungle because it gave him back his health at a time when he wasn't sure he would ever recover. Although he isn't religious, he considers his relationship with nature to be spiritual. He told me that after his health returned he made the decision to dedicate his life to the forest, conserving it, and teaching others to do the same. Guiding is his primary means to this end. Juan Ramon's dream is to one day see a tapir and a jaguar, hopefully on Hacienda Barú. 🐾

21

The Black-Hat Guy on the Bicycle

The Story of a Campesino Called "Tornillo"

During his years on Hacienda Barú, Daniel Granados (aka Tornillo) either planted or participated in the planting of over 20,000 trees, and he knows where each one is located. He remembers in the early 1950s when Maximo Cordero, administrator of Hacienda Barú, planted the mango trees around the Casona, now the Hacienda Barú Biological Research Center. Daniel himself planted teak trees in 1985, gmelina, acacia, pochote, and numerous fruit trees in the late 1980s; and over 5,000 trees of several endangered species like cedro bateo, manú negro, espavel, ceibo, javillo, cedro maría, lechoso, ron ron, ojoche, iguano, aceituno, and others during the 1990s. If you add to that all the living fence posts he planted on Hacienda Barú's 14 kilometers of fences, during the 55 years since he first began working here, Daniel can claim to have planted an enormous number of trees. Yet if you asked him what he did here, he will humbly tell you that he was a tractor driver and laborer, and probably won't even mention the trees.

Daniel Valverde Granados, son of María Granados López and Reynaldo Valverde Gamboa, was born in Palmares de Pérez Zeledón in 1944. He doesn't remember anything at all of life in Palmares, as his family moved to Caña Blanca, between Alfombra and San Juan de Dios, when he was less than four years old. His earliest memory of Caña Blanca was from the year 1948 when two armed men came to the house and took his father away at gun point. Three weeks later Don Reynaldo returned. Daniel remembers that his father was nearly naked with his sparse clothing torn and hanging on his emaciated body. It was the first time Daniel had seen his father with a beard. The two men had taken him to Pacuarito to fight in the civil war with the troops of Don Pepe Figueres. Don Reynaldo told them that there had been 25 men in his platoon and only 12 of them survived to return to their families. After the war there was a general feeling of insecurity in the countryside.

When Daniel was ten, his family moved to Dominical, and for the first time in his life he attended school. His first and only teacher, whom he remembers fondly, was Doña Marina Badilla. The school was in an old building that used to be the headquarters of the now-defunct Resguardo Fiscal (fiscal police). There were about 15 students in the school, six grades, and one teacher. About half of the students went to classes in the morning and half in the afternoon. Daniel always went to school in the morning. Since the Valverde family lived near Doña Marina, she was always happy to help him with his homework after the afternoon session was over.

At the age of 12 Daniel began working part time at Hacienda Barú in addition to his schooling. At first he helped with chores around the house, fed the pigs and chickens, and cleaned their pens. Soon, however, his responsibilities increased. Don Rafael Cruz, the owner of Hacienda Barú, had built a small dairy where they milked about 20 cows. Late every afternoon they separated the calves from the cows to keep them from nursing during the night. The cows would then have a full udder in the morning and be ready for milking. Each day at 4:30 a.m. Daniel brought the cows in for milking. His last job in the afternoon was to separate the calves from the cows and lock them in a small pen for the night.

After bringing in the cows every morning he had to feed the pigs and clean their pen, pick up the milk from the dairy and take it to Alcides Delgado in Barú, who sold it from his small general store, La Novia del Barú. Then Daniel hurried back to Dominical for three hours of school. After school, there was no time to play since he had to carry the workers' lunches to where they were working. After lunch, Daniel had a little time to study or help around the house, but then had to return to the job site with coffee and an afternoon snack for the workers, usually at 2:00 p.m. Sometimes, he would stay and help the workers, and on other occasions he would return home and do his homework until it was time to bring in the calves. He was a busy boy with little idle time for play or mischief. When he was 14, Manuel Angel began paying him a salary of 15 colones per week, so Daniel quit school and began working full time. By that time he was doing a man's job.

He worked with his brother-in-law on Hacienda Barú all during the early and mid-1960s. Then in 1967 Don Rafael Cruz sold Hacienda Barú to a LACSA pilot named Teorico Zamora, known to everyone as "Toco" Zamorra. At that time Manuel Angel Sanchez left Hacienda Barú and went into business for himself, while Daniel stayed at Hacienda Barú, working with Toco Zamora's new foreman, Alvaro Meza. In addition to being a commercial pilot, Toco was a partner in the local airline AVE. While flying one of AVE's small planes he crashed and was killed. After his death Toco's widow, Ana María Acosta, stepped into her late husband's shoes and took over the management of Hacienda Barú. Alvaro Meza remained as foreman, and Daniel was a laborer. It was during this time that one of Daniel's most-remembered life experiences occurred.

Daniel doesn't remember if it was Alvaro Mesa who felled the last *manú negro* tree on Hacienda Barú, but he was definitely the one who sent the workers to cut it into logs and split the logs into posts. Some people say that what happened that day was Alvaro's punishment for cutting down the last *manú negro* on Hacienda Barú. Others say it was the curse of an Indian shaman whose tomb Alvaro had opened. Regardless of why it happened, it was the worst experience of his entire life.

The year was 1971. Daniel Valverde, Nato and Challo Campos, and Arcele Arroyo followed Alvaro Mesa to the fallen tree, deep in the rainforest of the upper portions of the hacienda. On the hike up, Alvaro showed the men a pre-Columbian cemetery where he claimed to have found gold in one of the tombs. When they reached the fallen *manú negro*, Alvaro left instructions with Daniel and Arcele and took Nato and Challo with him to blaze the trail they would use to carry the posts out on their shoulders.

Daniel and Arcele got to work with axes. Chopping the large trunk into two-meter logs was their first task. Later they planned to split the logs into posts by driving iron wedges into the sturdy wood. The first time they stopped chopping to rest, they heard Challo's faint yell in the distance. "Come! Hurry! Alvaro's been bit by a *terciopelo*." [4]

"*Ya vamos*," hollered Daniel, setting off on the same path they had used earlier.

They found Challo at the pre-Columbian cemetery, intently watching the snake. "She's really pissed," he warned. "Keep your distance. God, you should have seen it. Alvaro slipped and fell over by the tomb. The *terciopelo* must have been lying right there. At first he thought a wasp had got him or maybe a thorn, but then he saw her, and he knew. We all did. It bit him a little above the elbow."

The *terciopelo* held its head high, level with Daniel's waist, looking from one side to the other, tongue flicking in and out, watching, waiting. It was the largest one Daniel had ever seen, well over two meters long. He cut a thin pole and held it out. The snake struck at the pole. Daniel swung and missed. The *terciopelo* advanced and struck again. Daniel's second blow caught the enormous snake behind the head. He hit it again and again. Finally he chopped it to pieces with his machete. "Let's go," urged Arcele. "We gotta find Alvaro."

---

4   A *terciopelo* is a pit viper sometimes called fer de lance (*Bothrops asper*).

A half hour later they found him sitting at the edge of the road in front of the hacienda. Alvaro didn't know who they were until Daniel spoke, when he seemed to recognize the voice. "Nato went to look for Don Marvin about the car," he said hoarsely, holding up a badly swollen arm. "Hey, help me get this watch off."

Daniel tried to unbuckle the watch. "I need a wire cutter to cut the band. I can't get the buckle loose." The swelling had engulfed the watch band in flesh. When Daniel gave up trying to remove it, his hands were covered with blood. It was oozing from Alvaro's pores.

Nato came running up, breathless. "Marvin said we can use the car, but Primo isn't around and nobody else knows how to drive."

"Daniel, get the tractor keys out of my pocket. I can't get my hand in it. You can drive the tractor, can't you, at least to get to Dominical and get some snake bite serum from Don Celso?" The policeman in Dominical always kept a vial of antivenin for snake bite. But Alvaro's entire body was swollen and Daniel couldn't get the keys out of his pocket.

Arcele's wife, Doña Irma, five months pregnant, came walking down the road to see how Alvaro was doing. Challo saw her first. "Here comes Doña Irma," he warned.

"God, no! Stop her! Don't let her get near me! If she gets too close I'll die on the spot." Alvaro couldn't see Arcele's wife, but the thought of her pregnant form was terrifying. It was a common belief that the proximity of a pregnant woman would kill a snake-bite victim. Daniel met Doña Irma on the road, blocked her path and explained that Alvaro didn't want her to come any closer. Tears filled her eyes, but she backed away, torn between concern for Alvaro and the belief that her presence might cause him harm.

"Listen!" called Arcele excitedly. "Is that a car coming?" The distant sound of a motor was barely audible, but growing louder by the second. After a few minutes an orange Willis Jeep came into view. Arcele looked at Nato. "Of all the people to come along at a time like this, Alvaro's worst enemy," he lamented.

"It doesn't make any difference," insisted Daniel. "He can't refuse to take Alvaro. He can't just let him die. We've got to stop him." He stepped out in the road and flagged the Jeep to stop. It hadn't come to a complete stop when Daniel ran around to the driver's side and blurted out. "Don Eliecer, Alvaro's been snake bit. We gotta get him to the hospital."

Eliecer Castro looked at the swollen form of Alvaro Mesa sitting at the edge of the road, blood dripping from his nose and dribbling down his shirt. "Come on, boys, let's get him in the car. We can't leave him here. Don't worry, I'll take care of everything." They loaded Alvaro, now incoherent, in the orange Jeep. He didn't even know who was taking him to the hospital.

Four hours after he was bitten, Alvaro Mesa arrived at the emergency entrance of the San Isidro hospital. Eliecer Castro found a phone and called Ana María Acosta, owner of Hacienda Barú. Arriving in San Isidro the following day, Ana María decided that Alvaro had to be moved to San Jose. The doctors at the San Isidro Hospital insisted that he would be fine with them. "If he is fine with you, then why hasn't he urinated since he's been here," she retorted. "Something is obviously wrong. I'm moving him to San Jose." And so she did.

Two days later, Alvaro was still mostly incoherent, but he remembers the doctors taking him into the operating room. "What are you gonna do to me?" he asked.

"We're going to fix you up," they told him. "After we're finished, you'll get better."

Alvaro did get better after the surgery, but he never understood they were going to amputate his arm, which had become infected, gangrenous and life threatening. It was quite a shock at first, but later he realized that the doctors had only done what they had to do to save his life.

One of the thousands of trees planted by Daniel on Hacienda Baru.

In 1984 Daniel returned to Hacienda Barú, again to work as a tractor driver. At first he lived in a house on the hacienda, but after several years acquired his own home in Platanillo. For the next 24 years Daniel made the daily ride on his bicycle. As the hacienda gradually phased out cattle ranching and farming and began catering to ecological tourism, the need for a tractor driver diminished. Daniel still drove the tractor when necessary, but he also became crew foreman, a job that he held until his retirement in February 2011.

Today, because of the work that Daniel and his fellow workers have done on Hacienda Barú, many of these trees will once again inhabit forests in the Path of the Tapir Biological Corridor. Daniel is happy to see that he and his companions are not alone. In recent years many school groups and environmental organizations have carried out reforestation projects within the corridor. He beams with pride when talking about all of these efforts. 🐾

Part Three

22

Clickity Clack Down the Track

Traveling Through the Jungle on a Narrow-Gauge Railroad

They called it the *carro salón* or luxury car, though it was anything but luxurious. I have also heard it called the "chair car" in English. Compared to regular passenger cars, the *carro salón* had comfortable seats with plenty of leg room, a relatively nice restroom, and a balcony on the back end. It had the distinction of being the last car on the train, right behind the caboose, so from the balcony passengers had a view on three sides. Beer and soft drinks were sold inside, and a short, fat lady with a checkered apron came through selling tortillas and empanadas. The wealthier people always rode on the *carro salón*, everybody else went in the regular cars.

All the trains had names. El Pachuco was the only train with a *carro salón*. It traveled between Limón and San Jose daily, as did another train known as El Pasajero. El Río Frio traveled between Turrialba and Río Frio, but Guápiles was the most important station on the far end of that line.

The cattle ranch where I worked was located in a corner so it bordered both the original narrow-gauge railroad line from Limón to Guápiles, *la linea vieja*, and the line from San Jose that joined it. The La Florida and the La Francia stations were both on the ranch, the former on the line from San Jose to Limón, and the latter on the *linea vieja.*

The few adventurous tourists who visited Costa Rica in the 1970s and wanted to see Limón always rode on the *carro salón.* I rode the train twice each week, once going out to the ranch at the beginning of the week and again when returning to my family in San Jose at the end. I met foreign tourists on the train about once a month.

One day in 1973, two couples from Chicago were on El Pachuco on their way to Limón. A couple of hours out of San Jose, several people were standing on the balcony talking. About the same time that the train slowed for a curve and a bridge, one of the men leaned against the boarding gate. Suddenly it unlatched and swung outward. The man fell from the train and landed on the hard gravel beside the tracks, just a short distance shy of a bridge spanning a deep ravine. The man's wife screamed.

Everybody stood staring over the railing off the back end of the car at the fallen man. The train clickity clacked on down the track, rocking slightly from side to side. His wife screamed louder. I ran to the next car forward, the caboose, and burst through the door to be met by the startled faces of the crew.

"Stop the train!" I yelled. "A man fell off."

On either side of the caboose was an open door where a crew member stood looking out. "Nobody has fallen from the train," declared one of them defensively. "We've been watching."

"No, not there," I blurted, desperately. "He fell off the balcony of the *carro salón.* You wouldn't have seen him from the caboose."

Not yet comprehending and still on the defensive, he again tried to explain. "We've been watching and...*carro salón*, did you say?" He pointed toward the end of the train.

"That's right! Stop the train."

The brake man pulled the emergency brake. The train slowed abruptly and screeched to a stop. He communicated with the engineer over the intercom, and El Pachuco began backing up, slowly. It took five minutes to cover the half a kilometer to where the shaken man was still sitting beside the tracks. Though a little battered and bruised, he didn't seem badly hurt and, with a little help, stood up and boarded the train. He seemed to be okay in spite of his traumatic experience. Nevertheless, an ambulance met the train in Turrialba about half an hour later and took him and his wife to the hospital. At the end of the week, when I returned to San Jose, a crew member told me that the injured man had been released from the hospital and continued his journey to Limón the following day.

There was never a dull moment when traveling the trains. Landslides often blocked the tracks, especially along the steep banks of the Reventazon River, between Turrialba and Las Juntas. Derailments were also common, but since the trains rarely traveled faster than 30 kph, this type of accident usually didn't result in serious damage to either equipment or passengers.

The Atlantic railroad, owned by the Northern Railway Company, was founded by industrialist Minor Keith, the man generally credited with accomplishing the gargantuan task of constructing Costa Rica's first railroad. The project was begun in the 1880s and completed in 1891. Partially financed by United Fruit Company, the railroad made banana production feasible in the Atlantic zone.

Keith soon found that Costa Rican workers had little resistance to malaria and yellow fever and would not be able to provide the labor for building the railway, so he brought in black laborers from Jamaica. The Jamaicans were good workers and had a long history of resistance to tropical diseases. Had it not been for them, the Atlantic railway might never have been completed. Nevertheless they were offered little in appreciation for their role in making the railroad possible. Even Jamaicans born in Costa Rica were, for years, considered to be Jamaican citizens and were not granted the same rights as Costa Ricans. At first, blacks were allowed to travel no farther west than Peralta, a small town between Siquirres and Turrialba. Later they were allowed to go as far as Turrialba, then Cartago, and finally to San Jose and the rest of the country. This restriction on their travel was apparently not a law, but rather some sort of social restraint or perhaps a policy of the Northern Railway Company, the only source of transport from the Atlantic to the rest of the country. Eventually those of Jamaican descent, born in Costa Rica, were given citizenship.

The Chinese also played an important role in the building of the railway and the economy which sprouted up along its path. At the end of the nineteenth century and the beginning of the twentieth, the immigration of Chinese to Costa Rica was prohibited by law. Laws, however, are often written for the common people and do not apply to the wealthy. In spite of the legal impediments Chinese were brought here to work as indentured servants in the households of well-to-do Costa Rican families. After a certain number of years of unpaid service, their debt was fulfilled and their freedom granted. Most took the last names of their former masters and eventually acquired Costa Rican citizenship.

I knew a Chinese man who lived at El Cairo on the *linea vieja*. He and his wife were betrothed as children and came to Costa Rica at the age of 10 or 11. After gaining their freedom by working 15 years, they moved into the jungles of the Atlantic, along the railroad, and proceeded to make their fortune. Hard work and thriftiness over the years brought the family a respectable measure of success. When I knew them in the early 1970s they were in their 60s, owned several businesses, and were considered wealthy. One of their daughters had gone to the University of Costa Rica where she met a Costa Rican boy whom she later married. Her marriage to a non-Chinese, as I recall, was the greatest family crisis in many years.

As the sole form of transport, the railroad was the key factor for all production in the zone. In the tropical lowlands banana production was the motor that drove the economy; in other areas it was cattle. The ranch where I worked comprised four farms that had been purchased separately and combined to make one 4,000-hectare ranch. Part of the land had once been owned by Goodyear Rubber Company and consisted mostly of rubber trees. The rubber trees were planted and the community of La Francia built by Goodyear during World War II. Part of my job in the early 1970s was to oversee the felling of those rubber trees and the planting of cattle pasture.

Everything was coordinated from the main office in La Francia, which in addition to being our business office, functioned as a railroad station. As such we had a railroad telephone. Some older readers may remember when party lines were the norm and a private telephone line a luxury. The railroad telephones were the epitome of party lines. Ours had 52 parties, each with its own distinct ring. We could call the other 51 parties on our line, but it wasn't possible to call outside of that line. Rather than dialing, we turned the crank the specified number of rings, long and short. A full turn of the crank was a long ring, and half a turn a short ring. Everybody on the line could hear the phone ring whenever someone made a call. Needless to say, our phone rang all day long. My ears never got attuned to the different rings, but the office staff jumped whenever ours sounded: three long—two short—one long—one short. Most of the staff could identify all 52 rings. One time in an emergency, Mario, an office employee, called Limón and convinced the station manager to hold the receiver of the railroad phone up to the receiver of a regular phone and patch the call through to San Jose, but this service wasn't available under normal circumstances.

I remember meeting the Cahuita school teacher while waiting for the train at Penhurst. He had recently arrived from Jamaica and spoke excellent and very proper English, but not a word of Spanish. Most of the local people spoke a dialect called Patois, which appeared to be a mixture of English, Spanish, and French. I could pick up a few English and Spanish words, but couldn't understand the conversations. Almost everybody spoke English and the younger people spoke excellent Spanish.

Due to the influence of the English language throughout the Caribbean, many of the Spanish-speaking people used words adapted from English. For example, a creek, which is usually called a *quebrada* in Spanish, was called a "creekay" on the farm where I worked. The brake man on a train on the Pacific railroad is called a *frenero* which comes from the Spanish word for brake, *freno*. However, on the Atlantic Railroad the brake man is called the *brakero*.

At that time I owned a fat, loose-skinned, sad-eyed basset hound named Pierre that I really wanted to take to La Francia. The railroad, however, had a regulation against taking pets on the train, supposedly because of the danger of bites and rabies. My friend and fellow worker, Harry, suggested that I drive him to Siquirres by road (jeep trail). "We'll figure out a way to get him on the train from there to La Francia," he said with a wink.

My wife Diane, seven-year-old daughter Natalie, two-year-old son Chris, dog Pierre and I drove to Siquirres. We parked the jeep next to a gas station where people who had gone on the train left their cars. We walked Pierre over to the train station on a leash. He was the center of attention. One boy, looking at the folds of skin on his face, asked, "Does that dog have eyes?" Somebody else remarked that we had better hold onto him tight or he would end up in the chop suey at some Chinese restaurant.

Harry and a bunch of his friends met us there. We boarded the train in a mob and shoved Pierre under a seat. During the short ride it was easy to keep him hidden with human bodies. When the conductor came by to collect the fares, everyone laughed and joked to keep him distracted. The conductor spotted Pierre as I was leading him off the train. "Hey, what's that dog doing here?" he blurted. "You can't bring a dog on the train."

I stepped from the train over to the boarding ramp, Pierre made the short leap with ease, glad to be out from under the seat and into the fresh air as Harry turned to the conductor and smiled, "Don't worry, we paid for his passage." He stepped off the train as it began to pull away. The conductor threw up his hands in defeat.

The Atlantic railroad was severely damaged in the earthquake of 1991. It continued to operate with limited service until 1995 when it ceased to function entirely. In 2013 service was resumed as far as Cartago in an effort to offer alternate forms of public transportation and alleviate the congestion of automobiles in San Jose. 🐾

23

La Casona de Hacienda Barú

A House Full of Memories

In the early 1970s the Inter-American Highway (also called the Pan-American Highway) was full of holes and had even more curves than it does today. It took Ricardo and I four hours to drive from San José over the 3,100-meter Cerro de La Muerte to San Isidro de el General. Pulling into town we filled the Land Rover with diesel at the Gasotica, one of two service stations in town. The other was the Texaco which was located where today there is a Pizza Hut. The highway was paved, but all the streets in San Isidro were gravel.

After buying some supplies at the central market, where today stands the cultural center, we drove through town and asked a man on horseback for directions to Dominical. He pointed us down the street that ran along the west side of the park. It took us past the airport, which stretched from where today we find the new central market, south past the soccer field, and all the way to the bar called Uno Mas.

Soon we were on the outskirts of town stirring up dust on a bumpy gravel road which eventually took us up some extremely steep hills and straight over the top of El Alto de San Juan. Even though the road was dry we wouldn't have made it up that hill without four-wheel drive. Two and a half hours from San Isidro, after passing through four small villages and fording four streams, we arrived at our destination, a place called Hacienda Barú. That was my first view of La Casona hidden behind a grove of mango trees a hundred meters from the road.

The house was obviously new. Though unpainted the wood had the color and brightness of recently milled lumber rather than the gray, dried look characteristic of older wood. The design reminded me of the banana company villages with the kitchen and open porch downstairs, and four bedrooms upstairs, one in each corner. There was an old blue Ford tractor parked on the first floor, taking up about a third of the porch area. Ricardo parked the Land Rover next to the tractor. After nearly seven hours of travel in the rough riding vehicle, we stepped out and stretched our weary limbs. The month was February, the year 1972.

The foreman, Daniel Valverde, one of three workers, walked up and introduced himself. He offered to show us the house. The kitchen, located directly in front of where we were parked, was long and narrow. There was a large concrete sink and a shower behind the kitchen, as well as a real oddity for these parts, a flush toilet. Most homes had only an outhouse. Unfortunately we had no running water, so the toilet wasn't much use to us. Daniel explained that the free-flowing spring always dried up in late January. We would have to go to the Barú River to bathe, and we were both wondering about other corporeal necessities. Fortunately the weeds were high in the pasture behind the house. There was no furniture of any kind, but we expected this and had come prepared. From the back end of the Land Rover we unloaded a couple of mattresses, folding chairs, a camp stove, some basic cooking and eating utensils, and a bag of candles.

We were standing under an almond tree with Daniel and his wife when several chickens walked by. "How much for that young rooster?" asked Ricardo, looking at Daniel's wife.

"Two colones," she replied, her eyes on the ground.

"If you'll cook him for us, it's a deal."

"Two-fifty cooked," came the answer in a low voice.

"You've got yourself a deal." Ricardo bent down, pulled a pistol out of his boot, and shot the rooster dead on the spot. "There. You don't even have to kill him," he laughed and put the pistol back in his boot. My lower jaw dropped several inches. Daniel and his wife didn't appear to be the least bit surprised.

It was late afternoon and we were tired and hot. "I can hear the waves, but I can't see the beach." I looked at Daniel. He explained how to get there, and away we went. When we returned a couple of hours later it was dark outside and our chicken dinner was ready.

During the next four years I split my time between the big ranch on the Caribbean side of the country, Hacienda Barú, and my family in San Jose. In 1976 I went into partnership with the owners of the hacienda, and began working there full time, spending only weekends in San Jose. A couple of years later in 1978, my wife Diane, our 13-year-old daughter Natalie, and Chris, our son of seven years, moved from the big city to Hacienda Barú. It was the beginning of an enormous adventure. Though we didn't know it at the time, Diane and I would live in La Casona for the next 16 years.

We weren't exactly city slickers. Both of us had grown up in rural environments in the United States, but she and the kids had been living in San Jose for the last eight years and were used to certain creature comforts that weren't forthcoming at La Casona. I'm talking about things like electricity, telephones, TV, supermarkets, doctors, and English-speaking neighbors. The adaptation process was tough on everyone, especially Diane.

We made a few changes to La Casona, the most important of which was enclosing the downstairs and erecting a separate roofed area to park the car and tractor. At first our downstairs walls were nothing more than wire mesh, but were eventually replaced with wood. "It was a great improvement when we enclosed the three open spaces with walls and opened the back area to make a large living space," said Diane. "After adding a bit of paint inside and out, and some furniture, the house started becoming a very comfortable home."

Expropriating a chunk of pasture to make a backyard was one of our first family projects. Our menagerie included everything from guinea hens to goats, a pig that Chris won in a raffle, and of course, cows. When asked about those early days, Diane recalls: "I had a fight with that pig over who was going to live in La Casona, but I won. Chickens, too, felt they had dibs in the kitchen—I won that battle too."

Surrounded by a multitude of modern gadgetry and mediums of entertainment, today's youth have a hard time imagining how kids could possibly deal with the boredom of living without electricity, computers, televisions, video games, or telephones. The truth is that boredom just wasn't part of our lives. In fact some of my happiest memories are of life in La Casona, and I think the rest of the family would agree.

The days were filled with work and there never seemed to be enough time to get it all done. A multitude of activities filled our evenings. We listened to Voice of America, BBC, and a load of other stations from around the world on a battery-operated shortwave radio. We read a lot by kerosene lantern, and we all became accomplished backgammon players. Cribbage was also popular.

My favorite evening entertainment was our monthly cockroach hunt. The roaches loved the dim lighting provided by kerosene lamps. Our weapon was a special fly swatter that consisted of a spring-loaded plastic pistol that shot a plastic disk about two meters, and hopefully smashed the prey. A roll of the dice determined who got to go first. The player had one minute to find, stalk, and kill a cockroach with one shot. Success resulted in the right to another shot. Failure ended the turn, and the pistol passed on to the next shooter. The first time the pistol made the full round of all the players and nobody killed a roach, the game was over. A good hunt ended with upwards of 100 kills. It took about a month for the cockroach population to reestablish itself.

Our weekly shopping trips to San Isidro always began on Thursday. Leaving before noon to avoid the rains put us in San Isidro at mid-afternoon. We'd check into the newest hotel in town, the Ama-

181

neli, and do a little shopping. On Friday morning we'd get up early
and head to the farmer's market to get first pick of the produce. After
breakfast we finished the shopping, and headed for the ice factory,
since the limited capacity of our butane refrigerator prompted us to
acquire a large ice chest that would hold an entire block of ice and
several kilos of meat. Lunch at Bahía Restaurant was followed by
the bakery, the butcher shop, and off to Hacienda Barú before the
afternoon rains.

The lack of telephones spurred us to look into amateur radio
as an alternate means of communication. Radios could be operated
with batteries, and we could charge a 12-volt battery in the car or the
tractor during the day, and use it to operate the radio at night. Diane,
Chris, and I studied, took the exams, and acquired our ham radio
licenses. My call sign was TI 8 JEE, which over the radio was often
pronounced phonetically as "Tango India 8 Juliet Echo Echo." At
first we only communicated within Costa Rica, but as our enthusiasm grew we moved on to more and more sophisticated radios and
antennas, and were eventually talking with people from all over the
world. Just before lunch we met with a group of hams from Panama,
in the evening with the New Zealand and Australia crowd, and on
really good nights with Antarctica.

We were totally captivated by the amazing world of amateur
radio. I recall that all of the Panamanians went off the air, took down
their antennas, and hid their equipment during Manuel Noriega's
reign, lest they be accused of revolutionary activities. A few came
back on air the day the US invaded Panama and the rest a few days
later when Noriega was arrested.

During Hurricane Joan in October of 1988 our radio was a life-
line between the community of Dominical and the Comisión Nacional Emergencias. I was out of the country at the time, and the CNE
put Diane in charge of the local emergency committee. I returned
home as soon as roads permitted. Dominical had been isolated for
five days. Diane was thin and tired but filled with the satisfaction
of knowing she had made a difference. Medical emergencies were

dealt with, lives were saved, and delivery of food and medical aid was coordinated via Diane's radio and our Chevrolet Blazer. The call sign TI 8 DEE was long remembered in the CNE.

The arrival of electricity in our area in 1986 was the beginning of a learning experience, or rather a relearning experience. We no longer had to trim the lantern wicks and get out the candle holders every afternoon at dusk. Nearly every weekly shopping trip brought a new electrical appliance to our home. First was the fridge, followed by the washing machine, blender, and toaster. It was with a twinge of sadness that we retired our old hand-cranked coffee grinder and the white cloth bags for straining coffee. It was like losing a treasured part of past years, a clear reminder that times were changing and would never again be the same.

Diane thought it was simply wonderful getting electricity: "With a flip of a switch the house lights came on—no more lanterns, candles or flashlights. But most exciting was the refrigerator with a frost-free freezer. Our old third-hand propane fridge, complete with scars from a long life, had done a great job for us, and even that was better than

Diane, Natalie, and Chris at La Casona, 1984.

the two big ice chests we had used. But an electric fridge…that was something good."

In 1994 Diane and I built our present home in another part of Hacienda Barú and moved away from La Casona. Cattle ranching was now part of our past, and Hacienda Barú was moving full force into ecological tourism. La Casona became home to guides, interns, and volunteers. A woman from Hatillo, Doña Leticia, moved in with her two kids and became the lady of the house, cooking and cleaning for the occupants. La Casona was demolished in 2011. In its place stands the Hacienda Barú Biological Research Center. I know that the new center will grow to be an important source of biological information and a great stimulus to research and conservation in the Path of the Tapir Biological Corridor, but I will always remember with great fondness those 16 years of life in La Casona. 🦐

The Hacienda Barú Biological Research Center has been built where La Casona once stood (shown here in 1998). *Photo: Jack Anderson*

24

The Power of a Thought

A Life-Changing Experience

Some people kill wild animals for food, others hunt them for trophies. I learned to hunt at a young age. We didn't need to hunt for subsistence, but we did eat most of what I killed, everything from doves to deer. I knew all about trophy hunting too, since my dad traveled to faraway places to shoot exotic animals and later hang their heads on his office wall. So the day Tonio, the Hacienda Barú cowboy, called me to come and see his trophy, I could relate to the feeling behind the proud smile radiating from his face. Yet when I looked down at the velvety spotted coat of the dead ocelot (*Leopardus pardalis*), I felt a pang of uneasiness in my guts, like sadness or pity. *What a shame*, I thought, *to have ended the life of such a marvelous animal.*

But then the hunter in my psyche slipped subtly into control. *I wonder if there is another one of these spotted cats up there in the jungle that I could kill*, I pondered.

Almost instantly, the absurdity of these two conflicting thoughts struck me. How could I feel remorse for the ocelot one moment and, a few seconds later, wonder if there might be one more that I could

185

kill. Thinking back on it now, 42 years later, I believe that what upset me most was the idea that I would even consider killing the very last ocelot in the jungle. I never hunted again. A couple of months later I posted "NO HUNTING" signs on the boundaries of Hacienda Barú. Eventually I hired a full-time forest guard to combat poaching.

Hacienda Barú had more jungle and more wildlife than any other place around Dominical, and in the 1970s, nobody could imagine a life that didn't include paca (*Agouti paca*) and peccary (*Tayassu tajacu*) meat. Prohibiting hunting was definitely not the way to win a popularity contest. I was threatened, insulted, and accused of thinking I was God. "You think you own the wildlife," yelled one angry hunter, waving his machete menacingly. "But God put the animals here so we can eat them and you have no right to stop us."

"I don't care what you do on your own land," I retorted, holding my ground. "But if you come onto Hacienda Barú to hunt, you can expect trouble."

But conditions often change in such a way that we see things from a different perspective. Public opinion about hunting changed a little in the early 1980s, but I believe the real turning point came with the completion of the paved road from San Isidro in 1986. Prior to that time a couple of vehicles a day would drive past our house, but easy access to the region brought in many people from outside. Several salesmen who made weekly visits to local communities carried rifles in their delivery trucks and shot every animal they saw. Weekends brought carloads of hunters from places like San Isidro and Buenos Aires.

In 1987 a group of men came to my house one Saturday afternoon. Looking over the familiar faces I felt a little uneasy, realizing that most were past enemies. All were hunters or ex-hunters. Eduardo, the spokesman, was the brother of the man who had threatened me with a machete. "Don Jack," he began, "we need your help. If we don't do something, these outsiders are going to kill all of our wildlife. Just imagine, our grandchildren may never know the paca or peccary."

What a change, I thought. *Fifteen years ago he was saying, "You think you own the wildlife."* Now Eduardo calls it "our wildlife."

The visit from those hunters got the ball rolling and a vigilante group called ANADO was founded. It later evolved into a nationally known environmental organization called ASANA that works to protect natural habitats throughout our region. There are now a lot more animals and a lot fewer hunters. Cattle ranches have been replaced by nature reserves and cowboys by naturalist guides. In fact, wildlife and tropical nature have become the major attraction for visitors to the region.

Los Amigos de la Naturaleza

When Eduardo asked me to help them stop the hunting, I readily agreed, but told the group that we needed to enlist the help of more people. Since most of the hunters were from the village of Hatillo, we decided that surely there would be people in the slightly larger village of Dominical who would like to help as well. So that's where we went.

The local policeman, Don Rodrigo, and the school teacher, Don Gredin, readily agreed to help form the new committee. Soon we had about 15 people interested in the idea and scheduled a meeting at the Dominical school for the following Saturday afternoon.

Surprisingly a number of other people who lived in Dominical attended the meeting. I was heartened by the citizen's outrage over the uncontrolled hunting. "There aren't even any iguanas in Dominical like there used to be," lamented one lady. "If an iguana shows its face around here you can bet there will be a bunch of little kids throwing rocks at it, and," pointing to Don Rodrigo, the policeman, "he will be right there with them trying to shoot the poor animal. What can we expect of our kids when we have him as a community leader that everyone is supposed to look up to?" The policeman looked down at the floor.

A number of people were furious with the driver of the truck who brought popular soft drinks into the area. He carried a .22 rifle in the truck and shot every animal he saw. "We should sign a petition and present it to the company," declared a bar owner. "Maybe we can get them to fire that driver. We don't want people like that around here."

At the end of the meeting we elected a board of directors. The president was a lady named Flor María Madrigal. Eduardo was vice president, Don Gredin was elected secretary, and I became treasurer. The new committee adopted several resolutions: the bar owner and the restaurant owner would call the soft-drink company and express the community's displeasure with their driver; the policeman apologized for shooting iguanas, agreed to stop, and promised to stop everyone else from hunting them as well; we all agreed to report all hunting incidents to the policeman, who in turn promised to pass the complaints on to the wildlife department; and we agreed to call ourselves Amigos de la Naturaleza de Dominical (ANADO). The meeting ended with great enthusiasm.

The following Saturday afternoon a man parked his jeep near a group of people on the street that passes by the soccer field in Dominical. "Hey guys," he called, "look what I have here." He opened the back of the vehicle and pulled out a dead monkey. "Shot him with this," he said proudly, and held up a .22 rifle. Over the next few minutes he pulled out a coati, several iguanas, a sloth, and a hawk, all of which he claimed to have shot. He also showed everyone another rifle and two revolvers. He seemed quite pleased with himself.

About that time an ANADO member joined the group and confidently told the man, "What you have been doing is illegal. Monkeys and sloths are endangered species, and you can't shoot them."

"Don't tell me what I can do and what I can't do," retorted the man, confidently resting his hand on the revolver strapped to his hip. "If I want to go hunting, I'll shoot what I want, and nobody is going to stop me, especially not you."

The threat in his voice was clear, and Geiner, the ANADO member, left and went straight to the police station. The building was closed, and Don Rodrigo wasn't there. Geiner found another ANADO member who owned a camera. The two returned to the jeep with the small crowd gathered around and started taking photos. "Hey, what are you doing with that camera?" protested the offender. The two ANADO members didn't answer and kept taking pictures until the film ran out. The man loaded everything in his jeep and left, obviously disgruntled by the camera.

By the time Don Rodrigo returned, several other ANADO members had heard about the incident and were outraged. Don Rodrigo said he couldn't do anything now that the man had gone, but suggested we call the wildlife department. A telephone call to that government agency was another dead-end. "You should have confiscated the dead animals as evidence," stated the official flatly. "Without evidence there is nothing we can do."

Pondering the situation several days later and frustrated with the lack of support from the police and wildlife department, I called my friend Juan, who worked for the OIJ, the judicial investigative organization. I knew that they only investigate violent crimes, but Juan was a fellow environmentalist and I thought perhaps he could give me some advice.

The first thing Juan asked me after listening to the story was if we knew the name of the man who had killed the animals. "We don't know his name," I replied, "But we have his license plate number." I gave him the number over the phone. "You're at the public phone in Dominical. Right? Stay right by the phone. I'll call you back in about 15 minutes."

Juan called back as promised. "Get the witnesses together and the photos," he told me excitedly. "We're going to have a look at the case. We'll see you at your house in a couple of hours."

We gathered up the two ANADO members, the photos, and two other sympathetic witnesses and went to our house. The agents brought a typewriter with them, took statements from the witnesses, and looked at the photos. They didn't tell us what they had planned, and it was hard to read their faces, but I got the impression that they were pleased with the evidence. They took the photos with them and returned to San Isidro.

"I bet they'll give that guy a really big fine," exclaimed Geiner, "and, after that, anyone who has any ideas about coming to Dominical to hunt will think twice."

A couple of days later I went to Dominical to make some phone calls, and Geiner told me excitedly that OIJ had arrested the man we had accused. The rumor was that they had gone to his house, confiscated his guns and his car, arrested him, handcuffed him in front of his family and neighbors, and taken him to jail. I never figured they'd come down that hard on the guy; I was totally shocked by the news.

A couple of weeks later I ran into Juan on the street in San Isidro. He had a big smile on his face. "I guess you heard what we did to the bad guy?" he asked.

I nodded affirmatively.

"I imagine you're wondering why we were so tough on him."

"Why don't you tell me?" I probed. "I'm dying to hear."

"Well...to begin with, the guy's name was Fabio and he was wanted for armed robbery. Otherwise we wouldn't have gotten involved. The problem was we knew he had robbed people at gun point, but didn't have enough evidence to hold him, and the incident in Dominical gave us everything we needed. You had photos of him and all of his guns. We confiscated the four guns in the photos and one more when we raided his house. None of the guns were registered and he didn't have a permit to carry any of them. First we charged him with having one non-registered gun. After 24 hours his lawyer was able to get him out of jail. We let him walk a block from the jail house and arrested him again. This time we charged him with the same offense for the second gun. This went on for a week. Fabio's out of jail now, and awaiting trial. He'll probably end up doing about three months of jail time."

"Absolutely amazing!" I smiled.

"All we really wanted to do," continued Juan, "was to take his guns away from him and teach him a lesson. Hopefully, when he gets out, he won't return to his old habits."

The story of what happened to Fabio spread all over San Isidro and the rest of the countryside, and, needless to say, ANADO got quite a reputation. After that, nobody would hunt anywhere near Dominical. The soft-drink driver even left his carbine at home.

Over the next couple of years ANADO had another success story which got everyone's attention. We sued the Highway Department (MOPT) for taking sand off the beaches to build roads. Everyone in the community knew by then that our future was in tourism and the sand on the beach was a limited resource. The Department of Mines and Minerals backed our campaign to stop the removal of sand, but MOPT kept on taking it anyway. Finally ANADO sued them, and, as a result of the suit, MOPT has never again loaded a single dump truck of sand on any beach anywhere in Costa Rica. ANADO's reputation continued to grow.

Three years after the founding meeting in the schoolyard in Dominical, all of the ANADO members got together again for a general membership meeting and election. About 50 people attended that second meeting, including people from Uvita and Matapalo. Everybody wanted to be part of the organization, but the objection was raised that the name ANADO was specific to Dominical, and if the organization expanded its territory the name should be more inclusive. We settled on the name Asociación de Amigos la Naturaleza de Bahía Ballena, Barú y Savegre, after the three districts that make up the territory covered by the organization. The acronym ASANA was adopted. Several years later the acronym was retained, but the name was changed again to Asociación de Amigos de la Natureleza del Pacífico Central y Sur. This name has stuck with ASANA to this day.

At that second meeting the lady who had first complained about the policeman killing iguanas pointed out that, as we talked, three young iguanas were sunning themselves in the tree tops that shaded the schoolyard. The association was off to a good start.

Several resolutions were adopted and ASANA took a slightly different course than ANADO. Up until that time the organization had really been little more than a vigilante committee with the sole purpose of stopping the hunting. Now the agenda became a little more positive. In addition to controlling illegal hunting, it was decided that volunteer members of the organization would visit schools and give talks to the students, and the association would take a hand in the marine turtle rescue project that, since 1984, had been carried out by the employees of Hacienda Barú. ASANA was entering a new phase.

Biological Corridors

By 1990 Hacienda Barú had become known as a private nature reserve and was doing a few tours. We were visited by a vacationing biologist named Bob Carlson who worked with the Caribbean Conservation Corporation (CCC), an organization best known for its pioneer work with turtle conservation in Tortuguero on the northern Caribbean coast of Costa Rica. They had also been involved with efforts to preserve the Florida panther, especially in the creation of biological corridors for these endangered felines, and lately had become active in the creation of biological corridors in Central America.

Bob explained to me the theory and importance of biological corridors. If two large natural areas are isolated from each other, their capacity to harbor a high level of biodiversity is severely hampered. However, if you can join them together by way of a biological corridor, you create the equivalent of a much larger natural area with a much higher level of biodiversity. "A biological corridor is what you need in this area," he explained. "You've experienced an astonishing amount of deforestation during the past several decades, and what you have left is a landscape that looks like a bunch of green islands—a few big ones like Hacienda Barú and a lot of little ones like those on some of the neighboring properties. If you can create natural corridors to connect these islands to one another, you will be amazed at the amount of wildlife that will return to the area."

I was fascinated by the idea. Bob went on to explain that CCC was sponsoring a major wildlife corridor called the "Path of the Panther" that would connect the vast rainforests of southern Mexico with the rest of Central America and Panama. The dream of the project was to restore enough natural habitat so that a large predator such as a jaguar or puma (panther) could walk the length of the isthmus without stepping out of a tropical forest. The CCC soon realized that the Path of the Panther was much too ambitious a project for a nongovernmental organization (NGO), so they worked to sell the idea to the governments of the countries that would be affected by the corridor. In 1996, the governments of Central America and Mexico adopted a resolution giving top priority to the corridor. They changed the name to the "Mesoamerican Biological Corridor." The countries abided by the resolution with varying degrees of enthusiasm, but the government of Costa Rica took it very seriously and created a national commission with the mission of creating the Costa Rican portion of the corridor. As of June 2014 that commission had made great advances in the creation of the corridor and is still working diligently to consolidate it.

Path of the Tapir

After Bob Carlson's visit, I presented the idea of a biological corridor to the board of directors of ASANA. They enthusiastically embraced the project. To the north was the Los Santos Forest Reserve and to the south, the vast mangrove forests of the combined mouths of the Sierpe and Térraba rivers. We needed to locate the large natural reserves between those two extremes and convince the owners to adopt permanent protection for their land. At the same time we needed to convince the owners of deforested land to create corridors across their property with the objective of connecting the larger parcels of forest together.

There is a largely unenforced law in Costa Rica that prohibits the deforestation of land along the rivers and streams. We decided to use this law as an incentive to ranchers to create natural corridors along the waterways that traversed their properties. The added bonus: doing what we asked would help protect their water sources from drying up. The landowners didn't have to invest any time or money; all they had to do was quit chopping the weeds along the edges of the waterways. Without constant weeding the jungle comes back with a vengeance. Several ranchers in key locations agreed to this proposal.

About this time a couple of ASANA board members, Don Walter Odio and Don Steve Stroud, spent a couple of days hiking across the Los Santos Forest Reserve from Santa Maria de Dota to Brujo. During the hike they saw lots of tapir tracks and were impressed by their guide's stories. Upon their return Don Walter suggested that we name ASANA's corridor Path of the Tapir. "We know there are tapirs in Los Santos and also at the other end of the corridor in the Peninsula of Osa. If we do a good job maybe they will return to our area as well. The day a tapir comes walking down a trail at Hacienda Barú we will be able to say that our project has accomplished its goal." The board voted unanimously to adopt the name "Path of the Tapir Biological Corridor" (PTBC).

For the next five years we worked at convincing people to quit chopping the weeds along their rivers and streams and let Mother Nature regenerate natural vegetation. These efforts helped a lot, but another unanticipated factor helped even more. The price of real estate skyrocketed in the area. At first glance a real estate boom would appear to work against the corridor, but, in this situation, it had the opposite effect. The new buyers were foreigners, and they weren't buying land to raise cattle. Rather they were looking for places to live. Some were building a second home and others a retirement home. But they all had one thing in common: they wanted to see monkeys and toucans, not cows. Property owners with the idea of selling soon discovered that jungle land was worth a lot more to the new buyers than open pasture. Sellers let the natural vegetation return to their pastures. This was probably the biggest single factor influencing the regeneration of rainforest within the Path of the Tapir Biological Corridor.

By 1996, when the national commission for the Mesoamerican Biological Corridor was formed, we already had three national wildlife refuges: Hacienda Barú, Rancho la Merced, and Hacienda Portalon; one national park, the Bahía Ballena Marine National Park; and about 15 informal nature reserves within the corridor. We were off to a good start. Then lots of doors opened to ASANA.

A donation from Steve and Mayra Stroud, matched by one from the United Nations Development Program (UNDP) allowed us to contract The Nature Conservancy to do a rapid ecological assessment of the corridor which would determine which species were present in the area and their relative abundances. This study produced very positive results and indicated the project was not only feasible, but well worth the effort it would take to accomplish its objectives. As the largest land mammal in Central America, and an animal that was once abundant in the area but now locally extinct in the PTBC, the tapir was the perfect symbol to represent the project.

About the same time another important source of funding became available to ASANA. Costa Rica created an agency called FONAFIFO which was charged with creating and implementing a system of "Payments for Environmental Services," known as PSA, the acronym in Spanish. The concept was simple: People who burn fossil fuels put carbon dioxide (CO_2) into the atmosphere. Trees remove the CO_2, use it to create wood fiber, and release oxygen in the process, thus providing a service. Therefore, those who burn fossil fuels pay those who protect forests and plant trees for the service of removing CO_2 from our air. In practice this was done by taxing gasoline and diesel and paying people to protect forests and plant trees. It became a compelling incentive for people to protect their natural forests and to plant trees on former farm land. Additionally, ASANA could finance many of its expenses by charging a commission for tackling the daunting amount of paperwork necessary for property owners to take advantage of PSA.

During the next 17 years ASANA received financial support from the National Commission for the Mesoamerican Biological Corridor, UNDP, AVINA, World Bank, Earth Island Institute, The Nature Conservancy, Debt for Nature Swap, and several private donors. We built an office on a lot donated by Hacienda Barú, hired an executive director, and have made great strides in consolidating the Path of the Tapir Biological Corridor.

Increasing Biodiversity

In the year 1947 a terrible epidemic of yellow fever ravished much of rural Costa Rica, hitting this region especially hard. As a result of the epidemic, all of the spider and howler monkeys died, and only the white-faced capuchins survived. Fifty years later, in 1997, a lone, male spider monkey appeared on the Hacienda Barú National Wildlife Refuge. At first we thought he must be a tame monkey that someone once kept as a pet and later released. But he acted like a wild monkey. The nearest place to Hacienda Barú where spider monkeys were known to exist was Dos Bocas, about 15 kilometers away, as the crow flies. We surmised that the corridor must be complete between Dos Bocas and Hacienda Barú. Six months later a lone female arrived, but traveled with a group of capuchin monkeys for almost a year before she went near the male. Finally the two got together and started having offspring. Over the years more spider monkeys traveled across the corridor and joined the ones already here. As of this writing, I estimate there are between 20 and 30 spider monkeys on Hacienda Barú and in the surrounding area.

The scarlet macaws, big red and blue parrots with impressive plumage, were all killed by hunters prior to the 1970s. They started reappearing sporadically in the area in about 2005, and are now well established in the Uvita area. A tapir appeared in Dos Bocas in 2008, and was seen by many of the people who live there. Tapir sightings are reported several times each year in the higher sections of the PTBC. And there have been three questionable tapir sighting on Hacienda

Barú and surrounding properties. I am waiting for one to appear on a trail camera before accepting that they have definitely returned.

In 2010 a jaguar was sighted in a place called Punto de Mira, about six kilometers from Hacienda Barú. In 2011 Dr. Cheryl Margoluis was walking with a group of students through the forest at the Firestone Center for Ecological Restoration when a collared peccary crossed the trail a couple of meters in front of her at a full run, squealing and obviously in a state of panic. A split second later a full-grown puma crossed in exactly the same place, hot on the tail of the peccary. It was the first absolute confirmation that large predators had returned to the corridor. Since then, many videos of pumas have been captured by trail cameras at the Firestone Center and on Hacienda Barú. The presence of large predators is a strong indication of a healthy ecosystem.

Though the tapir, jaguar, and scarlet macaw have appeared in the PTBC in different locations at different times they still can't be considered as permanent residents. The white-lipped peccary, mentioned in chapter 12, still has not been sighted within the corridor. Their return will probably be followed by the jaguar, the only predator of this large wild pig.

And what about the ocelot? Did Tonio kill the very last ocelot in the jungle? Definitely not. Notwithstanding their nocturnal and naturally secretive habits, ocelots are sighted a couple of times each year by Hacienda Barú guides, park rangers, and visitors. They have appeared on the trail cameras at every location. Males, females, and kittens have all appeared in the videos. There is every indication that a healthy population of these exceptionally beautiful spotted cats exists within the Path of the Tapir Biological Corridor.

And it all began with a thought. 🐾

25

Fat-Handed Cats

The Return of the Ocelots

With her chest and thick front paws on the log, her eyes peering over the top, the sleek, spotted cat waited patiently for a spiny rat or some other small rodent to scurry along. She had been there since moonrise, but so far no prey had ventured past. An uneasy feeling enveloped her body like a mist penetrating to the very core of her being. She waited and watched. A faint sound reached her ears, and soon she became aware of the source of the unpleasant feeling: dogs, their distant howls drifting on the cool night breeze. The unwelcome wail was not new to her ears; it signified the most fearful thing in her environment. The thought of climbing a tree briefly flickered across her mind, but if the dogs caught her scent and found the tree, she would be trapped, an easy target for the humans who always came with the dogs. The other choice was to put distance between herself and the howling dogs, but the forest wasn't that big, and she could only run so far. The female ocelot decided to wait and listen.

Maybe the feared canines would go a different direction. She crouched down to make herself smaller. But the sound kept coming closer, and it was time to make a move. The beautiful spotted feline

sprinted through the forest keeping well to one side of the approaching dogs' path. The terrain was familiar and she moved quickly and
easily, making a wide circle around the oncoming dogs. She crossed
their path well behind them, the area still strong with the dreaded
scent, and headed for the stream and the one tree that meant safety.
Crossing the swift current she came to the giant fig with the buttress

roots reaching to the water's edge. She climbed the trunk to an opening far above the ground, crawled into the hollow core, lay down on a ledge, and remained still, waiting, listening.

After a time the baying of the dogs turned into a frenzy. They had probably cornered a paca in its cave. The ocelot relaxed; she was safe for another day. Crouched in her hiding place, vivid memories flowed through her mind of a night long ago when her mother had hidden her and her brother in another hollow fig in a distant forest, and had then run away from the hiding place, intentionally leading the dogs astray. She remembered hearing three loud bangs that only came from humans. Her mother never returned. The following day she and her brother ventured down from the tree and into the forest. They were old enough to make it on their own, but life wasn't easy.

❈ ❈ ❈ ❈ ❈

Of the six species of wild cats in Costa Rica, only the jaguar and puma are larger than the ocelot. The jaguarundi, margay cat, and oncilla are all smaller. One biologist described the oncilla as the size of a small house cat, the margay and the jaguarundi the size of a large house cat, and the ocelot the size of a medium dog. A large ocelot will weigh 14 kilograms with a head and body length of 90 centimeters and a tail 40 centimeters long. The tail is relatively short in comparison with the head and body. In fact it is slightly shorter than the back leg. An ocelot front foot track can measure 7 centimeters across and 5 centimeters on the back foot.

The name "ocelot" is derived from the Náhuatl (Central American Indian language) word *océlotl* which refers to the same cat. It appears often in pre-Columbian art and lore and was an important totem in some indigenous cultures. Aztec priests who performed human sacrifices wore cloaks made of ocelot skins during the ritual. In folklore, confusion often arises between ocelots and jaguars because in some cultures the word *tigre* refers to an ocelot and in other cultures to the jaguar. Also, in some places the name "ocelot" means jaguar. In the local Borucan Indian language the cat is called *cvon kuas*. In Costa Rica the ocelot is usually called *manigordo* or "fat hand" because of its exceptionally thick front paws.

Ocelots are agile climbers and often sleep in trees, but most of their waking hours are spent on the ground. Unlike most cats, ocelots don't stalk their prey; rather they wait and watch, or wander stealthily around and kill what they come across. They hunt mostly small rodents, but have been known to kill animals as large as peccary. Occasionally they will kill birds, which they prefer plucked before eating.

In 1973, when Tonio killed the ocelot mentioned in chapter 24, all of the lowlands of Hacienda Barú—160 hectares—had been deforested and converted to cattle pasture. About 170 hectares of primary forest remained in the highlands. A few of the neighboring properties still had isolated parcels of jungle, but many had been totally denuded of trees. Hunting was rampant, and every year there was less forest and fewer animals to hunt. Most hunters used dogs, animals quite adept at pursuing and treeing ocelots. Once the cat was treed, it was an easy target for hunters' rifles. On top of all this hunting, ocelots had the unendearing habit of sneaking into farmyards and killing chickens, so they were largely considered pests that should be shot on sight. With odds like that against them it is no wonder that the ocelot population dipped very near to zero. But that was almost 40 years ago and many things have changed.

In 1979 we started restoring habitat at Hacienda Barú. Little by little over the next 20 years all the pasture land was turned back over to Mother Nature. Since 1985, which marked the peak of deforestation in the area that comprises the Path of the Tapir Biological Corridor, every year has seen an increase in forest cover.

Other factors contributing to the ocelots' recovery include ecological tourism which has become an important source of income in the area. Many people now realize they need to protect the rainforest and wildlife which brings visitors to the region. Also, a number of protected nature reserves—both formal, like National Wildlife Refuges, and informal privately owned nature reserves—have been created. Many owners of these reserves hire guards to protect the wildlife. Hunters with howling dogs are easy for the guards to locate. Some guards capture the dogs and turn them over to the wildlife department of the environmental ministry, MINAET, and others shoot them on sight. As a result many poachers have quit hunting with dogs and now use traps instead. The traps are designed to catch peccary and pacas, but not ocelots, a fact that has contributed considerably to the recovery of the spotted cats.

After that ocelot was killed in 1973, there were no more sightings at Hacienda Barú for 18 years. Then, in 1991, an ornithologist was sitting on a log watching and listening for birds in the primary forest of Hacienda Barú when a mature male ocelot came strolling past totally unaware of the human's presence. The following year my wife Diane was returning from a middle-of-the-night trip to the hospital with a sick employee when she spotted an ocelot along the road in the Hacienda Barú forest near the Barú River. It had some sort of prey in its mouth. A year later one of the park rangers saw an ocelot near

Caught on a Hacienda Baru trail camera, an ocelot with a small rodent in its mouth.

a self-guided trail in the lowlands of Hacienda Barú. Since that time there have been one or two sightings every year by guides, tourists, or park rangers. I have captured many videos of them with several trail cameras placed at different locations on Hacienda Barú. Recently a friend and neighbor, Cheryl Margoluis, was out on an early morning run when she came face to face with a female ocelot and two kittens. Obviously ocelot populations have recovered significantly over the last 40 years and there are now quite a few of them on Hacienda Barú and within the Path of the Tapir Biological Corridor.

Ocelots defend a fairly large territory, and even in a protected area the size of Hacienda Barú and the neighboring private nature reserves—a little over 500 hectares altogether—there aren't likely to be more than three males and seven to ten females. In addition to the low population density it is also important to take into consideration that ocelots are mostly active at night and are very secretive animals. All of these factors mean that even when populations levels are high, sightings are few.

On Saturday, April 28, 2012, two wildlife inspectors from MINAET came to Hacienda Barú with a cage in the back of their pick-up. In the cage was a young-adult male ocelot. The cat had been killing chickens at a farm near the village of San Juan de Dios. One night the owner of the farm managed to lock the culprit inside the chicken house. Rather than kill it, as would have happened 20 or 30 years ago, the owner called MINAET. The inspectors managed to get a noose around the ocelot's neck and maneuver it into the cage, but it acquired a few bumps and scrapes in the process. First they took it to the animal clinic in Uvita. My wife Diane happened to be there at the time, and helped distract the cat while Dr. Riera dabbed a little antiseptic on the abrasions with a long swab. He checked it over and told the inspectors the cat appeared to be healthy and in good condition and that in his opinion, there should be no problem releasing it in a suitable habitat. So they brought it to Hacienda Barú.

With the help of several workers and park rangers, they mounted the cage on a couple of bamboo poles and carried it about a kilometer up into the rainforest on the upper slopes of the refuge. There the ocelot was returned to its native habitat. Hopefully it will find a territory and settle into a normal life of hunting small rodents and other available prey. If it returns to its old habit of killing chickens, the next farmer may not be so forgiving. 🌶

Chicken killer released at Hacienda Baru in 2012. *Photo: Johnny Fajardo*

26

A New Mafia

Poachers Determined to Destroy Our Wildlife and Forests

Years ago when I posted the first "NO HUNTING" signs on Hacienda Barú, the prohibition was aimed at neighbors who loved to hunt. Most of game in the remaining parcels of forest in our area had been killed, but the hacienda still had plenty of healthy rainforest that harbored lots of wildlife. This is where everybody came to hunt, and prohibiting hunting was definitely not the way to win a popularity contest. Of course, nobody paid the least bit of attention to my signs. We often found them shot full of holes or chopped to pieces with a machete. Eventually I decided to hire a guard, a local man named Alejandro, who knew the forest well. Though having a guard didn't stop the hunting entirely, it helped a lot. Then one day a friend of Alejandro's convinced him to look the other way for just one afternoon: "Your boss always goes to San Isidro on Thursdays. I haven't eaten paca meat for months. Just let me kill one paca and I won't bother you anymore." Alejandro relented and let his friend hunt, "just this one time."

Pacas are large rodents weighing up to 10 kilograms and measuring 70 centimeters in length. Since their diet consists almost entirely of fruits and seeds, paca meat is delicious and considered a delicacy. Though hunters also hunted deer and peccary, paca was their favorite prey, but hunting had driven their numbers to local extinction in some areas.

Paca at Hacienda Baru.

Of course, Alejandro's friend wasn't satisfied with just one paca, and before long he and another friend were hunting every Thursday when I was in San Isidro. By the time I found out what was going on the situation was out of control. I dismissed Alejandro and hired another guard named Ignacio who was known for being mean and nasty, and had few friends. He wouldn't let anybody trespass or hunt, and I thought we had the problem solved. Then one day Ignacio's son José commented to my son Chris that they had eaten toucan soup the night before, and it was delicious. When Chris started questioning him further José got nervous and tried to say he was only joking. The incident put me on alert, and I started asking around. It turned out that Ignacio had stopped all hunting on Hacienda Barú, but his motive had nothing to do with any desire to do a good job. Rather, he wanted a personal monopoly on all of the game in the rainforest.

Over the years I have had many forest guards, and most have done an excellent job of controlling the poaching. Stopping 100 percent of the hunting was, and still is, next to impossible, but the guards did keep it down to a tolerable level. In the end it was a local policeman, Don Marcos, who came up with the solution to the poaching problem. "If you can stop the poachers from hunting with dogs you will eliminate most of the problem," he explained. "When the hunting dogs detect fresh paca scent they start baying, and you can hear them for several kilometers. The hunters can't keep up with the dogs

206

and are always several hundred meters behind, yelling at the dogs to keep them excited and on the trail. What you have to do is get in front of the dogs, catch them, and bring them to me. I will deal with the hunters," promised Don Marcos.

I was a little dubious about Don Marcos' idea, but decided to give it a try. About a week later we captured one of the two long-eared canines with the hunters. We took the dog to Don Marcos, and he locked it in a jail cell behind the small building that served as the police station. He almost never used the cell, but it was a good place to keep the hunting dog. The lock was to keep the hunters from sneaking in and liberating their pet. I left enough dog food to keep the animal well fed during its imprisonment.

It took the hunters a couple of days to figure out where their dog was. Three brothers went to Don Marcos' office and asked about a lost dog. "One of our dogs ran away from home. He must have gotten on the trail of a paca and got lost. We've been looking for him for two days. We heard that you've got a dog here and figured it might be ours."

"Well now," said Don Marcos. "It just so happens that I do have a dog here, but it can't be yours. Your dog ran away from home by itself, and this dog was with hunters who were trespassing on Hacienda Barú and hunting paca illegally. Your dog must still be lost."

"Couldn't we just have a look at the dog to make sure it's not ours."

"Naw. It would just be a waste of time. I've got things to do, and since you guys weren't hunting with your dog, this one couldn't be yours."

The conversation continued along this line for a while, but eventually the hunters admitted to hunting on Hacienda Barú.

"Here's what we're going to do," explained Don Marcos. "I'm going to type up a confession, and you're going to sign it. You're going to admit to trespassing and hunting paca out of season and without a license. You're also going to promise, in writing, never to hunt on Hacienda Barú again. In return, we're not going to press charges this time. But I'm going to file this confession, and if you break your promise, we're going to press charges for this time and next time too. How does that sound?"

Realizing that it was the only way they were going to get their dog back, the hunters signed the confession. Over the years we repeated this scenario many times. No one ever came up with a novel excuse for losing their dog, nobody readily admitted having been hunting, and no one ever broke their promise not to return to Hacienda Barú. Word got around quickly, and soon the hunting on the hacienda all but came to a halt.

Poaching Today

Most of the local people have given up hunting. The biggest source of employment in the area is tourism, and people understand how important the animals and birds are to the tourists. Taking the occasional paca for the kitchen table still happens, but rarely. Today we have a new breed of hunters: armed professionals who hunt for profit and are willing to resort to violence if necessary. The murder near Limon of Jairo Mora on May 31, 2013, in revenge for his work trying to stop the poaching of turtle eggs shook the nation and even made waves internationally. Six suspects were arrested and charged with murder. They were four men and two women from Limon who made their living poaching turtle eggs, dealing drugs, robbing people at gun point, and any other illegal activity where they could make a quick buck.

On August 29, 2013 two wildlife inspectors responded to a call about illegal hunting near a place called Aserri. They confronted the hunters and confiscated a dog. During the scuffle that followed one of the hunters stabbed a wildlife inspector in the leg, causing him to be hospitalized. The hunter was charged with illegal hunting and assault with a deadly weapon.

Not only are turtle egg and paca poachers becoming violent, there have been a number of incidents of violent behavior shown by timber poachers. The Attorney General of Costa Rica recently stated that the business of poaching the coveted Almendro tree, essential for the well-being of the great green macaw, is being run by a well-organized mafia.

Jehry Rivera

In early September of 2013, a group of tribal elders was meeting at the Terraba Indian Reserve in southern Costa Rica when they heard the faint whine of a chainsaw in the distance. The tribal environmental commission was called and set out to find the site where the poachers were cutting timber within the reserve. They found the location of the cutting, but the thieves had fled into the forest. The commission members tried to call the forestry department of the environmental ministry, but there was no cell phone signal. Young Jehry Rivera was sent to find a place where he could make the call. Several hundred meters from the site he encountered one of the poachers who attacked him and beat him so brutally with a stick that he required hospitalization.

Why are we seeing such a trend toward violent crimes against the environment? I believe it is because of the profitability of poaching. A nest of turtle eggs will sell for $40 to $60, double what the poacher can make per day at a regular job, and in the middle of the turtle season a poacher can easily steal two nests a night. A paca can be sold to certain restaurants for about $70. The trees that are being poached are worth up to $3,000 per tree. For that reason we are now seeing professional poachers replace the traditional local hunter of the past.

Costa Rica recently passed a law prohibiting hunting of any kind, anywhere in Costa Rica, and levying fines of up to $3,800 for poaching turtle eggs or wildlife. The same fines apply to restaurants that sell paca meat or turtle eggs. Everyone expected the new law to be a great deterrent to poaching, but in practice it isn't working that way.

If the person doing the poaching can convince the judge that he is poor and needs the meat or eggs to feed his family, he will go free. If a restaurant owner selling paca meat gets caught, he will claim he was lying about the meat being paca, and that it is really just chicken. The appearance of paca and chicken is similar, and DNA testing is not an option on the meager budget of the wildlife department. The restaurant owner will keep the paca carcass in some other location and bring only meat already cut into pieces to the restaurant.

With turtle eggs the ploy is a little different. There are two beaches in Costa Rica, Ostional and Nancite, where thousands of turtles come to lay their eggs. If left to nature, the second group to lay will dig up most of the eggs laid by the first group and the third group will dig up those laid by the second group. The exposed eggs will lie on the beach and rot, and, in the end, very few nests actually hatch. For this reason the environmental ministry allows the local people to harvest the first two batches of eggs on these two beaches. Bar and restaurant owners can buy these eggs legally and are given a certificate. After selling all of the legal eggs they will continue to buy from local poachers at reduced prices and use the same certificate they got with the legal eggs as proof that the eggs they have are legal.

Poaching is a serious problem worldwide and, in the not too distant future, could drive elephants, rhinos, tigers, and other species to extinction. Poaching is such a big business that it has even brought violence to normally peaceful Costa Rica. What is the solution? No one has figured it out yet, and I don't see any light on the horizon. All we can do is keep working on it the best we can, as we do at Hacienda Barú. 🐾

27

The Scream Maker

The Revenge of the Manglera

Nothing penetrates the consciousness like a woman's scream. I'm not talking about an ordinary run-of-the-mill scream, like when her husband spills coffee on the new tablecloth, or even when she sees her two-year-old standing on a chair, reaching for a pot of boiling water. I'm talking about one of those screams that pierces to the very center of your being—a scream of sheer terror. That's the sound that sent chills up and down my spine, shocked me out of my daydream, and snapped me instantly back into the here-and-now. A moment earlier the only danger to me and my family was the possibility of me dozing off at the wheel, but my wife's scream changed all that. Her first expression of hysterical panic was followed by yelling: "Jack, Jack, that snake, that snake." Without even looking, I knew what must have happened.

It was 1975 and one of the cowboys had recently captured a snake. He called it a *manglera* and cautioned me it was extremely poisonous. The head looked triangular to me, and I knew pit vipers always have triangular heads. Light greenish-brown in color with a fuzzy diamond pattern, the *manglera* was as long as I am tall and about as thick as a shovel handle. The last 20 centimeters of its tail curled up, reminding me of a hook. The cowboy had found it hanging by its tail in a mangrove tree. Knowing that snakes fascinated me, he brought it to the ranch house on the end of a long branch, and we managed to get it into a plastic bag.

A couple of weeks earlier, our family had visited the Clodomiro Picado Institute, where antivenin—serum for the treatment of snakebite—is manufactured. Mesmerized, we watched technicians hold large vipers securely, force their fangs into glass vials covered with rubber sheets, and "milk" them of their venom. This highly toxic venom, fully capable of killing an adult human, is the key ingredient in the production of lifesaving serum used for the treatment of snakebite. A white-coated scientist explained the process to the visitors. He mentioned that the institute was always in need of poisonous snakes from different regions of Costa Rica. For that reason, I decided that I would take the *manglera* to the institute. That weekend, it rode to San Jose in the luggage compartment of my jeep, still inside the plastic bag.

Upon arrival at our apartment in San José, I unpacked my things, but decided to leave the plastic bag with the snake where it was. The next day was Saturday, visitor's day at the snake institute and I planned to take the *manglera* and donate it to their worthy cause. That morning, however, the plastic bag was empty, and a limited search of the car revealed nothing. I wasn't about to peek under seats and dashboard. A friend of ours knew one of the snake handlers from the Clodomiro Picado Institute. He came to our house and searched every nook and cranny in the jeep, but the snake was nowhere to be found.

Common names of serpents vary from one part of the country to another and the name "manglera" wasn't familiar to the technician. His opinion was that the snake had already found its way out of the jeep, but recommended that we leave a door open all night. The snake would leave the jeep to search for food and water, he said. We left the doors open at night for a week and finally decided there was no chance the snake was still in the car. The mystery of the *manglera* became an interesting anecdote that was relegated to family history. But then one lazy Sunday afternoon, a scream that threatened to wake the dead, brought it abruptly back to the present.

Instantly awake and alert, my instincts took over and directed my adrenaline-charged body to simultaneously brake, pull over, and look to my right. Diane was leaning over, nearly in my lap, with Chris in her arms. The snake's triangular-shaped head with a short length of neck was sticking out of the ceiling liner of the jeep, close to where Diane's head had been a few seconds earlier. Its forked tongue was flicking in and out.

Our German shepherd began barking and halfheartedly attacking. Diane's screaming changed to yelling, urging everyone out of the car. We all jumped out of the driver's door. I ran around to the passenger side of the jeep, grabbed a stick from the side of the road and tried to drag the snake from its hiding place between the cardboard ceiling liner and the metal roof of the jeep. To my horror, it evaded my stick, doubled over, stuck its head back through the hole from which its body was protruding, and tried to return to its safe haven. Panicked that it would escape back to the inner depths of the jeep, I grabbed the *manglera* with my bare hand, pulled it free of the car, threw it on the ground, and beat it to death with the stick.

We all breathed a sigh of relief. The snake was dead. I examined the head more closely, wanting to see the fangs. To my dismay there were no fangs and no pit—a small, heat-sensitive depression between the nostril and the eye. Pit vipers always have this second opening, similar to a nostril. My *manglera* didn't have it. In spite of the triangular head, it was not poisonous.

The story about our Sunday afternoon outing was written up in *The Tico Times* the following week, and we finally did relegate the entire episode to history. But that didn't help me with my feeling of guilt over having killed the *manglera*, which had never intended the slightest harm to any of us. It was me who took it away from its natural habitat, starting the chain of events that ended with its death.

I was determined to learn more about the *manglera*, but in those days few books were available about the serpents of Costa Rica. My knowledge was slow in coming.

Near the end of the 1970s, when Diane and the kids moved to Hacienda Barú, everyone was comfortable around snakes. Diane didn't scream anymore when she saw them and we learned to accept them as part of our daily lives. A very special one lived in the ceiling of our house, where it happily made a meal of every bat and rat which crossed its path. We knew it was a boa, but weren't sure what kind. Content to remain in its lofty hideaway the snake never bothered us; the only indication of its presence was the occasional nocturnal squeal of an unfortunate rat. We took those noisy occasions as announcements that our attic boarder had just paid its rent. We even gave the snake a name: Agatha.

In those days, there were no cabins or hotels in Dominical so visitors to the area usually stayed in someone's home. Harvey, a biology student from California, once stayed with us for a couple of weeks. Shortly after his arrival, a family of Norwegian rats moved in.

Norwegian rats are big and smart. They will turn up their noses at even the most alluring rat poisons and are much too clever to be fooled by a rat trap. Their only weakness is being creatures of habit and routine. Experience had taught me that if a rat runs along a certain beam every night at a certain time, it will be so punctual that on future nights you can set your watch by it. My only successful method of exterminating them was to wait until a few seconds before the normal nightly run and aim an air-powered BB rifle at some point along its path where the rat habitually paused. Chris would watch and let me know when the rat appeared at the beginning of its run. I then began to squeeze the trigger, timing the release of the BB for exactly the moment the rat paused. If my aim was true and I killed the rat, all of its companions promptly left the house. If I missed, they just hung in there and varied their routine, making it nearly impossible to hunt them in the future. As astonishing as the Norwegian rat's intelligence may be, however, it was no match for Agatha.

It seems that the newly arrived Norwegian rats were making their nightly runs through the snake's territory, not ours. We would catch occasional glimpses of them, but not long enough for a clear shot with the air rifle. On the third night, Agatha scored. The scream from the big blue rat was comparable to Diane's on that Sunday afternoon when the *manglera* crawled out of the ceiling of the jeep.

Harvey decided to climb into the attic and investigate. His presence upset Agatha so much that she wouldn't eat her dinner, and instead let the dead rat drop. About 15 minutes later, one of the other Norwegian rats came across its dead companion's body. The second rat took off running and screaming. It was joined by the third member of the family, and both noisily ran off into the night, never to return.

Harvey captured Agatha, brought her downstairs, and stretched her out on a table to take notes about her physical attributes, things like the number of scales on her head. Seeing her clearly for the first time, I realized that Agatha was a *manglera*. Harvey explained that the end of her tail was curled up in its characteristic hook-like shape so she could easily hang from tree limbs. Serpents of her species spend most of their time in trees. With the help of a book on reptiles, Harvey was able to determine that she was a common tree boa (*Corallus ruschenbergerii*). After recording his observations, he returned Agatha to the attic, where she continued to live and eat bats, rats, and opossums for a number of years.

Common boa snake of Costa Rica.
Photo: Jeff Patterson

Today Diane and I don't kill any snakes on Hacienda Barú. We will move poisonous ones that consistently cause problems, like hanging out near people's homes or along the walking trails. Although our relationship with the common tree boa got off to a bad start, the whole family learned to appreciate the presence of our upstairs boarder. As a matter of fact, rodent control was only one of Agatha's functions around the house. She was also an interesting conversation piece, though we were careful not to mention her to our guests. After all, we wouldn't want the ladies to scream. But in all households, certain guests are less welcome than others, and a few stay longer than is polite. With guests like that, a casual comment at breakfast often served as a very effective hint.

"The snake hasn't come into your room at night has she? She's usually no bother at all, you know, but sometimes she just takes a liking to certain people and crawls right into bed with them." The unwanted visitors were invariably packed and gone by noon.

I have come to believe that it is best to let the snakes live, even the poisonous ones. In the overall balance of nature, they will do more good than harm. When you see lots of snakes, it is usually because something is out of balance. There might be an overabundance of rats, for example. Once the rat population diminishes, the snakes will go elsewhere.

Humans' innate fear of snakes induces us to destroy them, even those species that provide valuable services for us. Our fear is usually born of ignorance. Today, very good field guides are available for the identification of all living creatures. *A Guide to Amphibians and Reptiles* by Twan Leenders is an excellent source of information. Had it been available back in the 1970s, I would've been able to identify and learn about the *manglera* rather than mistake it for a dangerous serpent. Even so, it wouldn't have stopped Diane from screaming.

One evening in 2012 I was in the reception office of Hacienda Barú Lodge when an extremely agitated lady came in telling me to come quickly as there was a snake right alongside one of the trails. "It almost bit me," she whimpered. "I was just walking from my room to the restaurant, and I saw something move. I looked to my right, and there it was staring at me, flicking its tongue in and out, getting ready to bite me."

I went with her to as close as she would go to the bush where she said the snake was wrapped around a branch. As I approached I could see that the snake was a *manglera*. Though it offered no danger to anyone, I knew that other guests would be frightened and decided to capture the snake and release in a nearby jungle. I grabbed the *manglera* by one of its coils and tugged gently, trying to remove it from the bush where it was determined to stay. I pulled a little harder, and then grabbed a second coil, and tugged on that one. Finally the snake came free, at which point the head whipped around and bit my hand. The lady screamed.

The teeth were fine and sharp like fish bones, but stronger. The common tree boa's favorite prey is birds, and for that reason its teeth are longer than those of other boas. After releasing the snake in the forest near the trail that goes to the beach, I disinfected the bite with iodine. It itched and hurt a little for about three days, but healed up fine. The last *manglera* that touched my life left me with a tiny scratch, hardly a fitting revenge for the death penalty I imposed on that first *manglera* so many years ago. 𓆚

28

Bird Watching in the Killing Field

Here Come the Garzas

When the first settlers moved into the area around Dominical in the early 1900s, they found primary forests comprised of thousands of species of living organisms. Over time trees were felled and the highly diverse forests were replaced with several species of grass intended for the exclusive consumption of domestic animals that in turn would be slaughtered for human food. The deforestation of Costa Rica generally began in the northwestern province of Guanacaste and spread southward.

The ecosystem that evolved around this reality was much lower in biodiversity than the primary forest it had replaced. However, certain species that humans consider pests, such as vampire bats, ticks, lice, grasshoppers, and rats experienced population explosions; and, in the case of birds, the number of species increased significantly to include those that thrive in open spaces and near livestock.

At first glance it may seem strange that deforestation could trigger an increase in the number of bird species. Had the rainforest been eliminated entirely, the number of bird species would certainly have decreased, but this was not the case.

When Hacienda Barú was still a ranch, approximately half of the rainforest was undisturbed and the rest had been cleared and planted to pasture or crops. We kept about 150 head of cattle and a dozen horses which grazed in pastures fenced into sections that varied in size from two to ten hectares. As anyone who has lived in the tropics will attest, weeds literally grow like weeds. Keeping unwanted vegetation under control is a constant chore. Clean pastures produce more beef than weedy ones. Some ranchers used herbicides, but I preferred mechanical methods.

The most efficient method of cleaning lowland pastures is with a farm tractor and a mechanical mower called a bush hog that chops or mows everything down to a height of about 15 centimeters. Two or three times a year, after the livestock had completely grazed a pasture, we went in and chopped everything left standing with the bush hog, leaving a weed-free pasture. Cleaning pastures with this mower was my favorite job. It was also my first experience in bird watching.

One morning, bright and early, I started up the tractor, hooked up the bush hog, and headed out to a small pasture that was overdue for chopping. My son Chris rode on the fender of the tractor. It took nearly 20 minutes to cut a swath around the perimeter of the pasture. About half-way through the second round, Chris tapped me on the shoulder and pointed to the sky in the direction of the mangrove estuary. "Look, Daddy, here come the *garzas*." A group of white cattle egrets was breaking out of their typical V-shaped flight formation and descending, ultimately flaring their wings to land in the newly cut vegetation near the tractor.

At the time, these were probably the most populous birds on Hacienda Barú. Their history is fascinating and relevant to our theme of deforestation resulting in increased diversity of bird species.

The cattle egret is native to Africa. Ornithologists hypothesize that the first ones to reach the Americas were blown across the Atlantic in a storm. Furthermore, they believe that this may have happened on several occasions, but prior to the late 1800s, conditions in the Americas were not favorable for the egrets. The first officially recorded sighting was in Suriname in the year 1877. By then there had been sufficient deforestation and creation of cattle ranches in South America to support a viable population of cattle egrets. As ranching expanded, cattle egrets followed. They were first recorded in Costa Rica in 1954 and today are found as far south as Argentina and as far north as the United States.

Why is deforestation and cattle ranching essential for the survival of cattle egrets? You need only observe feeding egrets for the answer to that question. The handsome white-feathered birds with yellow beaks and legs stand about as high as your knee. Cattle and horses typically graze with heads down, moving slowly through a pasture and disturbing insects as they move their feet within the grass. Sharp-eyed egrets walk alongside, snatching grasshoppers, beetles, and other large insects that flee the large animals' scuffling hooves. If you pay close attention, you will notice that each egret defends a two-meter swath around a cow or horse. On occasion I have seen egrets pick external parasites, such as ticks, from the hide of a resting cow. I have seen them feed on caterpillars that attack pasture grass. Experienced rice farmers know that if inchworms attack the young rice plants, there is no need to spray insecticides, because the egrets will soon come to feast on the pests.

Our tractor and bush hog didn't move through the pasture on four legs, but it sure did stir up insects, and that's what the *garzas* liked. It moved faster than livestock and the birds constantly took to flight, moving ahead of the machine and jockeying for position, rather than trying to defend a territory. There was plenty to eat for all. Again, I felt a tap on my shoulder. "Daddy, there's that hawk, and look up there, the bone-breaker just arrived." Chris was referring to the crested caracara, named for its habit of carrying bones high into the air and dropping them on a hard surface, then landing to remove the nutritious marrow from within.

"Over there. Look at that rat. Uh oh, here comes the hawk." The roadside hawk dove for the rat, flaring its wings at the last moment and extending its talons. But the rat dodged, changed directions, and evaded the raptor. Out of nowhere the caracara plunged and snatched up the panicked rodent, then carried its prize over to a cleanly chopped area near the trees and ate it. The bone-breaker preferred the ground to an arboreal perch.

The roadside hawk lacked the skill to make a clean kill but instead, finished off rats, lizards, and frogs that the egrets crippled but didn't swallow. The egrets' strong, straight beaks worked fine for snatching insects, but they have no way of chewing and swallowing larger prey. One would occasionally try to gulp a frog, but was quickly plagued by companions pulling on the amphibian's legs, trying to steal a morsel. As larger prey fled the blades of the mower, the nearest *garza* usually delivered a powerful blow to the head with its sharp pointed beak and left the crippled animal for some lucky hawk or vulture.

As our work continued, the freshly chopped area of pasture increased and the brush-covered portion diminished. After a couple of hours an island of weedy pasture remained completely surrounded by a cleanly mowed swath several times its width. Straight ahead a large iguana made a break from the island. Egrets scattered, some taking to flight, as the large lizard barged through the flock and made a beeline to the trees at the edge of the pasture. Nothing intervened and the iguana safely reached its goal, a large *poro* tree where it took refuge in the upper branches.

On the next round of the machine a tyra slipped silently and almost nonchalantly from the opposite side of the island. "Hey, look over there," I nudged Chris' leg. "There goes a *tolomuco*" (the tyra's Spanish common name). This black member of the weasel family, about twice the size of a large house cat, didn't waste any time finding cover, but it certainly wasn't frightened. The bush hog was the only thing that could harm it. Its self-assured attitude, coupled with its agile body and sleek black coat, captured my admiration and respect.

The *tolomuco* turned slightly and looked back at us as it entered a brushy area at the edge of the pasture where we were working.

The hungry birds remained until the job was done. By then, both black-headed and turkey vultures had arrived to pick through the aftermath. The bone-breaker joined them. Although this magnificent bird is an adept predator, it is mainly a carrion eater and is often found feeding with the vultures. The large black birds generally defer to the smaller raptor.

The following morning I saw a female coyote with two pups nosing around in the chopped vegetation hoping to find a morsel. In addition to the numerous small organisms that the egrets and hawks had eaten there remained much that had been killed by the machine. Land crabs were the most prevalent, but lizards, snakes, and a few small mammals could be found as well. Within a couple of days nothing edible was left. The traces left uneaten by the carrion eaters were consumed by the ants. Nature leaves nothing to waste.

What is the point of this blood-and-guts tale? It is certainly not an experience of which I am proud, but it is part of my past which I cannot deny. I was in the business of raising cattle, and clearing overgrown pastures was a necessary part of ranching. Experiences like this helped spark my interest in tropical nature and influenced my decision to convert Hacienda Barú into a refuge for wildlife of all kinds. There are a number of lessons to be learned here:

One—With only a couple of months of overgrowth a weedy pasture becomes a haven for life of all kinds, from tiny insects to mammals. These species feed on one another and begin to develop a balance amongst themselves, which is the beginning of a well-functioning ecosystem. When we quit raising cattle on Hacienda Barú and allowed the pastures to return to their natural state, biodiversity increased rapidly. Now after more than 30 years, it harbors many times the number of species that existed in the overgrown pasture.

Two—Mother Nature recycles everything. All animals must eat. When one animal becomes injured or sick, it is easy prey for a predator or scavenger. Every living thing on this planet sooner or later becomes food for some other living thing. By mowing the pasture, I created a "killing field" and a feeding frenzy for the meat eaters.

Three—The success story of the cattle egret illustrates the concept of the niche. Though these impressive white birds may have been blown across the Atlantic on many occasions, there was no niche for them and they failed to establish a viable population. Once humans began the process of deforestation and cattle production, the *garzas* found their niche, and as the niche expanded so did populations. Cattle egrets evolved and found their niche in Africa, where humans evolved, and their success is closely tied to human activities.

Now that Hacienda Barú is a National Wildlife Refuge, 96 percent of the pastures have reverted to secondary forests, but the cattle egrets have not disappeared. They now come here to nest in the mangrove estuary, perhaps feeling shielded by the buffer of natural vegetation. Each day they fly out to feed in pastures and fields of neighboring farms and return to the refuge each night to roost.

The cattle egret found its niche in this hemisphere, and in little over a century, spread throughout North and South America. The roadside hawk, crested caracara, rat, tyra, iguana, coyote, vultures, and land crabs all occupy their niches. Without human intervention they, together with uncounted other organisms, will arrive at a state of dynamic equilibrium, constantly changing yet intricately balanced by the activities of all other organisms, each occupying its own special niche.

I often wonder about the human niche. What is our niche? Or do we simply run roughshod over every species that gets in our way and appropriate all the niches we want? Maybe that's why our planet is growing less hospitable. Maybe we should find our proper niche and learn to show respect for the millions of other species with which we share the planet. If not, I fear that Mother Nature may resort to more drastic methods of bringing the Earth back into her bosom. ꙮ

Cattle egrets hunting insects (top photo) and nesting.

29

Troubled Times in Costa Rica

Dinner with the General

The late 1970s and through the 1980s were times of turmoil in Central America. Costa Rica had been a stable democracy since 1948, had no army, and was the only nation in the isthmus not involved in some sort of internal conflict. Nevertheless, some of the violence from neighboring countries was bound to spill over. When I think back on those years, it seems strange that life could have once been so different in this small, peaceful nation where we live today.

For many years, Nicaragua had been a dictatorship ruled by the Somoza dynasty. The beginnings of internal resistance began to appear in the early 1970s. Then, in 1974, a major earthquake destroyed much of Managua and killed over 10,000 people. Financial aid poured into the country from all over the world. The Somozas are said to have kept most of the money for themselves rather than rebuilding the capital city. That was the final straw that broke the camel's back. It triggered the Nicaraguan Revolution, which ended with the ousting of Somoza in 1979.

Twelve different resistance groups had participated in the revolution, and each was given a seat in the new ruling junta or council, informally called the Group of Twelve. It soon became apparent, however, that only one of the twelve, the Sandinista Party, controlled all of the guns and thus all of the power. Daniel Ortega, as head of the party, and his brother Humberto, as head of the military, ran the country as they pleased with little regard for the wishes of the Group of Twelve. The junta members soon began resigning in protest, and within a year all pretense of government by consensus dissolved. Most of the former junta members eventually fled the country out of fear for their lives. Some of them ended up in Costa Rica.

Up until 1981, Costa Rica had not experienced any violent fall-out from the Nicaraguan conflict, but that was about to change. A bomb exploded in front of the Honduran airline office in San Jose, blowing out the windows, but not causing major damage or harming anyone. Costa Rican authorities suspected the involvement of the Nicaraguan Embassy. A few weeks later another bomb exploded in the hallway of an apartment building in Escazu directly outside the door of a Nicaraguan expatriate. The Nicaraguan wasn't home at the time, but the explosion also blew out the door of the apartment across the hall, seriously injuring the Canadian lady who lived there. Again Nicaraguan embassy involvement was suspected. There were other incidents, but one in particular got everyone's attention. A powerful bomb exploded in a downtown San Jose parking lot, killing two people: the two Nicaraguans who had been carrying the bomb in a suitcase. It was later determined that the device was intended to kill Alfonso Robelo, a Nicaraguan and former member of the Group of Twelve who had moved to Costa Rica, and whose office was located in the building right across the street from the parking lot. Unfortunately for the two Nicaraguans carrying the suitcase, it detonated prematurely.

After that bombing, Costa Ricans started getting a little nervous. Neutrality wasn't keeping the country safe. Then an interesting thing happened. In 1982, the rebel group called the "Contras" initiated their counter revolution against the Sandinistas in Nicaragua, and all the bombings in Costa Rica stopped. The Sandinistas were too busy fighting for survival at home to worry about exporting their revolution to the rest of Central America. However, a new problem evolved. The counter revolution began spilling across the border into northern Costa Rica.

In 1983, a worried Costa Rican President Luis Alberto Monge began a program called the Organización Para Emergencias Nacionales (OPEN), which trained private citizens who, in the case of an invasion from Nicaragua or elsewhere, would become a civil defense force. The people in charge of OPEN for the southern zone soon contacted me and asked if I had any military experience. I explained that I had never served in the military, and the only thing I had ever done that was even remotely related to the military was six months in the Reserve Officer Training Corps (ROTC) while attending Colorado State University, 20 years previous. "Wonderful!" they said. Before I knew it I was a Lieutenant in OPEN with a platoon of a dozen men under my command. My badge was number 100. At that time the slang word for a 100 colon bill (roughly $2.50 in 1983) was a "teja," and my nickname became Comandante Teja. Men eagerly joined my platoon and our training began with target practice, nocturnal jungle patrols, and rappelling off cliffs. When I think back on those days with OPEN, it seems like we were just a bunch of kids having loads of fun. At the time, of course, we all took everything dead seriously.

In February of 1985 our company of OPEN invited the Panamanian Armed Forces in David, Panama, to visit the livestock exposition in San Isidro and bring along their skydivers to do a demonstration. The invitation was innocent enough, and we didn't really expect them to come, but to our surprise, they accepted almost immediately. A day later we got another phone call from Panama. General Manuel Noriega, the Panamanian strongman, was coming with them. Panama had a president, but Noriega controlled the military, another example of: "He who has the guns makes the rules." The reason for the visit, we were told, was that the General's hobby was growing orchids and he wanted to see the orchid exposition.

The day of General Noriega's arrival, Costa Rican President

Monge came to San Isidro to greet him. Monge was chatting with our group of OPEN officers at the designated meeting place when the Panamanians arrived. Noriega and his entourage of a dozen body-guards flew in three helicopters and landed at a small airfield outside of San Isidro. We didn't see them until they arrived at the meeting with President Monge in three late model SUVs. We all walked out-side to greet our neighbors from the south. General Noriega was a small man in his mid-50s. He wore a traditional, white guayabera and a small, cream-colored Panama hat. Deeply scarred with pock marks, his face was quite ugly. The second I laid eyes on him I knew the origin of his nickname "Pineapple Face." In spite of this defor-mity, he seemed pleasant and smiled all of the time. The two national leaders greeted each other warmly and conversed briefly in private. After the meeting they both walked out to President Monge's older model car and said good-bye.

"I'll drive," said the President to his chauffeur. "You can relax for a while."

Noriega's personal guard found this incredible. "Where are his bodyguards?" asked one of them.

"The chauffeur probably has a pistol in his back pocket," joked one of my fellow OPEN officers.

Next came lunch with the General at a luxurious private rural home. The guests included notable people from around San Isidro, a high-ranking official from the Social Christian Political party, half a dozen OPEN officers from the southern zone, and about 20 of the General's followers, including his personal guard and press corps. Everything was very informal. At one point, a skydiver parachuted into the backyard, quickly released his parachute, ran up and smartly saluted the General.

That evening we dined at the Hotel del Sur. The mood was only slightly more formal than lunch, and everything was very cordial. Diane, our 18-year-old daughter Natalie, and I were seated directly across the table from the General and his young mistress. During the course of the evening Manuel Noriega invited both my wife Diane and my daughter Natalie to dance. Some of the Panamanian officers had previously danced with Natalie, but once she danced with the General no one else would go near her.

Something I noticed in particular was that he rarely spoke. I don't think I heard him utter a complete sentence in the presence of more than two or three other people, certainly nothing that could be quoted. But during the course of the evening each of the OPEN officers was very subtly maneuvered into a private conversation. When my turn came to speak with General Noriega alone, he was like a talking machine that couldn't be shut off. The following is a close approximation of what he told me:

"You probably know that I was in Managua two weeks ago visiting Danny Ortega. That guy's a mad man. If he happens to wake up in a bad mood some morning, he's just crazy enough to invade Costa Rica. He has over 50 Soviet tanks. I saw them. And he's itching to use them. Those tanks can drive to San Jose in six hours. He can take over the country without firing a shot. If that happens the US won't come to Costa Rica's aid. It will take the gringos a month to

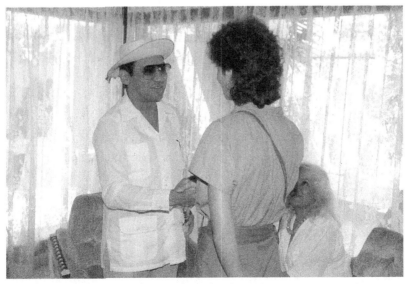

Diane Ewing meets General Manuel Noriega in 1985.

229

make up their minds. In fact Costa Rica has only one ally who can get here fast, and that ally is Panama. We can't make it in time to save San Jose, but we can save the south. I want you to be assured that Panama is Costa Rica's friend and, if Ortega invades, we will stop him at the Cerro de la Muerte."

In my opinion, what this really meant was: "Daniel Ortega and I made a deal. We're going to split up Costa Rica. He gets the north, and I get the south."

The next day a high-ranking OPEN officer came looking for Diane and I. "Where's Natalie?" he asked.

"She's still asleep at the hotel," answered Diane, with a little wrinkle in her brow.

"Don't bring her here today," he said emphatically. "The General likes her and if he decides he wants her he'll send a couple of his men to San Jose to kidnap her and take her to Panama. His intelligence officers will find out where she works, where she lives, and everything about her. Then when she least expects it they'll grab her and take her to Panama in the general's private plane. That will be the last you'll ever see or hear from her. General Noriega is ruthless, and he gets what he wants. Send her home or hide her today. If he doesn't see her, maybe he will just forget about her." Diane drove back to our hotel, woke Natalie up and took her to a friend's house. Once the general's party had gotten in their helicopters and returned to Panama, Natalie came down to the exposition for a couple of hours and then went back to San Jose on the last bus.

The OPEN officer who had warned us got in touch with the Costa Rican intelligence service Dirección de Intelligencia y Seguridad (DIS), and asked them to keep an eye on Natalie. A DIS agent met with her, explained to her how to tell if the Panamanians were snooping around, and gave her a number to call if she thought she was being followed.

When Diane and I returned to Hacienda Barú, we learned that one of the Panamanian helicopters had flown all over the property and even landed in a pasture near our house. They probably planned on making a base there at some point in the future. Fortunately, that never happened.

In December of 1989 the armed forces of the United States invaded Panama, arrested General Manuel Noriega and took him back to the US to stand trial on drug-trafficking charges. He completed a 20-year prison term in 2010 and was then extradited to France where he was convicted of money laundering. In 2011 the Panamanian government extradited him from France and plans to put him on trial for a multitude of crimes, especially the murder and dismemberment of opposition leader Hugo Spadafora back in the 1980s. As of this writing, the once strongman of Panama is in very poor health, and it is doubtful if he will ever stand trial.

Shortly after the invasion and removal of Noriega, a democratic government was elected in Panama. A couple of years later, elections were held in Nicaragua, and the Sandinistas were voted out of power by an overwhelming majority. Daniel Ortega stayed in Nicaragua, remained as head of the Sandinista Party and ran for president every election. Eighteen years later he was finally elected President of Nicaragua in free elections. Daniel Ortega is currently serving his second term as President of our northern neighbor. He has manipulated the justice system and the electoral system and harassed the opposition news media. Ortega was reelected in questionable elections in 2011.

Today, thinking back on those troubled times, it seems like all of this happened in another lifetime. In a way, I guess it did. 🐾

30

The Luxury of Living in the Third World

Life in Southern Costa Rica in the Good Old Days

Back in the late 1980s we still didn't have telephones in the coastal communities, and we were just starting to do some bird watching and ecological tours at Hacienda Barú. The lodge didn't exist yet. For booking the tours we shared an office with a travel agency in San Isidro and communicated with them by radio. One day I was at the phone company, which was also the electrical utility, seeing about getting an extra phone installed in the office. The whole process should have taken about ten minutes, but we kept having power outages. The clerk's computer didn't have a backup battery, so every time the power went out she lost all the work she had done up to that point. When the electricity returned, she had to start from scratch. The third time the lights went out she let out an exasperated shriek, "I can't stand this anymore. What the hell is wrong with the power?"

Her supervisor, who was standing right behind her, promptly smiled and said, "Don't sweat it, honey. This is just part of the price you have to pay for the luxury of living in the Third World." No sooner had those words escaped his lips than the lights came on and the clerk was able to complete her work.

In those days Costa Rica was still part of the Third World, and the southern coastal region was more underdeveloped than the rest of the country. Some of the coastal communities did have electricity, but there were no phones, and it took an hour and a half to drive from Dominical to Quepos down a rutted tooth-rattling road. I had been living in the region for 17 years managing Hacienda Barú which was well into the transition from cattle ranch to nature reserve and ecological tourism.

One day one of my workers came to our house and told me that there was a strange dog in the machine shed. "I don't know where he came from, but he's so damn mean he won't let any of us go in there, and I need some tools."

Having no fear of dogs I went out to have a look. Out from underneath a piece of machinery came strutting a purebred, male Pekingese with long reddish-brown hair, stub nose, tail half curled over his back, and a nasty attitude. Who knows where he came from and how long he had been lost. His right eye was in bad shape, protruding from his head and severely infected. For some reason, he and I hit it off from the beginning. He never offered to bite me, but raised his head and peered into my eyes with a forlorn look that said, "Are you going to save me?" With that he dropped his gaze, let out a ferocious bark, ran around me, and started nipping at the heels of the worker who had followed me into the shed. I picked him up, took him to the house, put some antibiotic salve on his eye, and fed him some dog food. He must have been starving, but he took a moment to lick my hand before he ate. This small gesture of gratitude totally endeared him to me.

He was the most thankful dog I've ever known and continued to be so for the rest of his life. Our other dogs, rather than lick your hand for feeding them, were more likely to take your finger off in their rush to get the food. My son Chris, who was home on vacation from high school in the US, christened our bedraggled new pet, Dead-eye.

The next day his eye had not improved, so I ham-radioed an operator in Quepos and had him patch me through to the only veterinarian in town. Though he was primarily a large animal vet he would do small animals when necessary, and it was hard to turn people with sick animals away. Reluctantly he agreed to look at the dog. "Bring him to Quepos," he said. "I'll get my instruments sterilized in case we need to do surgery." I drove, and Chris held Dead-eye in his lap.

When we got to Quepos, Jorge, the veterinarian, was just returning from treating a sick cow. He looked at Dead-eye's eye and shook his head. "I don't know why people let these things go so long," he said. "Now he's going to lose his eye."

"Don't look at me," I retorted defensively. "I never saw this dog until yesterday. I'm just trying to help him."

Jorge said that he hadn't had time to sterilize his instruments and to come back at three o'clock. We really didn't want to wait that long, but we had lunch and visited some friends. When we returned, the vet looked surprised to see us, and a little embarrassed. "I still haven't had time to get my instruments sterilized," he apologized, "but you guys have come a long way. Bring the dog in, and we'll see what we can do. Follow me." He took us to a room behind the office. "This is where we'll operate. Put him on the table."

Chris and I looked around the room. There was a cabinet and a table with a Formica top. Jorge wiped the table top with an alcohol-soaked rag. Out of the cabinet he took a stainless steel pan and poured it half full of alcohol. He took his surgical instruments out of a second-hand plastic bag that had once held rice and dumped them in the alcohol. "That ought to disinfect them enough for this operation," he explained. "Let's give him a little tranquilizer to calm him down before I try to put a needle in his vein to anesthetize him."

Dead-eye looked really sick and half asleep. I doubted if he would cause any problem. In fact, I was getting a little worried about him. But when Jorge stuck the needle in his leg to give him the tranquilizer, Dead-eye whirled around in a flash and bit his hand. "Son-of-a-bitch! That little bastard bit me!"

I grabbed Dead-eye's head and held him tight, muzzling him with my hand, while Jorge finished injecting the tranquilizer. In a couple of minutes he was real mellow. He didn't even flinch when Jorge stuck the needle in the vein. As the plunger on the syringe slowly forced the anesthetic into his vein, Dead-eye went sound asleep. When the syringe was about half empty the vet stopped and stared at the sleeping dog. "Damn! Did he stop breathing?" He reached down and touched Dead-eye's chest. "Oh my god, he's really skinny, he doesn't weigh half as much as I figured. I hope I didn't kill him."

All of our eyes were glued to the death-like form lying on the table. *Well, it looks like his suffering is over*, I thought. Not a word passed between us as we watched the ball of messy, tangled, reddish hair on the table, willing him to twitch or wiggle an ear. It was about 30 seconds later, but seemed a lot longer when Dead-eye's rib cage rose and fell once. Then again. And finally settled into a slow, but steady rhythm. "Whew! I guess I shouldn't give him the rest of this," said Jorge looking at me. I didn't think he really wanted an answer, so I kept my mouth shut. He looked back down at the unconscious dog and pulled the syringe out of his vein. "That was a close one! He's all hair. He doesn't weigh anything at all."

From this point on Jorge got down to the serious business of removing the damaged eye. The eye was a horrible mess protruding from the little Pekingese's head and badly infected. It even smelled bad. I could understand why Dead-eye was so listless and sick looking. The pain must have been intense, and fighting the infection had really worn him down.

The surgery went well. Chris and I assisted, holding Dead-eye when necessary, and handing the vet the surgical tools he asked for. Jorge removed the bad eye and severed the optic nerve with a scalpel. Once the eye was out he used a soldering iron to cauterize the optic nerve and several little vessels that were oozing blood. It was old and rusty, but he cleaned it off with a wire brush, and I doubt if any bacteria could live on the red hot iron anyway. Before sewing up the incision he dabbed the eye socket with gauze soaked in a mild antiseptic and squirted a big blob of antibiotic cream into the hole, a cream normally used for the treatment of mastitis in cows. Then he sewed the eyelids together, seven stitches in all, neat and clean. I could imagine how much better Dead-eye would feel when he woke up.

Before we left, Jorge gave Dead-eye an injection of antibiotic. This time the Pekingese was out like a light and in no condition to bite him. He gave me a small vial of antibiotic, a disposable syringe, five antibiotic capsules, and instructed me to give the dog another shot the next day and a capsule every day until they were all gone.

Dead-eye never moved a muscle all the way home. In fact, he didn't move until 3:30 the next morning. Chris and I took turns checking on him once each hour, and it was my turn when he finally regained consciousness. He was still pretty groggy, but awake. He wasn't interested in food, but stood on wobbly feet and drank a lot of water. Before drinking he took a second to lick my hand. Then he went back to sleep and rested peacefully the rest of the night. The next morning he was happy and hungry

That day Diane returned from touring with her family. My father-in-law, a veterinarian, was fascinated and a little horrified as Chris and I recounted the story of Dead-eye's surgery. He commented that from all outward appearances it had been a total success. I wouldn't have minded if Dead-eye had bit my mother-in-law, but unlike my brother-in-law, he seemed to like her just fine.

The incision healed with little problem. It was still slightly swollen when I finished with the capsules. I had to go to Quepos anyway for some horse medicine so I picked up four more of the antibiotic capsules. A week after the surgery Diane and I removed the stitches. Eventually hair grew over the incision and Dead-eye could even wiggle his eyebrow. The surgery was a total success.

Dead-eye's ordeal is a perfect example of the luxury of living in the Third World. We may not have the best conditions, but we get the job done with what we have available. And the cost? Jorge charged me a total of $12 for the surgery, including the antibiotics and another

$1 when I returned for more antibiotic capsules. I think he gave us a better price because he was a little embarrassed about almost having killed the patient. I had expected that he would charge us $25 which still would've been a bargain.

Today, 25 years later, Costa Rica is no longer part of the Third World. I don't believe there is a term for Costa Rica's present status, somewhere in between the emerging south and the developed north. Today the same surgery would be done in a spotless room on a stainless steel table with instruments sterilized in an autoclave and with a qualified veterinarian assistant helping the surgeon. They would weigh the dog prior to anesthetizing him, and would use a specialized surgical instrument to cauterize the incision. Everything would be done very professionally. The cost would be about $400, a lot more than the cost of Dead-eye's surgery, but not quite developed-world prices. In the US, this operation would be called an enucleation rather than an eye removal, and it would cost $800 to $1000. The results, with a little luck, would be the same as with our Third-World surgery.

We who live in Costa Rica can now hold our heads high and be proud that we have emerged from our former state and are well on our way to becoming a developed nation. We can now boast more professionalism in everything we do, higher wages, more gadgets, and much higher taxes. But all of this progress has a price. The price is that we can no longer enjoy the luxury of living in the Third World.

Dead-eye is no longer with us, but we have five other dogs, all of which were once strays. We keep them at our home at Hacienda Barú National Wildlife Refuge. Each dog has its own story. 🐾

31

Top Predators

Pumas in the Path of the Tapir Biological Corridor

In the rainforests of Central America the jaguar (*Panthera onca*) is at the pinnacle of the food chain, and the next largest feline, the puma (*Puma concolor*), is one step below. There isn't much that will confront a jaguar except the larger crocodiles lurking in some of the rivers. The presence of these magnificent spotted cats in a rainforest is a strong indication of the biological health of the ecosystem. It means there is enough for them to eat, and enough for their prey to eat. It suggests that the ecosystem is well balanced and productive. It also means that hunting is under control.

The last jaguar reported on Hacienda Barú was shot by a hunter in 1955. It had killed one of the hunter's dogs several weeks earlier, and he was so furious that he pursued it with his remaining three dogs until one day they treed it and he shot it off a limb. This was 15 years after the onset of the massive deforestation of the region. Much of the jaguar's habitat had been destroyed, and its prey base of white-lipped peccary had been seriously depleted by hunters. As a result the big cat had resorted to killing dogs and domestic pigs in order to survive. The people who lived in the area applauded the killing of the beast.

The deforestation continued into the early 1980s as did the uncontrolled hunting in most areas. At Hacienda Barú, we prohibited hunting beginning in 1976, and hired a forest guard to enforce the ban, although some hunting continued. One of my cowboys killed an ocelot in 1974, and a neighbor killed a jaguarundi a couple of years later. In the following years I heard of several sightings of cats, mostly ocelots and jaguarundis, but nothing larger.

Near Matapalo, about 12 kilometers from Hacienda Barú, a man named Eliecer Castro also had a large rainforest reserve in which he prohibited hunting. Don Eliecer had some white-tailed deer in captivity. He had acquired them from a friend in Guanacaste and trucked them to his ranch in Matapalo. Most of the deer were fenced in, but from time to time a few escaped. Eventually Don Eliecer released them all. They thrived in the rainforests and pastures of the surrounding area and established a breeding population. Many of the descendants of those original Guanacaste imports are around. At the time Don Eliecer never imagined that his deer would one day become important prey animals for large cats.

In 1987 we started offering several different ecological hikes through the rainforests of Hacienda Barú, including an overnight camping tour. In the dry season of 1989 a papaya tree with mature fruit stood in the middle of a cleared area around the jungle campsite. Every day, in the late morning, a large group of coatis appeared in the clearing and fought over the nearly ripe papaya, tearing them to pieces and gobbling up the sweet, orange fruit. Then, one day all of the coatis disappeared from the area, and the fruit ripened until it either fell off the tree or was eaten by birds. At the same time we found claw marks on a tree near the camp, and a very large paw print at the edge of a nearby stream. A few days later, the neighbors on a bordering farm observed a large tan-colored cat at the edge of a pasture where cattle were grazing.

From then until 2010 there were sporadic reports of puma sightings and puma tracks. After a puma was sighted on a farm near Matapalo, people quit sending their kids to school for a while for fear the large cat would attack them. For many years, it appeared there was only one puma roaming the area from Matapalo to Hacienda Barú, preying mainly on deer in the Matapalo area and collared peccary around Hacienda Barú. A couple of times each year, always when lots of peccary were in the area, we would see puma tracks, but we never actually saw one of the cats. We did, however, put them on our species list, along with four other felines: ocelot, margay cat, jaguarundi, and little spotted cat.

In North America the large cats known as mountain lions or cougars are the same species we call the puma in Costa Rica, though the ones we have here are slightly smaller. The difference in size is probably because those that reside in the temperate climates of the north prey primarily on larger ungulates such as mule deer and elk, and, over many years, natural selection has tended to favor larger cats. An adult puma in Costa Rica will average 110 centimeters from the tip of the nose to the base of the tail, and weigh about 50 kilograms. White-tailed deer, which weigh about 30 kilograms, and collared peccary, which weigh only about 20 kilograms, are the largest prey a puma is likely to kill. A large part of their diet consists of considerably smaller animals such as coatis, raccoons, and opossums. Pumas climb well and have been known to leap onto tree branches as high as five meters above the ground.

Studies in Corcovado National Park indicate that all four species of monkeys are consumed by pumas as well as both species of sloths. Once while hiking through Corcovado with a local guide we heard a terrible racket some distance from the trail. Our guide told us the sound was the extreme alarm call of a troop of spider monkeys, and the only thing that would frighten them enough to cause such commotion would be a puma nearby. The next time I heard a spider monkey give that same call of alarm was on Hacienda Barú in the year 2012.

In the late 1990s herpetologist Mason Ryan stayed with us at Hacienda Barú for about six months, spending most of his time wandering around the jungle at night looking for frogs and snakes.

One night while working in the highland rainforest of Hacienda Barú, Mason got the feeling he was being followed. Then he heard what he described as a puma's snarl from up on the hill. A few seconds later he heard a similar snarl from the downhill side. He stopped what he was doing and returned to the house. It was the only time in six months of walking around the jungle alone at night that Mason became frightened enough to return to the house. I asked him if he was sure it was a puma's snarl. "I worked in the

Captive puma. *Photo: Alan Olander*

Bronx Zoo as a volunteer for five years," he replied. "Part of my job was to clean the puma's cage, and I'll never forget that snarl." The next day one of our guides went to the location looking for tracks. He didn't find any tracks, but did find blood and peccary hair on the ground. During the years that followed there were sporadic sightings at Quintas la Guapil and the Firestone Center, both of which border Hacienda Barú National Wildlife Refuge.

Finally in 2011 we had a definite sighting on Hacienda Barú. Pierre and Michele, two serious ecotourists, spent Saturday, April 23, walking on the nature trails of Hacienda Barú National Wildlife Refuge and enjoying the flora and fauna. About 3:30 p.m., less than 500 meters from the lodge, they found themselves face to face with two large, tan-colored cats. One of the cats was standing, and the other was crouching, its black-tipped tail straight out the back and raised. The crouching cat hissed at the two hikers. Pierre wanted to get the camera from the backpack and take a photo, but Michele just wanted to leave. The couple stayed close together and slowly backed away. Once they were out of sight, they turned and hurried back to the lodge where Hacienda Barú guide Ronald Alpízar opened the gate for them. Breathlessly they told him their story. Ronald returned to the spot with the couple, but the cats were gone. They did, however, come across a large group of collared peccary close to where the encounter took place. When questioned further Pierre and Michele described the behavior of the crouching cat as aggressive, but not threatening. The standing cat, which they estimated to be 60 centimeters tall at the shoulder, was quite passive.

It is interesting that there were two pumas, because they are normally solitary animals. When you find a pair there are two possible reasons. When a female comes into heat she will be together with a male for about a week. They mate often, as many as 70 times a day. Biologists believe that this is because frequent copulation is necessary to stimulate ovulation. A mating pair of pumas will be anything but calm. The female yowls from time to time and the male can be irritable and aggressive.

The other possibility of seeing two pumas together is that they are cubs recently separated from their mother. The female nurses her newborn offspring for about four months, at which time she weans them. Nevertheless, they remain with her and are partially dependent on her for up to another 18 months. At that time the mother will separate from the nearly full-grown cubs. The cubs will often stick together for a month or more, before each going its own way. I believe the pair of pumas seen by Pierre and Michele were siblings recently separated from their mother. A week after that incident two pumas were sighted about three kilometers from Hacienda Barú. The local man who saw them described them as grown cubs, making it likely that they were the same pair.

On July 5, 2012 two pumas side by side were photographed by a camera trap at the Firestone Center for Restoration Biology. The camera was located about five kilometers from the location where the pair of cubs was seen by Pierre and Michele the year before.

Three months later, in October of 2012, residents of Punto de

Mira, six kilometers from the Firestone Center, were awakened at two o'clock in the morning when the motion-sensitive security lamps lit up the front of their house. They got up to see what had activated the lamps and, to their surprise and delight, discovered two pumas in the yard. These are probably not the same cubs as those caught by the camera trap, because it's unlikely they'd still be together after three months.

All of these sightings have taken place in an area of about 40 square kilometers, but it doesn't necessarily mean this group of pumas' movements is restricted to that area. Since there have been three sightings of puma pairs, all more than three months apart, it seems likely there are at least three sexually mature females in the area, along with at least one male, and they have produced at least six offspring in less than two years. One male will normally defend a territory of 75 square kilometers or larger, sharing this territory with two or three females. All of this leads me to believe that we have a high density of these magnificent predators in the area around Hacienda Barú. This is really wonderful news because it is a strong indication that we have a thriving ecosystem.

Currently four park rangers work to protect Hacienda Barú and some of the surrounding properties. Several other neighbors also actively protect their properties from hunters, so there are a lot more peccary here than anywhere nearby, as hunting is rampant elsewhere. It is probable that the high density of pumas in this area is due to the large peccary population.

According to studies in Corcovado National Park, pumas eat many different animals, but their preferred prey is the coati. In the absence of coatis, the collared peccary becomes their primary source of food. Those who live in the area around Dominical and Hacienda Barú know that in 2009–2010 we had an overpopulation of coatis. There were so many that they would come up to people and beg for food. People would stop at the fruit stand near the bridge and buy bananas to feed the coatis, and large groups of them would gather there to take advantage of the free hand-outs. Nowadays we seldom see a coati. Disease may have reduced their numbers, but I'm sure a large part of the population fell prey to the pumas, since the beginning of the decline of coatis coincided with increased puma sightings. We still have lots of collared peccary at Hacienda Barú, but with the high density of pumas in the area, their numbers have already noticeably declined and will surely continue to do so. This brings to mind the question of what the pumas will eat when there aren't enough peccary to feed them.

Most likely some of the pumas will migrate out of the area. Those remaining will resort to killing more of the smaller animals for food, animals such as opossums, armadillos, monkeys, sloths, iguanas, agoutis, and pacas. I have often wondered why we have such a high population density of sloths in this area. On a three-day visit to the Corcovado National Park a few years ago we didn't see a single sloth, suggesting that in Corcovado they are heavily preyed upon by the pumas. I think eventually we can expect problems with puma attacks on domestic animals like dogs, cats, pigs, goats, calves, and colts. Hopefully there won't be any attacks on people, but this has happened on rare occasions in Corcovado and could happen here.

It is very nice to know that we have a healthy ecosystem that will support large predators, but it is important we recognize that this situation may bring certain problems, and we must be prepared to deal with them. Mother Nature will deal with the situation in her own way, and we have no way of predicting what that might be. 🐾

244

32

Surviving Joan and Caesar

Hurricanes in Southern Costa Rica

When she opened the freezer and the putrid odor of rotting meat seeped into the room, Doctor Jiménez pinched her nostrils and stepped back. Giving the restaurant owner a sidelong glance, she pulled out her citation book and began writing.

"You don't have to do this," he pleaded. "Give me a break. With the hurricane and all it's been tough getting supplies. We have to take what we can get."

"Sign here!" she ordered. "That meat came from a dead bull that washed up on the beach. Witnesses saw you cutting it up. Others saw you serving it to your customers. I'm taking that rotten packet of frozen meat as evidence."

During and after Hurricane Joan in late October of 1988 at least 67 dead cattle washed up on the beaches between Uvita and Matapalo. The health ministry ordered local communities to bury them. Most were interred one way or another, but some were left to the vultures, and a few were cut up, cooked, and served in homes and at least one restaurant. Apparently a herd of cattle near the Terraba River was stranded by rising waters and carried out to sea.

Joan was predicted to hit Limon, and much of Costa Rica's Caribbean side was evacuated. At the last moment the monster storm veered north and made land in Bluefields, Nicaragua, about 250 kilometers to the north. The clouds east of the continental divide were sucked into the depression, leaving Limon with fair weather. As Pacific cloud cover moved toward Hurricane Joan, it collided with the central mountain range, dumping horrendous amounts of rain on the south-central Pacific region of Costa Rica. Hacienda Barú's weather station recorded 1,715 millimeters of rain that month, taller than an average-sized man. However, our rain gauge overflowed three times, and there is no way of knowing how much rain went unrecorded.

As Joan was making her way toward Hacienda Barú and Dominical, Diane was talking on the ham radio. Right after her friend said "OVER," a third party interrupted with the word "BREAK," meaning they had something to say.

"Go ahead BREAK," she answered, "this is Tango-India-8-Delta-Echo-Echo."

T-I-8-D-E-E this is T-I-2-C-N-E. I'm calling from the Command Center of the National Emergency Commission. My name is Oscar. Hurricane Joan is on the way, and we need information about Dominical. Will you help us? Over."

"You needn't worry. We're having beautiful weather. Over."

"Not for long. Now I need your QTH [radio talk for location] exactly. How far from the river? How far from the beach? Any danger from landslides? Do you have a backup battery for your radio?"

She answered these questions and more. "Good," replied Oscar. "It sounds like you'll be a safe and reliable contact. Now listen carefully. I am placing you in charge. The safety of that region is in your hands. Is that clear?"

Stunned and more than a little frightened by the enormity of her responsibility, Diane hesitated, "QSL," she replied. "It's clear, but I don't think anyone will believe me. Over."

"You're going to have to convince them. You still have some time, but we don't know how much. Tell everybody to get livestock away from the rivers and onto high ground. People who live near water must move. Oh, I almost forgot, we need a census. Get it and call me back tonight. Over."

"QSL. I understand. T-I-8-D-E-E over and out."

Diane got in her red Blazer and drove to Dominical. Memo and Marita were sitting at a table in front of Rancho Memo's. Diane jumped out of the Blazer and hurried to them. "We've got to alert everybody," she exclaimed. "Terrible rains are coming. We have to evacuate the people near the river, get everyone to move their cattle away from the water, and we don't have much time."

"Wait a minute Doña Diana, slow down," soothed Memo. "The sun is shining. Don't believe everything you hear on the news."

What she was saying was barely believable even to herself, but Oscar had been convincing. Diane figured that if she could convince Memo, the rest of the community would go along. A small crowd formed. Mon Marìn was there, so were Misa Arroyo, several of the Cherepos, Don David Venegas and Emilio Vargas, the policeman. Diane explained the situation to everyone, this time clearly and deliberately. The faces of her friends and neighbors were concerned yet full of doubt. "Wait a minute, let me try something." She pulled a hand-held radio from her bag. "T-I-2-C-N-E, this is T-I-8-D-E-E; do you copy?" Oscar answered almost immediately. Diane explained that the sun was shining in Dominical, and it was hard to believe they were in danger. She asked him to explain.

Oscar's voice came loud and clear over the small radio in Diane's hand. He explained about Joan and emphasized they were experiencing the "calm before the storm." When he finished the crowd was dead silent. "Now, I want everyone to know the National Emergency Commission has placed Doña Diana in charge of your region. She will communicate directly with me and I will give orders through her and everybody will follow them. You need to evacuate everybody who lives near a river or stream. If they don't want to leave their homes, get the police to drag them out and move them to a safe location like the school or church. Now, is everyone clear about the seriousness of this storm?" All those present looked at Diane and nodded. She told Oscar that the message was clear. "Good," he replied grimly. "You best get to work. Joan is coming."

I returned from a business trip to Venezuela a week later, flew to Quepos, and hired a 4x4 taxi to take me to Dominical. It was the first vehicle to make it through in four days. The road to San Isidro was still closed by landslides and wouldn't open for another two days. The rains had subsided to about 100 millimeters per day. The worst was over. The big task was getting food into the isolated communities. I only had to sleep with the Commander-in-Chief one night before Diane stepped down and gradually eased back into normal life.

For days afterwards I listened to Diane's stories of people who were threatened by the storm, working together to protect property and human life. One memorable ordeal was a two-car medical cara-van, three days into the storm; the patients included a badly bruised elderly woman whose house had fallen in, a girl with a severe case of asthma, and three men, all with broken or mangled limbs.

"The biggest challenge for me was traversing a broken bridge while evacuating the injured people," said Diane. "One side of the bridge was torn away but after checking underneath, Olman Cas-cante and I decided we could drive over it if he walked ahead of me, making sure the left tires did not go off the edge. I took a deep breath and drove slowly, watching his hand signals until I reached the other side. I waited for the second car to cross as I did, then we drove on to meet two waiting ambulances. After seeing them leave for the hospital, I gave a huge sigh of relief and called the National Emergency Commission on my radio to say 'mission accomplished'."

Two days later, with roads still under water, a woman in labor was evacuated by boat. Later still, food aid arrived and had to be distributed. Those who came together to survive Hurricane Joan share a common bond that is still evident today.

One thing about the emergency was truly amazing, a miracle actually. Neither the electricity nor the only telephone in Dominical went out during the entire ordeal, not even once!

In July of 1996 Hurricane Caesar caught everyone by surprise and dumped a lot of water on the region in a short time. Just one afternoon and night of torrential rain was enough to flood all of the rivers between Dominical and Quepos, wash out numerous roads, destroy the bridge over the Hatillo Nuevo River, bring down about a dozen landslides between Dominical and San Isidro, and knock out the electricity and phones for six days. So many trees washed up on the beach that it was possible to walk for several kilometers just stepping from one trunk to another without touching the sand. We had a group of students staying at Hacienda Barú Lodge who had to catch a flight a couple of days later. There was no hope of getting them out by road, but we did manage to get them out on a boat.

By 1996 a few people in Dominical had cell phones, so we weren't totally dependent on radios, but we did use them a lot. Without electricity, there was no way to charge the phones, so we were limited to brief calls.

Several people were killed by a landslide in the Uvita area. In Dominical the biggest emergency was with a woman named Hania who went into labor early in the morning the day after the rains stopped. She and her husband, Luis, lived in a village called San Miguel, far from the nearest road. Luis and some family and neighbors carried Hania to the small town of Hatillo on a stretcher made with a couple of blankets and two sticks. There they found a cattle truck to take her over an extremely rough road to Dominical where they hoped to find help.

A couple of Lagunas residents, Lisa and Donn, were on their way to Dominical over nearly impassable roads when they heard about the incident over their CB radio. They intercepted the truck, and Lisa, a registered nurse, asked a few questions and discovered that Hania had been in labor most of the night. "Let's get her to Dominical," said Lisa. "We need to find someplace more sanitary than this."

My wife Diane arrived in Dominical about the same time as Donn and Lisa, and the two women took charge of the situation. They converted a local real estate office into a makeshift clinic and

Lisa gave Hania a preliminary examination. Furrows appeared on Lisa's brow as she proceeded to examine the exhausted, expectant mother. Looking at Diane, and then back at Hania, she said, "We need a doctor here. The baby is turned sideways. I can't do this."

That same morning a helicopter brought medical supplies and food, but no doctor. Diane was in charge of the radio and called the National Emergency Commission and the hospitals in San Isidro and Quepos several times. All said they didn't have a doctor or a means of transport available. The day wore on. Hania was enduring great pain and suffering, but never once did she cry out or complain. Finally, about three o'clock, Diane and Lisa decided that the time had come, and something had to be done. "It's just you and me girl," said Lisa. "The mother's and baby's lives are in our hands. I can't turn the baby, and she can't wait any longer. Maybe a doctor can give us instructions over the radio."

Just at that moment came a knock on the door. "What now!" exclaimed Diane in an exasperated voice. She opened the door and stood dumbfounded, looking at two doctors and a medical assistant. One doctor and his assistant had come from Quepos in a boat. They were wet to their waists where they had landed on the beach in Dominicalito. The other doctor had been trapped at the clinic in Platanillo when the rains hit and had ridden on horseback across several landslides until he met a man along the road who had given him a ride the rest of the way on the back of his motorcycle. By pure chance both doctors arrived at the scene of the emergency at the same moment.

"Boy, am I glad to see you!" Diane cried.

"Who is it?" called Lisa.

"Three angels," was the reply.

The doctors were able to turn the baby, and, in a short time, Hania gave birth to a healthy baby girl. They named her Erica. Everybody thought Caesar would've been appropriate had the baby been a boy, but no one knew the feminine version of Caesar. 🦅

33

A Great Name for an Elephant

Growing Up in a Bilingual Environment

When our children were young, and we had only lived a short time in Costa Rica, I used to wonder how growing up in a household where two languages were spoken would affect their communication skills and if they would confuse English and Spanish. I think lots of parents wonder the same thing, as the topic often came up for discussion on social occasions. When reflecting on this question, one memory stands out above all others. My son Chris was sitting in a highchair, scattering bits of food here and there while jabbering away in his own version of two-year-old dialect. Everybody else had to decipher what little they could of his meaning from the few identifiable words that emerged from the babble. He seemed to be talking about an elephant, which we all assumed was an imaginary friend of his.

"Does your elephant have a name?" asked Diane.

"Yes," was the enthusiastic reply, accompanied by vigorous head-nodding.

"Well. Are you going to tell us?"

More head nodding.

"Well, what is his name? We want to know."

Silence with a pensive frown.

"Come on, Chris. Tell us your elephant's name."

"Bodega."

"Bodega. Wow, what a great name for an elephant."

To an adult, bodega—a Spanish word which can mean anything from a small storeroom to a large warehouse—seems an unlikely name for an elephant. But to Chris' two-year-old mind it was perfectly logical. I imagine he wasn't sure exactly what a bodega might be, but had heard the word and sensed that it was something big, like an elephant. When he was pressed to come up with a name, what better name for an elephant than something else that is big, like bodega.

Was this a confusion of English and Spanish on Chris' part? I'm sure it was not. It was a mixing of languages, which is quite distinct from confusion. Chris knew "elephant" was a word that belonged to the language his Mommy spoke, and "bodega" belonged to the language the housekeeper spoke. There was no more confusion than if my wife had said to our daughter, who was seven at the time, "Natalie, please go get the *escoba* out of the bodega and sweep up the *basura* on the floor around Chris' highchair." It is clear which words in the sentence belong to the Spanish language. Bilingual people mix languages all the time. We call it Spanglish. Some words just seem to fit better regardless of the language being spoken, as do some idiomatic expressions, like *ticos* (Costa Ricans) or *Pura Vida* ("that's great" or "everything is wonderful").

Growing up in a two-language household gives kids a tremendous advantage academically. It also seems to give them self-assuredness and maturity, due in large part to the insight into another culture that comes from speaking and understanding a second language. Spanish-speaking people not only speak differently than English-speaking people, they think and act differently, and many cultural distinctions are reflected in the language. This understanding of other cultures allows kids to grow up knowing that people everywhere are different, and no one is right or wrong. Having this knowledge gave both of our kids a big edge over their classmates when they went to the United States to attend high school.

Our daughter Natalie had never come in contact with the Spanish language before coming to Costa Rica. Nevertheless, her four-year-old mind was wide open, and she learned the language in a very short time. All of her friends spoke Spanish, and learning the language was necessary if she wanted to play. This, of course, made it a top priority. Her grammar was good, and she even spoke without an accent. Diane and I were in our late twenties when we started learning the language, and found ourselves at a distinct disadvantage. Even though we have spoken Spanish for 44 years, we still make lots of grammatical errors and our gringo accents are all too noticeable.

Natalie's early schooling was at a private, English-speaking grade school called the Country Day School. The classes were all in English, but after school, all of her friends spoke Spanish. By the time we all moved to Hacienda Barú she was ready for junior high, where she attended the Colegio Tecnico Profesional de Matapalo located about 12 kilometers from our house. There she completed seventh and eighth grades.

Surprisingly she adapted rapidly and loved her new environment. She rode an old yellow school bus the kids called the "tin can." Among other defects, it lacked brakes, and no repair parts were available. Other than that it was in pretty good shape, considering its age. The driver would honk the horn a couple hundred meters from the house, so Natalie could dash from the house to the road. The driver slowed down as much as possible while she ran beside the bus and leapt onto the first step, a simple task for a healthy young teenager. Getting off the bus, basically the reverse, was also no problem, but occasionally provoked a fall and a skinned knee.

Convincing Natalie to leave her new school and friends and move to Greeley, Colorado, for high school was a major battle. We didn't exactly have to hog-tie her and carry her to the plane, but neither did she go willingly.

In Greeley, most of her friends were from the Hispanic community. Her upbringing in a bilingual environment and her general life experience gave her an entirely different outlook on life than her fellow students. On one occasion her social studies teacher made mention of the poor people in Greeley. Genuinely confused, Natalie asked, "What poor people?"

"Well," fumbled the teacher, "Most of the people who live on the other side of the tracks are below the poverty level."

"Those people are my friends," retorted Natalie, feeling slighted. "They aren't poor. They have refrigerators, televisions, and cars and get plenty to eat. You want to see poor people, come to Costa Rica. I'll show you people who live in shacks with dirt floors and aren't sure where their next meal is coming from. The women are all barefoot and pregnant, and have half a dozen naked kids running and crawling around the house. But I haven't seen any poor people here."

The teacher didn't know how to answer.

After high school Natalie couldn't wait to return to Costa Rica. To her mother's dismay she didn't return home to live, but got a job in San Jose, shared an apartment with another girl, and started taking several university courses. In 1985 she was offered a job with a travel agency called Costa Rica Expeditions where she has worked to this day.

In San Jose Natalie speaks English only with clients. All of the rest of her professional and personal life is in Spanish, which she speaks flawlessly. Her two years at Hacienda Barú, when she spoke rural Spanish, known as *campesino* Spanish, didn't affect her at all. When her brother, Chris, would come from the farm and spend a few days with her in the city, she was always embarrassed by his *campesino* dialect. "He sounds ridiculous," she lamented. "A great big, good-looking kid, obviously a gringo, speaking Spanish like a country hick. *Que verguenza.*"

Today, after 30 years of living, working, and socializing in San Jose, Natalie's Spanish is so perfect that it tends to confuse people. Though she looks somewhat like a gringa and has a gringa last name, her mannerisms and speech are that of a *tica*. *Ticos* who meet her for the first time don't know quite what slot to fit her into. She is as adapted to Costa Rica as a non-Costa Rican can be.

Seven-year-old Chris entered the first grade at Barú, five kilometers from La Casona. He shared a classroom with 27 students from six grades all taught by the same teacher. Class began at 7:00 a.m. and everyone went home at 11:00. Sometimes he rode his horse, but occasionally we took him and a few neighbor kids in the jeep. The Dominical school was closer, as the crow flies, but there was no bridge over the Barú River.

Chris loved every minute of his schooling at Barú, but he hated the home study in English every afternoon; more interesting things were happening outside, like riding horses, working with cattle, talking with the workers, and fishing. He graduated from the Barú elementary school in 1984 and began two years of junior high school by correspondence. That was definitely tougher on Diane and me than on Chris. In the end it all worked out fine. He eventually graduated from the eighth grade with an accredited correspondence school, and went to Colorado to live with family and attend Golden High School. To everyone's surprise he made excellent grades, and, along with his other courses, studied German for three years. Upon graduation Chris was given a special award for being the only trilingual student at Golden High. He said that after already speaking two languages fluently, learning German was a "piece of cake."

When he first began attending GHS, Chris did have a problem making friends. One of his teachers told my wife that because of his high level of maturity the other students distrusted him, thinking the narcotics department had planted him in the school to spy. Once they realized the folly of their suspicions, Chris made friends easily.

Diane says boys are adventurers and girls are nest builders. To Chris, who grew up in the jungle, going to the states and living in a city was a big adventure. He thrived in his new environment and never returned to Costa Rica to live. Today he is an architect, married with two kids, and living in Boulder, Colorado. When asked about his time in Costa Rica, Chris had this to say:

"*My greatest take-away from being raised in rural Costa Rica is the ability to find the positive when events do not unfold according to plan, an attitude embraced by few Americans when their plans unravel. I am often commended in my professional life for bringing a sense of calmness, optimism, and at times, even confidence during times some consider a crisis.*

"*There is no doubt I learned this at an early age when few, if any, plans came together as originally intended, but despite the change, ended well. Whether the bus was a couple of hours late, the river crossing was flooded and impassable, the tide was too high, the gas tank fell off of the truck while driving down the rough dirt road, the cows were in the rice field, the bus caught on fire, or someone you were meeting didn't show up, you just adapted and found the next best alternative which usually involved using the change of plans as an opportunity to find food and coffee.*

"*The norm was that nothing went as planned, but everything always seemed to work out just fine. The common Costa Rican phrase* Pura Vida *sums it up best; loosely translated to 'It's All Good', it can be used as a question or general statement to indicate you understand, as in '10-4' or 'Roger'. 'What? Traffic is stopped and we have no idea when they will clear the landslide? No worries, Pura Vida. I needed to get off this cramped bus and take a piss anyway, then we can go find some food and coffee.' (And yes, someone would be selling food and coffee along the road.) The reality is that nobody waiting for you will really care if you didn't show up on time, and they will likely use it as an opportunity to go find food and coffee.*

"*During a college spring-break trip to Costa Rica, I visited a remote national park with my sister, niece and nephew. On our return we caught a plane ride out in a small six-seat puddle jumper. I was getting dropped off at a small landing strip about an hour and a half north of my parent's home where someone would pick me up; the rest were continuing on to San Jose. The flight was uneventful and we landed at a modest landing strip, with no buildings in sight and just an empty dirt road alongside it. And there was nobody waiting* to pick me up. The pilot jumped out, tossed my duffle down on the runway, and got back into his seat to quickly turn the plane around since he had a load of tourists to pick up in San Jose. My sister gave me the concerned maternal look she has given me since my earliest memories and said, 'Well, this isn't the first time we've left you along a jungle road to fend for yourself.' No it wasn't and I was thrilled!

"I carried my duffle over to the dirt road and sat on it under the shade of a palm tree. Coffee was going to be tough to find, but I was sure there was a mango or guava tree somewhere nearby. After 30 minutes of swatting the occasional mosquito I heard a vehicle making its way down the road. A few minutes later my dad's truck came into view. As he came to a stop, I threw my duffle in the back and climbed into the cab. While he maneuvered a three-point turn, I asked what had happened. 'A rice truck was stuck on the bridge at El Pasito.' He said as if it had been a fender bender during the five-o'clock rush hour. What more was there to know? We stopped at the next town; he got a diet soda and I got a coffee and some cookies.

"I still live in Colorado where I work as an architect managing the design and construction of research buildings for a large academic institution. I receive panicked calls on a weekly basis from clients who need to be talked off of the ledge because for whatever reason they believe we are in the midst of a disaster. I listen to their concerns and run through my mental checklist of what would be classified as a disaster in rural Costa Rica: 1) Are children and/or mothers in harm's way? 2) Did anyone get bit by a poisonous snake? 3) Did anyone get badly cut with a machete? 4) Did the national soccer team lose to a rival Central American team? 5) Did the cows or pigs get into the watermelon patch? No to all? Okay, this is not a disaster, just a change in plans, I say to myself since of course I can't say it out loud. Instead I say, 'Wow, I can see why you're concerned. Why don't you meet me down at the coffee shop in five minutes? I could use some coffee, and have you tried their new poppy-seed bread? Let's grab some coffee and bread, and figure out how we're going to solve our problem.' *Pura Vida*." — Chris Ewing ☕

34

Costa Rica Moonshine

Contraband Liquor in Rural Costa Rica

I haven't had a drop of any alcoholic beverage since May 17, 1977. I quit drinking because I figured that I had already drunk enough to last me a lifetime and it wasn't necessary to drink any more. Prior to that date, I was quite an expert on all things relating to alcoholic beverages, including Costa Rican moonshine, known locally as *guaro contrabando*.

My first taste of *guaro contrabando* came about a week after my arrival in Costa Rica in 1970. With only a rudimentary knowledge of the Spanish language, I asked one of my fellow workers, a man named Luís, where I could get a bottle something to drink. The only kind of liquor I knew how to say in Spanish was *ron* meaning rum and pronounced like the word "roan" rather than the abbreviation for Ronald. Luís took me to a *pulpería*, a small, family-owned, neighborhood general store, which has unfortunately faded from the Costa Rican tradition, only to be replaced by the mini supermarket. The *pulpería* sold everything from sewing machine needles and saddle parts to rubber boots, food stuffs and *guaro*, both the legal stuff and the *contrabando*. Luís and the owner of the *pulpería* highly recommended the latter. At the time, I didn't quite understand that what I was buying was illegal, but I had a pretty good idea that *"mas fuerte"* meant that it was stronger. That's what I bought. I remember it was so cheap that I thought they made a mistake and undercharged me. I also remember that it packed quite a wallop, in spite of being pretty tasteless.

As I built my Spanish vocabulary I rapidly learned those words common to all regular drinkers, enabling me to acquire exactly the kind of liquor I wanted. I still bought a bottle of *contrabando* once in a while, but I always got it at a *pulpería* or a cantina where I was known. Most places wouldn't sell it to a stranger.

Prior to 1940, before there were any roads into the Dominical area, homemade stills, known as *sacas*, were the only source of liquor, and there were lots of them. Nobody was secretive about them because there really wasn't a law against them. Bringing liquor or beer into the area on pack horses was not practical and didn't make sense when people could easily make hard liquor for themselves. Someone in every village had a *saca* for making moonshine, keeping everybody in the neighborhood happy. Moonshiners even competed over who had the best product.

By the time I arrived in Costa Rica, homemade stills were against the law. The products legally manufactured in Costa Rica were reasonably good quality and priced considerably less than the imported brands which carried very high import taxes. Nevertheless, the National Distillery had a monopoly, and they took advantage of the lack of competition by pricing their *ron, ginebra* and *guaro* high enough to give them a substantial profit. It also priced them out of the market for many working class people. Those were the golden years for the *contrabandistas* who found a ready market for their *guaro contrabando*.

As the years passed, import taxes were reduced on many products including liquors and wines, and this tended to also drive down the prices of the products from the National Distillery, making them affordable for blue-collar workers. At the same time the quality of the national products improved to the point that many of the Costa Rican liquors are today nearly indistinguishable from the imported competition. This, of course, was bad news for *contrabandistas* and most went out of business. There are still a few *sacas* operating in remote places, but the business today doesn't leave enough profit to make it worth the risk of getting caught.

Out in the bush, stories of moonshiners outwitting the police abound. To listen to them you would think nobody ever got caught, but I'm sure that wasn't the case. It is more fun to tell the story when the *contrabandista* comes out smiling and the policeman ends up looking like a fool. Memo, a moonshiner I once knew, left a small tree with a big wasp nest in the middle of the trail that went to his still. Some branches from another tree blocked the view of the nest, shrouding it from the eyes of the unwary. Memo was always careful not to touch the tree when he went past, but uninvited visitors weren't aware of the nest and usually bumped the flimsy trunk, shaking the nest and inciting the wrath of the angry wasps. Few uninvited visitors made it past that point. One day the local constable and a couple of deputies showed up at Memo's house and started nosing around.

"Whadaya think you are doing, Miguel?" asked Memo. "This is private property. I got rights. You can't just come in here and start snooping around."

"We're lookin' for your *saca*," came the reply. "Everyone knows you got one, and I'm gonna find it."

"There ain't no *saca* on this land, Miguel. Why don' you guys just leave. Go bother someone else."

"Hey, Miguel," shouted one of the other policemen. "There's a trail over here goin' back into the jungle. Ya wanna see where it leads? I bet it'll take us to the *saca*."

"You can follow it if you want," said Memo. "That's just an old huntin' trail. Don't go nowhere. Just the jungle."

All three policemen started off on the trail, confident they were going to find the clandestine distillery. It wasn't long before they returned in a big hurry.

"I told you there ain't nothing on that trail," called Memo. "But you wouldn't listen."

The three guards hurriedly got in the pickup and left.

Memo laughed like crazy when he told the story. According to him, Miguel had stopped to urinate almost directly under the wasp nest and leaned against the tree. I'm sure you can guess the first place he got stung.

Back in the early 1970s when I worked on the Caribbean side of Costa Rica, I was friends with a *campesino* named Javier who owned a small farm and a few cattle. We became big drinking buddies. He told me all about how *guaro contraband* is made. He even showed me a diagram of a *saca* done by a nephew for a science project at the local high school. Javier told me the first *guaro* that flowed out of the still, called the *cabeza* or head, was the best. He claimed the first drops of liquid to drip from the tube were so high powered that if you collected half a shot glass and threw it into the air, it would just go poof and disappear.

Though pure *contrabando* was nothing more than alcohol and water, the moonshiners sometimes did certain things to embellish the product. Some would add *nance* fruit to the finished *guaro* for a slightly sweet taste that took away the bite. Another way to modify the *guaro* was to add coconut cream and a little condensed milk. This concoction, called *leche de burra* or burro's milk, was very sweet.

I was still curious so Javier offered to take me to his uncle's *saca* out in the jungle. We rode to a *pulpería* in a rural settlement called La Alegría where we left our horses. Javier's uncle Guido was a little distrustful at first, but Javier vouched for me and assured him I was very tight-lipped. We walked for almost an hour until we came to a small, crystal clear stream. I remember thinking I could never find the place again if my life depended on it.

"There she is," commented Guido. "Ain't much to it."

I surveyed the scene, trying to make sense of it. There was a wooden trough that could have been used for watering livestock. It appeared to be fashioned from a dug-out log about two meters long and 40 centimeters wide. It looked like it would hold around 30 gallons. The trough was covered with a piece of galvanized tin, and from it emanated the smell of fermentation. Guido explained it contained a mixture of corn, water, and crude cane sugar called *tapa dulce*. It had been fermenting for about three days and was ready to be cooked. He said that some *contrabandistas* would substitute sorghum or oats for the corn, but other than that, there wasn't much difference. The fermented mixture inside the trough was called *chicha* and could be drunk in that state. I sampled the chicha and guessed its alcohol content to be about the same as a sweet wine. It tasted a little like home-brew beer but stronger.

Right next to the trough was a hearth. On top of the hearth was a tank made from half of a galvanized, 55-gallon drum. The cover over the drum had a narrower cylinder sticking up in the middle, in which a bronze tube was inserted. The other end of the tube went through a smaller trough where a constant stream of cold water flowed.

Guido retrieved a bucket from a hiding place within the buttress roots of a fig tree and began scooping the liquid out of the trough and pouring it into the drum. The last of the liquid that Guido scooped out of the trough was quite cloudy. He left the thick soupy solids in the bottom, explaining it would help get the fermentation started on the next batch.

While Guido transferred the *chicha* from the trough to the drum, Javier gathered firewood and started a fire in the hearth. After about ten minutes a trace of vapor began to rise from the drum. The two men put the lid on top so the vapor was forced to escape through the bronze tube. Guido placed a glass bottle at the end of the tube and soon a clear liquid began to drip into the bottle. The drip gradually increased to a dribble and then a weak stream. Remembering my high school science classes, I figured out the steam coming off the boiling *chicha* escaped through the bronze tube. Alcohol boils at a lower temperature than water, so the first steam was almost pure vaporized alcohol. In the cold-water trough the steam cooled, condensed into a liquid with high alcohol content, and drained out the end of the tube. This was the principal of the homemade distillery. We sat down to wait.

While we were waiting, Guido told us a story about a new recruit to the local police. The chief sent him off on foot to deliver a summons to somebody who lived about two hours from the police station. As he was walking along, the rookie policeman noticed a trail going off into the jungle. Curious and a little suspicious, he followed the trail, which eventually led to a *saca*, and caught the moonshiner with a fire under the still and *guaro contrabando* dripping out of the tube.

"Well, it looks like you caught me red-handed," exclaimed the *contrabandista*. "I suppose you gotta take me in. This batch is just about finished. Why don't you just sit down and let me collect the last few drops and shut the whole thing down. I ain't gonna put up a fight. I'll go along with you in a few minutes."

The policeman remembers feeling a thump on his head, then everything went black. When he regained consciousness he was in the same place, but everything was gone, the tanks, the trough, the still and everything. His clothing was all wet and stank of *chicha*. Somebody had dumped the dregs from the trough all over him. When he returned to the station with a splitting headache and smelling like *chicha*, the chief didn't believe his story and berated him for not completing the task he had been sent to do. The moonshiners laid low for a while and then set up the still in another location.

By the time Guido finished the story, the first bottle was full. He replaced it with another and put a cork in the bottle of crystal clear liquid. "*Pura cabeza*," he said, with a grin. Javier and I went off to explore the jungle, while Guido tended the still. Several hours later, when we returned, he had a five-gallon container almost full. Javier hefted the container to his shoulder and we left Guido to bottle the remaining five gallons.

Javier told me that another uncle of his had almost been caught. The police stumbled onto his still, but couldn't prove it was his. They destroyed the still and confiscated a few gallons of *guaro contrabando*. When asked if anyone ever went to jail for operating a still, he said he hadn't heard of any. Instead, most people just bribed the police, who in addition to the payoff confiscated all the *guaro*, which in Javier's opinion, they either drank or sold.

I recently asked around about *sacas* and *guaro contrabando* in the area around Dominical. It appears there are a few operating stills around the countryside, but these days they are few and far between. It is no longer the thriving business that it once was. Nevertheless, it will long be remembered as an integral part of the rural Costa Rican tradition. 🐾

35

The Land of Small Hotels and Big Parks

The Birth of Ecotourism in Southern Costa Rica

In 1982 the Costa Rican government began work on the coastal highway from Dominical to the south. At the same time, there was talk of building a bridge across the Barú River and bringing electricity into the area. The prospect of new infrastructure got me to thinking about tourism and the future of Dominical and Hacienda Barú. The words "ecotourism" and "ecological tourism" never entered my mind. In fact, they were not even yet part of the English lexicon. The closest thing to them was the term "nature-based tourism," but even that was seldom heard. It was thought of as a specialty type of tourism that appealed to a few oddball tree huggers. Bird watching, of course, had been around for a long time, but ecotourism as we know it today didn't exist.

Although Hacienda Barú was primarily a cattle ranch where we also raised rice and cacao, the property had three kilometers of beach frontage. The partners had always assumed it would one day be developed for tourism. The promise of improved access and services to the zone seemed to make that possibility a little more real. At the time, my concept of tourism was pretty limited. The image that came to mind was one of hotels and other tourist businesses lining the beach, Acapulco-style. To me, this meant cutting down the forest, filling in the mangrove estuary and replacing those natural areas with concrete structures. "I don't think I could bear to see that happen," I told Diane. We would move away from Hacienda Barú before the development began.

Several days after uttering those words, I was riding my horse along the edge of the mangrove, on my way to a pasture to check the cattle. Upon approaching a large strangler fig tree, its branches laden with ripe fruit, I first heard and then saw a group of white-faced capuchin monkeys (*Cebus capucinus*) jumping from branch to branch, gobbling up the small red figs as fast as they could stuff them in their mouths, dropping half in the process. Half a dozen chestnut-mandibled toucans (*Ramphastos swansonii*) were scattered among the leafy fronds, snatching mouthfuls of fruit in their enormous beaks, tossing back their heads and swallowing the figs whole. In the lower branches was a lone male coati (*Nasua narica*), meticulously picking and eating the small round fruits one by one. Just watching him, I could imagine how delicious they must be. I knew that after their feast, all of these birds and animals would move out into the mangrove and bordering forest. Later in the day they would defecate, and in this manner, disperse the fig seeds. Some of the seeds would fall to the ground, but many would find their way into the cracks and crevices of trees where germination would take place, and a new strangler fig would begin its long life cycle. After a while I rode on, marveling at the sight I had just witnessed.

The pasture and group of grazing cattle soon came into view. Riding through the herd, I found myself thinking about Mother Nature rather than paying attention to the cattle. A thought struck me: *Why can't we build cabins in places like this pasture, where the forest is already gone? Why not conserve the mangroves, wetlands, and rainforests and bring tourists here to see the birds and animals? Surely there are other people in the world who enjoy nature as much as I do.*

I had just glimpsed a vision of what would one day be called ecological tourism. I was later to learn that many other people in Costa Rica were having similar thoughts and visions. A concept was starting to germinate in people's minds. It seemed like people with similar ideas gravitated toward one another. We met, we talked, we exchanged ideas. The concept grew and gained more adherents. Eventually it ripened, like the fruits on the strangler fig, until it was ready to pick. Some of us began putting the concept into practice. At Hacienda Barú the stimulus to do so came from friends of friends who were visiting from Switzerland. One day Diane and I, our friends Beatrice and Martin, and their two friends all went hiking through the rainforest. For three hours we had a great time exploring the wonders of the most diverse habitat on the face of the planet. When we returned to the house, one of the visiting Swiss friends asked me how much they owed us for the tour. "You don't owe me anything," I replied. "We do this because we enjoy it. It isn't a business."

"You must accept something," she insisted. "We don't have anything like this in our country. We have traveled to many places, always looking for something different. Usually we just find the same old thing: pretty beaches, palm trees, and hotels. An experience like we had today really is different." She stuffed two $20 bills in my shirt pocket, kissed me on both cheeks, said "Thank you so much!" and waved good-bye. Little did she know what she had just set in motion.

I decided that if our Swiss visitors would pay for a walk in the jungle, there must be others. We began offering a six-hour hiking tour we called "The Rainforest Experience," and a shorter three-hour hike called the "Mangrove Walk." I typed up a single sheet of paper describing each tour on my old mechanical typewriter. I took the paper to San Isidro, got about 50 photocopies, and took one to each of the two restaurants, three cabin rentals, and two general stores in Dominical. I even left one at the gas station. Before I knew it people were coming to go on rainforest hikes. As I remember, we sold about $300 worth of tours that first year, 1987. The following year we sold that many tours in the month of January alone and about $1,500 for the year. That trend continued for five years, and then

A canopy tour at Hacienda Baru.

the growth rate settled down to about a 25 percent yearly increase for a few more years. Eventually, it leveled off at about 15 percent annual growth. In the years that followed, our offering of tours expanded until today it includes two kinds of canopy tours, four hiking tours, one camping tour, three birding tours and seven kilometers of self-guided trails. Other ecological tourism destinations have had similar experiences. The time for ecotourism in Costa Rica had obviously arrived.

In 1984 the word "ecotourism" was coined by the International Union for the Conservation of Nature (IUCN). Six years later the International Ecotourism Society was founded. Today many countries have their own national ecological tourism organizations. Costa Rica has the Camara Nacional de Ecotourismo (CANECO). There are hundreds of web sites that promote nature-based tourism.

I once heard the southern zone of Costa Rica called the "Land of Small Hotels and Big Parks." I have come to believe that most of the people who live here share the desire to live in a place where nature takes top priority. I have always believed the people who live in a place make it what it is. The southern zone is in the initial stages of tourist development. It is rapidly gaining a reputation for great natural beauty and biodiversity. It is up to those of us who live here to protect those natural treasures that make our region so attractive to visitors. Ecological tourism and bird watching in Costa Rica are already extremely popular activities. This region has the potential to become the epitome of nature-based tourism.

The Swiss woman was right. People really do want something different. They are looking for the "Land of Small Hotels and Big Parks." 𝒞

36

A Place Where Biodiversity Is Increasing

Sustainable vs Biodiverse: Why Can't We Have Both?

The word "sustainable" has been in use for a long time, at least since 1727 according to *Merriam-Webster.* It means that when a resource is used, it is taken in such a fashion that the resource can replenish itself. In recent years, with increased interest in our environment and concern over the rate of depletion of our natural resources, the word has come into popular usage. Information about how to live sustainably is readily available, as are products for sustainable ways of doing things. Energy and water conservation and efficiency are of utmost importance, followed by social responsibility and general environmental friendliness.

In environmental terms being sustainable means that we don't use resources faster than they can be reproduced. Our actions are sustainable if they do not cause the environment to deteriorate. If we are sustainable we can continue to do things in the same manner indefinitely and the environment will remain pretty much the same or improve. The word doesn't necessarily mean the environment is in great shape; it only means it is not getting any worse.

Another word that relates to this same idea is "biodiversity," a fairly new word that didn't enter the language until 1985. It means biological diversity in an environment as indicated by numbers of different species of plants and animals. When our activities destroy living species, biodiversity decreases; when they promote an increase in the number of species, biodiversity increases. In reality biodiversity increases when humans leave nature alone. The only human action that can promote an increase in biodiversity is the protection of land so it can't be degraded by exploitation. Mother Nature does the rest.

Many of the original property owners around Dominical homesteaded their land in the 1930s and 40s. Costa Rican law allowed a person to acquire title on up to 100 hectares of wild and unclaimed land if they could demonstrate they had worked the land for a minimum of ten years and made it productive. When I first came to this area in 1972 there were many small landowners with farms of slightly less than 100 hectares, all of whom had acquired their land through the homestead program. Don Rodolfo García was typical among the property owners.

He, his wife Doña Inéz, and their seven children, varying in age from 2 to 17 years, lived in a humble wooden house. The wood for the home had come from their land. Their energy consumption was minimal. There was no electricity. The family cooked with wood, and used candles and kerosene lanterns for light. Don Rodolfo owned a small diesel pickup which he drove to San Isidro about twice a month. They didn't consume any energy pumping water because it was gravity fed. Their home had a shower and a sink with a single faucet which was constantly running. I once asked Doña Inéz why she didn't turn the water off when she wasn't using it. "What difference does it make?" she asked. I didn't have an answer for her. There was only one house using the water produced by a free-flowing spring originating on their property. Everybody had enough water, and it really didn't make much difference if the faucet was on or off. The unused water ran down the drain into a ditch and eventually ended up back where it would have ended up had it never been diverted into the family's water system in the first place.

Waste water discharged from the house contained soap suds and bits and pieces of food washed off the cooking and eating utensils. It ran from the sink into a shallow drainage ditch. Doña Inéz' chickens were the first to pick out morsels of edible waste, and once the water was far enough from the house wild birds could occasionally be seen scavenging in the ditch. By the time the water reached the stream it was fairly clear and didn't visibly affect the stream quality. Nobody worried about not having enough water, and nobody worried about contamination. The family toilet was an outhouse built over a hole in the ground, and when the hole was full, they simply dug another a few meters away and moved the small wooden house over there. A tree or some bushes were planted over the old location. The environment could deal with the impact of the family's everyday activities and was not deteriorating. At that time the Garcia family's home was sustainable.

Don Rodolfo had homesteaded 80 hectares of forested land in the late 1930s. He worked hard to clear the land and plant pasture. Sometimes he grew a crop of beans on each newly cleared parcel, and he grew corn for his pigs on one hectare of reasonably flat land on the lower slopes of the farm. Two years after homesteading the land Don Rodolfo borrowed 1,500 colones from his father-in-law, and purchased nine cows and a bull. By 1972 when I met the Garcías, his herd had increased to about 60 animals, a few more than the farm could comfortably support. At that time only the steepest part, about eight hectares, was left in forest. The spring that produced the water for the livestock and the house was located in this small patch of jungle. The land that had once supported a forest with many thousands of species of plants, animals, insects, and other life forms had been converted into a pasture that supported little more than grasses, weeds, and cows.

The neighboring farms were much the same. Only the steepest parts still in forest harbored a few wild animals. All of the spider and howler monkeys had been killed by an epidemic of yellow fever in 1947. The last white-lipped peccary was shot by a hunter in 1952, a jaguar was killed in 1955 and nobody saw another one after that. The last sign of tapir was when one of Don Rodolfo's neighbors saw the distinctive three-toed tracks near a salt lick in 1957. The scarlet macaws disappeared from the area in the mid-1960s.

Although the situation was bad ecologically, by 1970 the land had reached a point of stability because biodiversity was no longer diminishing. The farm produced enough beef year after year to provide the García family with a reasonable standard of living and the environment remained unchanged. Don Rodolfo and his family didn't feel like they were living in a degraded environment. They were happy with their lives, and it seemed to them and their neighbors that everything was all right. In view of the way the word sustainable is used today, it seems odd to say the Garcia farm was sustainable. But it did fit the strict definition of the word. Even though biodiversity had diminished to an all-time low, the farm was producing and the environment was no longer deteriorating.

Things went well for the García family for the next 15 years. The kids grew up, and most of them left home. Some went to the city to work. One of the boys got a part-time job with a rice farmer in the area and lived at home. He also helped work the family farm. The youngest daughter had not yet married and still lived with Don Rodolfo and Doña Inéz.

In the 1980s the price of beef dropped considerably, and the Garcías had to tighten their budget. Don Rodolfo was nearing 70 years of age and had been dreaming about how nice it would be to move to the city, buy a small house, and retire. But no matter how he figured it, there was no way they would be able to manage financially. The couple had pretty much resigned themselves to the harsh reality that they would live their final years on the family farm and never experience the comforts of the city.

One day a gringo came to Dominical looking for property to buy. After several trips to look at three different farms, the buyer purchased a farm similar in size to the García's farm. Don Rodolfo had never thought about selling the family's land, but the gringo had paid extremely well for the nearby property. The farm that sold belonged to the heirs of a neighbor who had died seven years earlier. The children weren't interested in managing the farm, so they sold the cattle to get some quick cash and pretty much abandoned the land. When the foreign buyer came along it was almost totally overgrown with secondary forest. Only the area around the house had been kept clean. Don Rodolfo reasoned that if an abandoned property like that would sell for $40,000, a productive farm like his, with well-kept pastures, should be worth at least twice that amount, more than enough to retire on. He went and talked to Jorge, the caretaker of the newly purchased property. Jorge told him the gringo wasn't interested in buying any more property, but some of his friends were, and they would soon be arriving in the country looking for land to buy. He promised to tell them that Don Rodolfo was interested in selling.

When the new buyers came to look at the García property, they didn't seem very impressed. Don Rodolfo couldn't understand what they said to each other, but he got the idea they liked the flat hilltops. They did make an offer, but it was only $25,000. Later Jorge told him they wanted land with jungle. They weren't interested in raising cattle, but rather wanted to build houses in places where they could see the ocean and observe lots of wildlife. *That's crazy,* thought Don Rodolfo. *Why would anyone live up in those hills when there is flat land down here by the road? And why would they want to be around wild animals? We don't even live near the forest, and the tayras and jaguarundis still come around and kill Doña Inéz' chickens. What would it be like if we lived right next to the jungle?*

Even though he thought it was crazy, Don Rodolfo made the decision to let all of the upper pastures regenerate into secondary forest. If that's what it took to get a good price, that's what he would do. In the long run it was better he hadn't sold right away because land values kept escalating. Four years later the García property sold for $280,000. Don Rodolfo was 73 and Doña Inéz was 64. They gave their children some money, bought a house in San Isidro, and got to live their dream.

Today, on what used to be the García farm, there are four large beautiful homes with swimming pools, one on each of the four hill-tops. There is an access road that allows the owners to get to their homes when they aren't flying back and forth to North America or Europe several times each year. Each home has its own well from which the inhabitants pump water for domestic use, the pool, and watering the lawn. Each home has a septic tank and drain field for the treatment of waste water. All of the owners have at least one gas guzzling SUV, and some have two. The homes all have numerous electrical appliances that consume considerable amounts of energy, and three of them have air-conditioning. The families that live in them consume hundreds of times more energy than the Garcías who once occupied the property. In no way can these homes be considered to be sustainable.

Biodiversity is another story. Of the original 80 hectares, 72 of which had been pasture, all but four have returned to nature. White-faced capuchin monkeys and chestnut-mandibled toucans are a common sight. Spider monkeys and squirrel monkeys are seen occasionally. Several of the homeowners have heard howler mon-keys in the distance, but have yet to sight any near their homes. One homeowner saw a puma crossing the access road, and a jaguar was sighted about five kilometers away. Scarlet macaws have begun visiting the area a couple of times each month, and peccary, coatis, and raccoons are so numerous that some people consider them to be pests. In addition, there are a multitude of smaller species of reptiles, amphibians, insects, fungi, and plants that are less obvious than the species mentioned above. Biodiversity has been increasing steadily over the last 20 years and is continuing to do so.

Which situation is preferable, high sustainability and low bio-diversity or vice versa? Which situation do you prefer, that of 1972 or that of 2014? Of course the ideal situation would be a totally sustainable lifestyle in an area of high biodiversity. But that is not what we have, and neither did the García family.

The other day I was talking to a group of students, and a very bright young girl asked me if Hacienda Barú is sustainable. I answered with an explanation of all of the measures we take to make our operation environmentally friendly, energy efficient, water efficient, and socially responsible. "That is all important," she replied. "But you said that 17,000 people visited Hacienda Barú last year. If you factor in all of the fuel that was burned transporting those people from their countries of origin to Costa Rica, and the in-country transportation to Hacienda Barú you probably aren't very sustainable at all."

I had to admit that her point was well taken. Of course, I did point out that on Hacienda Barú we protect 160 hectares of primary forest, and, over the last 32 years, have allowed Mother Nature to regenerate over 170 hectares of secondary forest. All of this natural habitat absorbs a tremendous amount of carbon while, at the same time, producing oxygen and contributing significantly to biodiversity. She smiled and admitted that it would take a better mathematician than either she or I to determine if Hacienda Barú is truly sustainable.

If I had to choose between the situation in 1972 and that of 2014, I wouldn't hesitate to say that I prefer the high biodiversity we have today. But neither biodiversity nor sustainability alone is enough. If we want to leave a healthy planet to future generations we need to strive for both. 🐾

37

Hacienda Barú

From Rainforest to Cattle Ranch to Wildlife Refuge

The first pioneers to settle in this region didn't own land as we understand the concept of ownership today. They only possessed it temporarily, felled a parcel of rainforest, burned the fallen trees and other vegetation, grew crops on it for several years, and moved on to another parcel. This procedure, known as "slash and burn," was described earlier. Later, as more people moved into the area, those who worked the land began claiming rights of possession to designated parcels, often by chopping a four-meter wide swath around the claimed land. Anyone who saw the swath knew that the parcel had already been claimed by someone else. Prior to 1940 there is no record of anyone claiming ownership to any part of what later became known as Hacienda Barú, and none of the pioneers I interviewed remember anyone who worked the land. Nevertheless, there were probably people who slashed and burned different areas, farmed them for a few years and moved on.

The first written record of ownership is an application for title to 80 hectares of land filed by Garfield Fitzgerald Burrows on April 23, 1950 (probably the same person referred to in chapter 15 as the owner of a bar on the Dominical side of the Barú River). The document shows that Garfield acquired the rights of possession to the land from Eliecer Sibaja Lobo for the sum of 1,000 colones (about $2 at today's exchange rate). In July of 1952 Garfield sold the land to Mercedes Fernandez Porras for 1,750 colones. She sold it to Rafael Cruz Ramón for 3,000 colones in March of 1958. We also know that Don Rafael acquired the rights to several adjoining properties, which, taken altogether, form Hacienda Barú as we know it today. The record shows that Don Rafael Cruz owned the land for about 10 years and sold it to Ishmael Mata. In September of 1970 it was sold again to Teorico Zamora who shortly thereafter died in a plane crash. His widow, Ana María Acosta, inherited Hacienda Barú, owned the property for about a year, and in 1972, sold it to a company called Tennessee Land and Cattle Company S.A. owned by a group of investors from Nashville, Tennessee. Shortly after my first visit to Hacienda Barú in February 1972, the owners realized that the name of the company was not appropriate for Costa Rica and changed it to Finca Barú S.A.

The six partners of the company were successful businessmen who had invested in other projects together. They had heard a new coastal route of the Pan-American (now called Inter-American) Highway was in the works, and it would pass through the middle of Hacienda Barú. Their plan was to wait for the highway, which would cause land prices to escalate, and sell at a profit. In the meantime, they wanted to spend as little money as possible keeping the farm active, so they leased the land to Central American Meats, my employer at the time.

Central American Meats was in the business of fattening cattle on various ranches in Costa Rica, slaughtering them, and exporting the beef. In the 1970s three big export businesses in Costa Rica brought in most of the foreign exchange: beef, coffee, and bananas. The beef was fattened on grass rather than grain, and the meat was tough and lean. It was exported as a product called boneless beef, mostly for the fast-food industry in the United States where it became hamburger.

With beef production and its export so important to the economy, government policy urged people to cut down the rainforest and convert the land into pasture for cattle, and so much of Costa Rica was deforested in the 1960s and '70s.

The investors were happy with the lease arrangement with Central American Meats. It brought in a little income and relieved them of the expense of caring for the land while waiting for the highway to be built. In 1974 a new president came into office and promised that the highway, called La Costanera Sur, would be done during his four years in office. This further fanned the hopes of the owners of Hacienda Barú. Had they known that every president for the next 36 years would make the same promise, they certainly would have tempered their optimism with a dose of realism.

In 1975 Central American Meats made the decision to quit raising their own cattle. They terminated their leasing contracts with all of the ranches, including the two I managed, leaving me without a job. It also left the Tennessee investors without an option for caring for their property. They asked if we could meet, and two of them flew to Costa Rica. I imagined that I would be offered some kind of a deal to take care of Hacienda Barú, but what Glen and Irvin proposed was totally unexpected. In addition to the job of managing the property, they offered me an equal share of the stock. I readily accepted the offer, and, in January 1976, began working full time at Hacienda Barú. I traveled to San Jose on weekends to be with my family, and worked at Hacienda Barú during the week.

Working at Hacienda Barú changed me. Little by little I began thinking of the property as a nature reserve rather than a cattle ranch, and noticed I was giving higher priority to protecting the flora and fauna than to making money for the company. Nevertheless, the ranch didn't do badly. Raising cattle was our primary activity, followed by growing rice and cacao.

Since Central American Meats took all of their cattle when they left Hacienda Barú, we bought a herd of cows that had been poorly fed and cared for. Though thin, some were very good quality animals.

We vaccinated and wormed them all, put them on good pasture, and selected 50 of the best to keep as breeding animals. We bought two imported Charolais bulls to breed the cows. The bulls suffered tremendously in the hot, humid climate, and spent most of the day in the water hole. They apparently came out and grazed at night, because they looked good and gained weight. After several months, Orlando, the foreman, told me he didn't think we were going to have any calves. "I have never seen one of those bulls breed a cow. This breed just won't work here," he declared. "What you need is a good Brahman bull." Several neighbors, who felt sorry for me, told me the same thing. "These cattle are nice and pretty," they advised me, "but they just won't work in this climate."

A little over nine months after we put the Charolais bulls with the cows, Orlando appeared one morning and said, "I can't believe it, Don Jack. Come and see the beautiful bull calf born to the number 33 cow. He's like nothing I've ever seen." Two more calves were born the next day and one the day after. Word got out fast and the neighbors started coming around to see the beautiful white calves. Everyone was amazed, and I was relieved. They had almost convinced me that we weren't going to have any calves. I jokingly told everybody that Charolais bulls are embarrassed to breed cows during the daytime.

On my very first visit to Hacienda Barú I had noticed a steep, badly eroded hillside pasture between La Casona and the Barú River. After several years of raising cattle on the hacienda, I realized that we weren't getting any monetary return out of that pasture. The type of grass growing there wasn't very nutritious and the cattle didn't like to climb the hill to graze. Mostly they just hung out near the fence along the road. To make things worse, the soil was eroding badly, and brown, muddy rivulets of water rushed down its slopes with every heavy rain. Taking into consideration the cost of keeping that pasture weed-free, and the small amount of return we were getting, I decided to look into other ways to use that land. Though I knew nothing about it, reforestation seemed to be a strong option.

With the idea of learning something about reforestation, I paid a visit to the Forestry Department, part of the Ministry of Agriculture. In 1979 tree planting was practically unknown in Costa Rica, and the government foresters weren't much help. One of them, however, gave me the name of a man in San Jose who worked for the Organization of Tropical Studies.

"That hill is much too steep for traditional reforestation," he declared after one look at the aerial photos. "Normally thousands of trees, all the same species, are planted close together in rows so they will grow tall and straight. That would shade out all of the undergrowth and create worse erosion than you already have." He recommended that I simply quit chopping the weeds and let Mother Nature bring back the natural vegetation in her own way. I took his advice. We planted a few endangered species of trees, widely spaced, and abandoned the land to the forces of nature. This was the beginning of a trend at Hacienda Barú and an education for me in the ways of nature.

Within a year the ground was covered to a height of a couple of meters with vegetation ranging from wide-leafed banana-like plants to brush. Fast growing trees like balsa and cecropia were emerging from this thick undergrowth. Wildlife invaded the area. In the second year a couple of large members of the weasel family called tyras started sneaking out of the budding jungle a couple of times a week and killing Diane's chickens. Each year the secondary forest grew and evolved. As trees came to dominate the area they created shade, which favors some kinds of plants and hinders others. Today, 35 years later, that hillside is covered by an impressive, mature, secondary forest. I suspect it will take 100 years before it is indistinguishable from primary forest. It will always be remembered as the first step in the regeneration of natural forest on Hacienda Barú.

In 1979–80 we planted cacao trees which produce the basic ingredient used to make chocolate. Within three years the trees started producing and in five years were in full production. By the mid-1980s the cacao business was so good that it precipitated massive planting in countries like Brazil and Malaysia. In the late 1980s the price plummeted from a high of $3,300 per ton to less than $700 a ton. Cacao production is labor intensive; machines can't do the multitude of tasks involved in growing, maintaining, harvesting, and processing. Countries like Costa Rica that require employers to pay workers a fair wage can't compete with countries where labor is shamefully cheap. The price we were paid for our production wouldn't even cover the cost of harvesting the pods and processing the seeds. We had to abandon our cacao venture. As told in *Monkeys Are Made of Chocolate*, Mother Nature made good use of the plantation, and it soon became one of the most diverse habitats on the hacienda.

From the mid-1970s we had raised a little rice ourselves and also leased some of the rice land to neighbors. We stopped all rice production in 1985. I was becoming more and more environmentally conscientious and had noticed several undesirable side effects caused by the use of large quantities of chemicals applied to the rice fields. We always had lots of mosquitoes, but one year when we didn't grow any rice their numbers diminished considerably. The following year, when we leased the rice land to a local farmer, the mosquitoes returned. I surmised that the pesticides were killing many of the natural enemies of the mosquitoes, such as frogs and geckos.

I chose to switch from rice farming to tree farming, so I went to the Forestry Department and asked their advice. "Plant teak on the flatland and pochote on the hillsides," they told me. So that is what I did. We planted eight hectares of teak trees in a former rice field and about the same amount of pochote trees in a former pasture. Though local native species would've been better for the environment, I have never regretted the decision. Today we use teak wood in everything we build. We have a policy of not buying any wood that comes from natural forests.

The road from San Isidro was paved in 1986 and electricity arrived the same year. In 1987 and 1988, as described earlier, the bridges between Dominical and Quepos were built, and about that same time we began offering tours on Hacienda Barú. The tours rapidly became popular, and though they weren't yet producing enough income to interest my partners, they did help with expenses and I enjoyed guiding them. At the same time there was an influx of real estate customers into the area. Land prices were increasing, and more and more Costa Rican farmers and ranchers began putting their land up for sale.

In 1990 my Tennessee partners decided the time had come to sell. It didn't look like the highway would be built anytime soon, but with the recent appreciation in land values, they could probably sell at a nice profit. I really didn't want to leave Hacienda Barú, but my opinion didn't count for much. We listed the property with a real estate agency. Shortly afterwards we sold all of the cattle.

Several developers looked at the property in the first few months. Then one day a young man rode down the lane to La Casona on a bicycle and inquired about buying property. I told him Hacienda Barú was for sale and he showed some serious interest. Steve Stroud and I soon discovered our interests were quite similar. Steve was looking for a nature reserve with beach front suitable for ecological tourism. He was especially interested in creating a destination for student groups who were interested in tropical nature. Hacienda Barú filled all of his needs.

Steve was a cautious buyer. He looked at many other properties in Costa Rica, but always kept returning to Hacienda Barú. One day he asked me, "If I buy Hacienda Barú, would you be willing to stay on as my partner?" This, of course, was my best-case scenario, and I told him so. "Good," he said. "Let me talk to your partners and we'll see what we can do."

After extensive negotiations Steve ended up buying my partner's shares in the company rather than buying the land. The deal was signed and sealed in April 1993, and Hacienda Barú began on the course that would make it the internationally known nature reserve it is today.

We began by looking into ways to show our guests the rainforest canopy and teach them about it. Steve knew Dr. Donald Perry, the biologist who figured out how to climb into the treetops and thus pioneered canopy exploration in Costa Rica. Donald came to Hacienda Barú and taught us how to climb trees. Ornithologist and former Peace Corps volunteer Jim Zook became our first tree-climbing guide. We soon came to realize that lots of people either couldn't or didn't want to expend the amount of energy necessary to climb a tree, but were still interested in seeing and learning about the canopy. We built a platform 34 meters above the rainforest floor in the umbrella-shaped crown of an enormous tree. Guests were hoisted into the tree with an electric winch. This soon became our most popular tour.

In 2000 we added the Flight of the Toucan, a zip-line tour. From the very beginning it was obvious this would replace the canopy platform as our number one tour. It became our bread and butter. Later we added three bird watching tours, a short nocturnal hike, and a pre-Columbian tour of petroglyphs and indigenous cemeteries.

Once we gave up ranching we had no further need for a cowboy or a fence fixer. These employees left Hacienda Barú and found work in other places. We refurbished their houses and started renting them to tourists. By the beginning of 1995 we had a total of six cabins, a restaurant, and five tours to offer to visitors. The final stage of

Author Jack Ewing climbs trees whenever he gets the chance.

expansion didn't come until 2008 when we built six new rooms and a swimming pool.

One of the most important events in the history of Hacienda Barú took place in 1995 when, after a tremendous amount of paperwork, President José María Figueres signed the presidential decree creating the Refugio Nacional de Vida Silvestre Barú. Though this national wildlife refuge status limits the type of development we can implement, the limitations were no more stringent than those we would impose on ourselves. One helpful benefit: being placed on the map with all of the national parks.

The most recent noteworthy development on Hacienda Barú has major significance for the future of the Path of the Tapir Biological Corridor. With the construction of La Costanera Sur Highway, the government expropriated about 10 hectares of land from Finca Barú del Pacífico S.A.; Steve then invested that money in a biological research center for promoting research on Hacienda Barú and other places within the PTBC. The center was built near the ASANA office at the location where La Casona used to be.

Hacienda Barú National Wildlife Refuge has long stood as an icon for environmental restoration and protection in the Path of the Tapir Biological Corridor, and its continued protected status is of utmost importance to the corridor and the well-being of innumerable inhabitants of the area. It is a legacy that will be carried forward by future generations of stewards who will be charged with the responsibility of its protection and the recording of its evolution.

It is immensely satisfying to have been a participant in the adventure to this point. The culmination of that satisfaction will come the day that tapirs and jaguars return to the rainforests of Hacienda Barú. 🐾

Acknowledgments

I would like to thank the following people for their assistance in making this book a reality…

Pamela J. Herring for many hours of editing and encouragement, and for writing the foreword. Jan Betts for creating the wonderful pencil drawings and the amazing cover artwork. Veronica Czerny for reading the manuscript and making helpful suggestions. Ray and Sue Krueger Koplin of Toucan Maps, Inc. for their detailed map of this area, and Jakob Spatling for his technical assistance with the other maps. Vanessa Pereira, Karen Lazaro, and Shirley Cascante for their help in translating the original essays into Spanish. Ignacio Campos for editing the Spanish edition. Ana Lyons, Pat Cheek, and Marcel Pfister for publishing the original articles in the magazines *Quepolandia* and *Dominical Days*. Rex and LaVonne Ewing of PixyJack Press for insightful suggestions, all of the time and hard work they put into editing, and for pushing me when I needed to be pushed.

A very special thanks to all those who shared their personal stories with me. Without the information provided by the following people it would not have been possible to piece together an accurate picture of the pioneer days: Margarita and Marina Morales, Hipolito Villegas, Cristino Rios, Jose Maria (Nitos) Gómez, Braulio Jimenez, Evelyn King, Emilio Vargas, Lencho Espinosa, Benjamin Cedeño, Guillermo Astua, Manuel Angel Sanchez, Blanca Valverde, Porfiria Gómez, José Artavia, Juan Ramon Segura, Daniel Valverde, Lisa Svenson, and Arnold Leiva.

And most of all, my wife Diane and our children, who made this journey into the jungle with me. And what a journey it has been.

Metric Conversion Chart

Distance
millimeters x 0.039 = inches
centimeters x 0.39 = inches
meters x 3.28 = feet
meters x 1.093 = yards
kilometers x 0.62 = miles

Area
square meters x 10.76 = square feet
hectares x 2.47 = acres
square kilometers x 0.39 = square miles

Weight
grams x 0.035 = ounces
kilograms x 2.2 = pounds
metric tons (or 1,000 kilograms) x 1.1 = tons

Speed
kph (kilometers per hour) x 0.62 = mph (miles per hour)

Liquid / Volume
liters x 0.264 = gallons

Author Jack Ewing

The cattle business may have brought Jack Ewing to Costa Rica, but his love of nature kept him there.

In 1970 Jack and his wife and young daughter ventured to Costa Rica for a 4-month job. They never left. Although life in the jungle with few modern conveniences was a far cry from his native Colorado roots, his ever-growing fascination with the rainforest soon prompted his transformation into environmentalist and naturalist.

Hacienda Barú National Wildlife Refuge—a former cattle ranch and now a well-known ecotourism destination on the southwest coast of Costa Rica—was the result of Jack's decades of dedication to forest ecology. His expertise on biological corridor projects is much sought after, and he is currently president of two environmental organizations, ASANA (Association of Friends of Nature) and FUNDANTA (Foundation for the Path of the Tapir Biological Corridor).

A natural-born storyteller, Jack's articles have appeared regularly in Costa Rican publications, and he often speaks to environmental, student and ecological traveler groups. His years of living in the rainforest have rendered a multitude of personal experiences, many of which are recounted in his first book, *Monkeys Are Made of Chocolate.* Jack and Diane, who recently celebrated 50 years of marriage, live at Hacienda Barú.

Jack and Diane Ewing, 2014

HACIENDA
BARU

Hacienda Barú National Wildlife Refuge and Ecolodge is located on Costa Rica's southern Pacific Coast—a region of distinct natural beauty, where forest covered mountains rise up from the dramatic Pacific coastline. A fantastic variety of habitats, from wetland and secondary forest in the lowlands to primary forest on the highland coastal ridge can be found on 330 hectares. Several kilometers of trails and pristine beach are waiting to be explored, as are the orchid and butterfly gardens. Our mission is to protect the wildlife habitats of Hacienda Barú, while educating our visitors about its biological wealth.

HaciendaBaru.com

ASANA — Association of Friends of Nature
asanacr.org

To contribute to the Path of the Tapir Biological Corridor,
search for "ASANA" at **globalgiving.org**

100% solar & wind powered since 1999
PIXYJACK PRESS INC

WHOLESALE ORDERS WELCOME
PixyJackPress.com   *info@pixyjackpress.com*
PO Box 149   Masonville, CO 80541 USA

Made in the USA
Las Vegas, NV
23 April 2023

71011695R00173